Social Work and Antisemitism

Carole B. Cox • Dana B. Marlowe

Social Work and Antisemitism

Issues and Interventions

Springer

Carole B. Cox
Graduate School of Social Service
Fordham University
New York, NY, USA

Dana B. Marlowe
Graduate School of Social Service
Fordham University
New York, NY, USA

ISBN 978-3-031-72770-2 ISBN 978-3-031-72771-9 (eBook)
https://doi.org/10.1007/978-3-031-72771-9

This Springer imprint is published by the registered company Springer Nature Switzerland AG
The registered company address is: Gewerbestrasse 11, 6330 Cham, Switzerland

In honor of the victims of October 7, 2023;
may their memory forever be a blessing.

Foreword

As written by Professors Carole B. Cox and Dana B. Marlowe in their Preface to this book: "This is a book that never should have been written as there should be no need for it." I only wish it was so; obviously there is a great need for such a book today. In a world in which "20% of Americans between the ages of 18 and 29 think the Holocaust is a 'myth,' and almost a quarter believe the Holocaust has been 'exaggerated'" (*Somin, December 9, 2023*), and students, including those in schools of social work, are among those chanting "from river to the sea," there is a desperate need for this timely book.

One of my most vivid childhood memories was running very fast to get into my apartment where my parents were. I was running in a very large, enclosed courtyard in the center of an apartment complex in Lodz, Poland in the mid-1950s trying to get away from a bunch of Catholic kids my age who were after me, calling me a version of "dirty Jew." I made it home and locked the door behind me before they were able to catch me. I don't remember the specifics of why they were after me, beyond the fact that I was Jewish. I don't think I told my parents about it, but I do remember being very scared, at the same time feeling proud that I could outrun many kids, including boys who were much bigger than me.

I had not thought about this incident for years until, not that long ago shortly before my retirement (and one of the factors leading me to my retirement in 2021), I was sitting in a large circle with my university colleagues with a leader from the office of Equity, Diversity and Inclusion. The reason for this meeting was to discuss the faculty's feelings of divisiveness after a faculty member sent an email asking the "non-white" faculty to secretly get together to discuss how to take over the "old" (and "white") leadership of the school. When I tried to share some of my feelings about being excluded and having a history of being attacked for being Jewish (more than just the one incident mentioned above), only one or two other faculty members responded with a supportive gesture. The clear message was that my shared feelings of discrimination were not appropriate in an environment where everything was viewed in terms of "black/colored vs. white" and I was in the "white" camp (even though members of my extended family include "black Jews" from Yemen and "brown Jews" from North Africa and I never considered myself as a "white

American"). As pointed out in a recent *New York Times* article "…the real problem lies with some of the main convictions and currents of today's academia: intersectionality, critical theory, post-colonialism, ethnic studies and other concepts that may not seem antisemitic on their face but tend to politicize classrooms and cast Jews as privileged and oppressive. If, as critical theorists argue, the world's injustices stem from the shadowy agendas of the powerful and manipulative few against the virtuous masses, just which group is most likely to find itself villainized?" (Stephens, June 25, 2024).

Years prior to this meeting, as I chaired, at different times, both the Human Behavior and Social Environment (HBSE) area as well as the Social Work Practice area in a major school of social work, I was responsible for updating the curriculum in these areas for our Master of Social Work students. It was evident to me that while we, as faculty, tried to keep up to date with the various readings related to social work, social justice, and racism, the issue of ethnoculture and religion, especially as it related to Jewish clients, was missing. This was especially relevant as many of our students worked with elderly clients, some of whom were Holocaust survivors, and some of their younger clients who were children and grandchildren of survivors of the Holocaust. Students were taught about cross-generational trauma focusing on American, Canadian, and Australian Native populations, even on Cambodian and Vietnamese refugees and their children, but there was little in our reading list in relation to their Jewish clients. Looking to find such literature to incorporate into our HBSE and Practice bibliographies became a frustrating task; with the exception of two or three, mostly older, articles, such literature just did not exist in the United States.

Thus the crucial need for this textbook. With its clear discussion of antisemitism in the context of human rights and social justice; the historical background of this concept and its role in the Holocaust; the history of Palestine, Israel and Zionism; the current manifestation of antisemitism and its impact; and how to intervene with individuals impacted by it, this is a book that should be on the required reading list of every school of social work in the United States.

I applaud Springer Nature for publishing this book. It is not a topic that many publishers, or even readers, welcome no matter how important it is today. And I applaud the authors, Carole B. Cox and Dana B. Marlowe, for giving us this book.

New York, NY, USA Shulamith Lala Ashenberg Straussner, PhD

Shulamith Lala Ashenberg Straussner, PhD, DSW, LCSW, is Professor Emerita at New York University Silver School of Social Work. She is the Founding Editor of the *Journal of Social Work Practice in the Addictions*, was inducted as a NASW Social Work Pioneer, and is a Board Member of the Fulbright Israel Interest Group after being selected as a three-time Fulbright Senior Scholar to Israel, Ukraine, and the Czech Republic. She is the author/editor/co-editor of over 25 books and numerous book chapters, referred journal articles, and other publications. She is the author of a chapter on "Jewish substance abusers: Existing but invisible" in Straussner, S.L.A. (Ed). *Ethnocultural Factors in the Treatment of Addictions* (2001) Guilford Press, and the main researcher of a 2015 national survey "Social Workers' Self-Reported Wellness Study" (https://wp.nyu.edu/socialworkers), which includes a large sample of Jewish social workers.

References

Somin, I. (2023, December 9). *New Survey Showing Public Ignorance About the Holocaust Among Young Americans. Reason Foundation.* https://reason.com/volokh/2023/12/09/new-survey-showing-public-ignorance-about-the-holocaust-among-young-americans/

Stephens, B. (2024, June 25). Should American Jews Abandon Elite Universities? *The New York Times.* https://www.nytimes.com/2024/06/25/opinion/jews-ivy-league-antisemitism.html

Preface

This is a book that never should have been written as there should be no need for it. Social work is the one profession that is focused on securing socially just societies where human rights and dignity for all are recognized and supported and where all groups are able to participate fully and equally.

Antisemitism, hatred, and discrimination against Jewish people and Jewish institutions are perhaps the oldest forms of oppression. In the Old Testament, Jews were tyrannized as they would not forsake their God to worship idols. Throughout the Middle Ages, they were segregated in societies and frequently blamed for any misfortune impacting society, including the Black plague of the 1300s. Throughout history, as with other oppressions, myths and stereotypes to substantiate antisemitism were developed and many remain today.

The belief that the Jews were responsible for the death of Christ fed such antisemitism and violence against Jews. Although Jewish responsibility for the death of Christ was refuted by the Church during the Second Vatican Council, the beliefs and myths that underlie and contribute to the oppression remain. Discrimination always finds a way to vilify the oppressed, and in the case of antisemitism, Jews have been treated as a menace to society that needs to be eliminated in order to maintain the social order or a powerful force that could in itself overtake the society. They become either the oppressed or the oppressor, thus justifying antisemitism.

And as a result, Jewish people suffer. If they are too successful, they are ridiculed for their success, and if they are in need or harassed, they are ignored as it is justified. In 2021, during COVID, I (Cox) became concerned about outbreaks of antisemitism around the country, including remarks by political figures that the Jews were responsible for the virus, reminiscent of the claims of the Middle Ages. My research (Cox, 2021) found that social work, a champion of social justice, concerned about fighting oppression, had written little about antisemitism since the 1990s. Subsequently, my article on social work and antisemitism generated a great deal of interest from the community of Jewish social workers. Particularly important was the involvement and support of NASW/New York State, which formed in 2021 the Jewish Social Workers Interest Group that continues to meet regularly.

Unfortunately, antisemitism has not decreased; it has steadily increased across the globe. The attacks by HAMAS on Israel in October 2023, the deadliest assault and murder of Jewish people since the Holocaust, led to an unprecedented rise in antisemitism. This new form sees all Jewish people, including students, as responsible for the policies of Israel. Concomitantly, social work, which has played a formidable role in fighting oppressions, has tended to ignore antisemitism and its impact, having done little to combat it or deter its increase and impact.

This book aims to fill an important gap in social work education as it focuses on this one specific form of oppression. It discusses its history, impact on individuals and society, the role of the Holocaust, contemporary manifestations of antisemitism, and its impact on individuals and societies. It also includes a teaching guide for use in social work curriculum that can be adapted as needed.

As was said in the beginning, it is truly regrettable that this book needs to be written. At the same time, we are hopeful that the book will fill an important gap in social work education and in the profession. Social work cannot continue to ignore the impact that antisemitism has had and continues to have. Combatting and dismantling it is critical for both Jewish people and institutions, the profession, and for the entire society.

We want to thank Springer Nature for their interest and eagerness in producing this book, for NASW/NY State for its consistent collaboration and assistance, and the members of the Jewish Social Workers Interest Group for their encouragement and thoughtful help. With all your support and involvement, social work can surely make Never Again, NEVER AGAIN.

New York, NY, USA

Carole B. Cox
Dana B. Marlowe

Contents

About the Authors

Carole B. Cox, MSW, PhD is a Professor at the Graduate School of Social Service, Fordham University, where she teaches in the Policy Sequence. She is a Fellow of the Gerontological Society of America, a Fulbright scholar, and a representative of the International Association of Gerontology and Geriatrics (IAGG) to the United Nations. In 2023 she was appointed to the Advisory Council on Family Caregiving of the Administration on Community Living, focusing on Kinship Families and Grandfamilies. Dr. Cox is the author of 10 books and more than 75 journal articles dealing with aging, human rights, caregiving, human trafficking, and social policy. In 2022 she received the CURA Award for Kincare Champion from the NY State Kincare Coalition. Since 2020, she has focused on antisemitism and social work education and practice and has done research, presentations, and articles on the subject. Her 2021 article on antisemitism and social work led to the development of the NASW/NYS Jewish Social Workers Interest Group which she continues to co-chair.

Dana B. Marlowe, PhD, LCSW is a Clinical Professor and the Director of Academic Excellence and Teaching Innovation at the Fordham University Graduate School of Social Service. Dr. Marlowe teaches across the curriculum, teaching classes in clinical social work and social policy. She specializes in innovative pedagogy and works with faculty and adjunct instructors to enhance their teaching skills. She has published several book chapters on active learning strategies and articles on teaching evidence-based practice. She also specializes in trauma treatment, with a focus on EMDR. In 2021, she became involved in researching antisemitism and social work, resulting in presentations at national conferences, workshops, and publications. She also co-chairs the NASW/NYS Jewish Social Workers Interest Group.

Chapter 1
Introduction: Human Rights, Social Justice, and Social Work

Background

Human rights and social justice are pillars of the social work profession. Unique to social work is its emphasis on the individual in society and the importance of societies in promoting security and support for all people so that their human rights and dignity are assured and respected. As such, the profession is responsible for challenging all discrimination and oppression that obscures the actualization of these rights and acts as a barrier to individual well-being. The importance of these goals is recognized through the three principal associations that represent the profession.

The International Federation of Social Workers (IFSW)

The International Federation of Social Workers (IFSW) is a professional organization composed of social work associations throughout the globe. Its definition of social work includes principles of social justice, human rights, and respect for diversities which are central to the profession (IFSW, 2023). Among its nine principles are:

1. Recognition of the inherent dignity of humanity.
2. Promoting human rights.
3. Promoting social justice.
4. Challenging discrimination and institutional oppression.
5. Respect for diversity.

As a human rights profession, IFSW (2023) social work is the profession that works for social justice and human rights for everyone challenging discrimination and institutional oppression. Advocating for and protecting the human rights of all

C. B. Cox, D. B. Marlowe, *Social Work and Antisemitism*,
https://doi.org/10.1007/978-3-031-72771-9_1

is core to social work. Social work has the responsibility of promoting social justice and challenging discrimination and institutional oppression while respecting diversity and working toward inclusive communities.

National Association of Social Workers (NASW)

The National Association of Social Workers (NASW, 2022) emphasizes social works' commitment to social justice for all and to ending racism, discrimination, and prejudice against any group as they are damaging to the social, emotional, and economic well-being of the affected group and society. A key principle of the profession is to challenge social injustice while promoting sensitivity to and knowledge about oppression and cultural and ethnic diversity (NASW Code of Ethics, 2021). The profession's ethical responsibilities call upon social workers to be culturally aware and understanding of diversity and oppression as it occurs in many forms, including race, ethnicity, sex, sexual orientation, gender, status, ability, and religion (NASW Standards and Indicators for Cultural Competence, 2015).

The Council on Social Work Education (CSWE)

The Council on Social Work Education (CSWE), the accreditation body for schools of social work in the United States, specifies nine competencies expected of graduating students. All nine focus on the purpose of social work to promote human and community well-being. This includes respect for human dignity which is realized through social work's concerns for social, racial, economic, and environmental justice that facilitate the realization of human rights (CSWE, 2022). Among the nine competencies, Competency 2 and Competency 3 particularly focus on socially just societies supportive of diversity and free of oppression.

Competency 2: Antiracism, Diversity, Equity, and Inclusion (ADEI)

Social workers understand how diversity and difference characterize and shape the human experience and are critical to the formation of identity. Such diversity includes many dimensions including race, ethnicity, and religion. Social workers are knowledgeable about the impact that these diverse factors may have in excluding, discriminating, and oppressing persons and groups.

Competency 3: Advance Human Rights and Social, Economic, and Environmental Justice

Every person has fundamental human rights. Given their knowledge and understanding of oppression and human rights, social workers are expected to these rights while working toward eliminating barriers that oppress and impede their realization.

Both competencies attest to the role of social work in supporting diversity and combating forces that would marginalize, oppress, and negate the dignity and security of individuals and groups. Such efforts are integral to ensure that all persons are respected, and their basic rights of human dignity and security are assured.

The Profession of Social Work

Social work is a helping profession in the same category as psychology, medicine, or nursing. But in contrast to these other professions, social work has a broader focus than just the individual client or patient, it is a profession of change that recognizes that change is frequently dependent upon the environment. It is these environments that are often the cause of the concerns and problems affecting the individual. Thus, oppression and discrimination, which target groups can have, perverse impacts on several levels ranging from psychological well-being and security to policy and programs' availability of resources.

Social work's concept of helping encompasses helping the individual to cope with and alter environments as well as direct actions to change offensive and restrictive policies and practices. Biases and stereotypes that characterize specific groups are the foundations for discriminative and oppressive practices and policies. Consequently, it is critical that social workers are able to recognize them and engage at the micro, mezzo, and macro levels of practice to assure that they are challenged and replaced.

Given these goals which emphasize human rights, social justice, and respect for all groups, antisemitism, hatred against Jews and Jewish institutions, which serve to discriminate and oppress, must be a target for the profession. However, as will be discussed in this book, to date the profession has tended to ignore antisemitism in education, practice, and the community. As a prelude to the book's focus on antisemitism, we are offering a short description of human rights and social justice and the pivotal roles they place in the profession.

Human Rights

The Universal Declaration of Human Rights was adopted by the United Nations in 1948 at the end of World War II. It was enacted in response to mass atrocities and "barbarous acts that outraged the conscience of mankind" during World War II (United Nations, n.d.). Underlying the rights is the concept of human dignity which is the foundation for freedom, justice, and world peace.

The 30 Articles that compose the Declaration specify the means that nations must take to ensure the rights of all people. It is equally important that the rights are indivisible, no one right is more important than another. Moreover, violating one right impacts all rights. Signing the Declaration commits member states of the United Nations to strive to promote the rights and freedom of their citizens. The foundation of the rights is the concept that all human beings are born free and equal in dignity and rights.

The UDHR rests upon five core notions: the importance of human dignity; non-discrimination; civil and political rights; economic, social, and cultural rights; and rights to solidarity (Wronka, 2017). Together these rights contribute to societies where all people have the same opportunities, protections, and supports. These rights, as they affirm the value and worth of the person, their autonomy, and their right to make their own choices form the basis of a rights-based approach to social work practice (Androff, 2015). Equally important is the fact that the UDHR is also used to inform empowerment-based assessment and social work interventions with vulnerable populations to ensure their full participation in society (Wronka, 2017).

Articles of the UDHR
Article 1: Right to Equality
Article 2: Freedom from Discrimination
Article 3: Right to Life, Liberty, Personal Security
Article 4: Freedom from Slavery
Article 5: Freedom from Torture and Degrading Treatment
Article 6: Right to Recognition as a Person before the Law
Article 7: Right to Equality before the Law
Article 8: Right to Remedy by Competent Tribunal
Article 9: Freedom from Arbitrary Arrest and Exile
Article 10: Right to Fair Public Hearing
Article 11: Right to be Considered Innocent until Proven Guilty
Article 12: Freedom from Interference with Privacy, Family, Home & Correspondence
Article 13: Right to Free Movement in and out of the Country
Article 14: Right to Asylum in other Countries from Persecution
Article 15: Right to a Nationality and the Freedom to Change It
Article 16: Right to Marriage and Family

(continued)

Article 17: Right to Own Property
Article 18: Freedom of Belief and Religion
Article 19: Freedom of Opinion and Information
Article 20: Right of Peaceful Assembly and Association
Article 21: Right to Participate in Government and in Free Elections
Article 22: Right to Social Security
Article 23: Right to Desirable Work and to Join Trade Unions
Article 24: Right to Rest and Leisure
Article 25: Right to Adequate Living Standard
Article 26: Right to Education
Article 27: Right to Participate in the Science, Arts, & Cultural Life of Community
Article 28: Right to a Social Order that Articulates this Document
Article 29: Community Duties Essential to Free and Full Development
Article 30: Freedom from State or Personal Interference in the Above Rights

Source: United Nations (n.d.) *Universal Declaration of Human Rights*

Social Work and Human Rights

Social work can be viewed as grounded in human rights as it focuses on the importance of individuals being able to participate and live with dignity in secure and nourishing societies. It emphasizes the value of each person, their worth, and the importance of a just society free of oppression and discrimination.

As discussed by Wronka (2017), human rights are the thread that weaves theory into integrated practice. Such a society based on human rights can be visualized as one in which each person is recognized for their own self-worth and has access to a just society composed of individuals living in supportive environments where, free of oppression, and with the resources needed, all regardless of race, color, sex, language, religion, birth, or other status are entitled to the same human rights.

Rights-based approaches to practice are based on the dignity of each person and thus entail respecting self-determination, appreciating, trusting, and empowering their ability to make their own decisions (Mapp et al., 2019). In addition, rights-based practice is non-discriminatory, focusing on inclusion and promoting relationships, particularly among those who are subject to discrimination and exclusion. It requires that persons participate in decisions that affect them, and that social workers and their agencies are transparent so that they generate trust and are accountable in that they advocate and organize against those violating human rights. As such, social workers are also responsible for assuring that societies permit and even foster individual human rights.

The rights-based perspective contrasts with the often-used needs-perspective. Needs, such as food, shelter, housing, and income are easy to identify but at the same time, as they are assessed by individual practitioners in varying societies, they can reflect subjective perspectives (Ife, 2012; Wronka, 2017). In contrast, human rights that are indivisible apply to everyone and are not reflective of unique societies or values.

Applying a rights-based framework to practice is essential for empowering individuals and communities. It is based on the underlying values and principles outlined by the United Nations (2015). Fundamental to the framework is the respect for all persons, the intrinsic value, dignity of all, and the duty of governments (duty bearers) to their citizens (rights holders) to protect and respect their rights. Consequently, we are all responsible for assuring that the rights of each person are recognized. At the same time, the rights-based framework influences social work by giving the profession the responsibility to ensure that these rights are not threatened or terminated.

The six major principles of a human rights framework are: (1) universality, (2) non-discrimination, (3) the indivisibility and interdependence of rights (political, civil, social, economic, and cultural), (4) participation, (5) accountability, and (6) transparency (Cox & Maschi, 2023).

(1) The principle of *universality* states that human rights belong to everyone, and there are no exceptions for any individual. The mere fact of being human entitles every human to have political, civil, social, economic, and cultural rights.
(2) The principle of *non-discrimination* assures access to rights for everyone. In an ideal world, there should be no intentional or unintentional discrimination of national and international laws, policies, or practices.
(3) The principle of *indivisibility and interdependence* guides governments to ensure political, civil, social, economic, and cultural rights to everyone. For example, suppose a government does not recognize a social right, such as the right to health and well-being. In that case, it challenges citizens' access to achieving other rights, such as the right to education, and safety and protection from violence and discrimination.
(4) The principle of *participation* refers to everyone's rights, especially those most affected, to participate in decisions that may infringe upon the protection of their rights. In the ideal situation, governments should engage, support, and provide a platform for the participation of civil society on political, civil, social, economic, and cultural issues.
(5) The principle of *accountability* suggests that governments are responsible for creating a mechanism of accountability for the enforcement of equal rights, including monitoring and evaluating the implementation of laws and policies that protect rights.
(6) The principle of *transparency* means that governments should communicate to civil society all information and decision-making processes affecting human rights. Society's members should be educated on becoming informed decision-makers and actively participating in making significant decisions that affect their rights. Such major decisions are at the national and international levels and at institutional levels such as social services and other institutions needed to protect such rights, including the right to social equality and education (United Nations, 2015).

Human rights practice involves interactions at all levels, micro, mezzo, and macro. At the micro level of practice, needs are translated into rights and individuals are respected as the experts in their own lives. This type of intervention demands that social workers respect and understand the views of the individual and their experiences. It also requires that practitioners recognize their own biases and values that may impact their clear understanding of the clients' experiences. Consequently, in dealing with discrimination or oppression, practitioners must be responsive to the harassment and attacks experienced by the individual and be aware of their own beliefs and stereotypes that might distort their understanding.

The mezzo level of practice involves attention to the systems and structures with which individuals interact and their responsiveness to these individuals. With human dignity at the core, services must be non-discriminatory and accountable. Sensitivity to cultures and how specific groups may interpret and respond to providers and agency policies and practices is critical for services to be effective and accepted. Being knowledgeable about cultures and how cultural diversity may influence individual responses, including service providers and clients, is critical for service effectiveness. Interventions at this level may include education and advocacy for changes in practice that increase their acceptability.

The macro-level focuses on policies and how governments and institutions support or violate human rights, thus impairing groups' well-being and involvement in society. Macro-level interventions include advocacy and social action to bring about necessary systemic change. The Black Lives Matters Movement is an example of how advocacy contributed to macro policy changes in law enforcement and policies in support of dignity and security.

Social Work and Social Justice

The pursuit of social justice has been a common thread throughout the history of social work. Human rights are important to promote and achieve social justice for individuals, families, and communities (Wronka, 2017). Basically, social justice ensures the following:

- The values of fairness in the assignment of fundamental rights and duties.
- The economic opportunities and social conditions.
- The equal worth of all citizens and their equal right to basic needs.
- The importance of spreading opportunity and life chances to as many people as possible (Reisch, 2012).

Using a social justice lens helps reframe issues generally viewed as individual in origin to include broader social, political, economic, and cultural understandings. These open possibilities for new solutions for individuals, families, groups, organizations, and communities. It also focuses on social change efforts that extend from a solely national to a global or international perspective (Maschi, 2016; Maschi &

Leibowitz, 2017). With this framework, oppression, such as antisemitism, clearly falls under the social justice lens.

The Social Work Dictionary defines social justice as an ideal condition in which all members of society have the same rights, protections, opportunities, and social benefits (Barker, 2003). The International Federation of Social Workers (IFSW, 2023) asserts that the principles of social justice, human rights, collective responsibility, and respect for diversities are central to social work as they reflect its core values and principles. Building upon this foundation, IFSW developed a new Global Agenda that stresses the future of social work as a profession that shifts from providing to people in crisis to becoming agencies of social transformation that prevent social crisis (IFSW, 2023). Consequently, it calls upon social workers to advocate for policies and systems that challenge oppression, support diversity, and support and engage all people. Given this social justice perspective and the ensuing Global Agenda, antisemitism, oppression against Jewish people, must be a target for the profession.

Antisemitism

Antisemitism has been called "anti-Jewish racism" as it operates in multiple ways, can be intentional or unintentional, and expressed in stereotypes, coded language, and in conspiracy theories (Waxman, 2022). It is an ancient form of oppression that has existed for thousands of years and is attested to in the Passover Haggadah, the book read by Jewish people at Passover, with the passage, "In every generation they rise against us to annihilate us."

Throughout history, Jews have been targeted by societies that perceive them as the cause of all problems, resulting in their expulsion or destruction (Prager & Telushkin, 2016). Reasons for this hating or targeting include economic factors, need for scapegoats, ethnic hatred, xenophobia, resentment of Jewish success, and religious bigotry (Prager & Telushkin, 2016). In addition, Jewish laws based on the belief that they are chosen people and ethical values that the laws dictate have continued to distinguish them as a group. Such values, including a stress on education and professional success, have often provoked envy and hostility in non-Jews (Prager & Telushkin, 2016).

Antisemitism, hatred against Jews, rests on caustic stereotypes and tropes that contribute to hate and oppression while denying Jewish people both their human right of religious freedom and their ability to fully participate in society. Antisemitism is based on lies that Jews control the media, and finances, and that Jews are part of a global cabal to control the world. Thus, antisemitism permits Jews to be ostracized and attacked simply because they are Jews. Having been targeted for millennium, they present a simple explanation for any of societies' ills, ranging from the Black Plague in the Middle Ages to COVID-19 to economic depressions.

> Jews have been hated both for what they were and at the very same time, what they were not. They were persecuted and reviled because they separated themselves, and because they assimilated; because they practiced ancient traditions and beliefs, and because they were unrooted and believed nothing; because they were poor and because they were rich; because they were communists, and because they were capitalists; because they were exiled and stateless, and because they returned and reclaimed their state (Contler-Wansh, 2023).

Unfortunately, as stereotypes and beliefs are transmitted and circulated throughout societies, they assume a measure of truth that denies any need for validation, they are simply accepted.

Although Jews comprise only 2% of the US population, they account for 60% of all religious-based hate crimes, with antisemitism reaching historic levels in 2022 (DOJ, 2023). Since the October 7th, 2023, attacks on Israel by the terrorist group, Hamas antisemitism has seen an unprecedented increase globally, targeting Jewish students, people, and institutions (Anti-Defamation League (ADL), 2024).

Social Work and Antisemitism

According to the NASW Code of Ethics (2021), the profession is committed to social justice for all and ending discrimination and prejudice against any group as they are damaging to the social, emotional, and economic well-being of the affected group and society. As such, the profession has been active in combating racism and oppression. At the same time, it has been passive in its dealing with antisemitism (Cox, 2021). This lack of attention to antisemitism and its impact on Jewish people and Jewish institutions suggests that there may be a hierarchy of oppressions and that some are more valid than others.

The absence of antisemitism in the social work curriculum has long been noted. Soifer (1991) wrote about the need to infuse content about Jews and antisemitism into the curriculum while Gold (1996) advocated for content on antisemitism in schools of social work along with suggestions for incorporating it with other antiracist content. The subject appeared to lay dormant until Cox (2021) discussed its absence, impact, and the need for its inclusion.

Oppression that denigrates and harms any specific group should be challenged as such actions impede the lives and rights of individuals while undermining social justice and human rights. As a targeted group in society, Jewish people should be entitled to the same respect and support as others struggling with prejudice and hostility. Given the mandate of the profession to challenge oppression that acts as a barrier to the fulfillment of human rights and social justice, the profession is obligated to combat antisemitism.

To date, the profession has failed to include teaching about antisemitism in the curriculum and has been reticent to take a stand against it in the community. The absence of attention to antisemitism is noticeable in its impact on Jewish students and practitioners. A national study of antisemitism in the profession found students being discriminated in classes and targeted in agencies, often being told they were White and did not have a problem (Cox & Marlowe, 2023).

Supporting Jewish people and working to assure their rights and security does not diminish the rights of other groups or their security. Supporting Israel and its right to exist and the security and well-being of its people does not negate the security and well-being of the Palestinians. Consequently, among all professions, social work must recognize and address the many factors that contribute to oppression and specifically, antisemitism, and thus obscure the rights and security of people and the creation of a socially just society.

Given the dramatic increase in antisemitism and its impact on individuals and society, social work cannot continue to ignore it. It presents both challenges and opportunities for the profession (Cox, 2021). The overriding challenge is to combat it in all its forms and at all levels of practice, from the micro to the macro. The opportunity is to be able to achieve justice and security for all Jewish people with antisemitism no longer a concern or a barrier to their well-being, participation, and security.

The chapters in this book address the history, aspects, and current manifestations of antisemitism, the many issues associated with it, and interventions to combat it with the history and its contemporary manifestations discussed in depth. Models for teaching about antisemitism are offered as well as a Teaching Guide for use in Schools of Social Work. Chapters cover the trauma associated with many forms of antisemitism and how practitioners can deal with it in clients.

It is important to recognize that any type of oppression that prevents people from living fully and freely in society is divisive and harmful. Moreover, oppressions never rest with just one group but proliferate to other marginalized populations. Consequently, rather than ignoring antisemitism, social work must take steps at all levels to combat it. We hope that this book can assist in that work.

Conclusion

As discussed in this introduction, antisemitism must be an issue for the social work profession. Social work's mandate to combat oppression and establish socially just societies that support the human rights of all people, enabling them to freely participate with dignity and without fear, demands it work toward the elimination of antisemitism. This book explores antisemitism in-depth and presents interventions at all levels to deal with it.

Antisemitism is one of the oldest forms of oppression. Recently, since the Hamas attacks on Israel in October 2023, it has had an unprecedented increase globally (US Embassy, 2024). Although antisemitism begins with the targeting of Jewish people, it is often the prelude to attacks on other marginalized groups as it tends to ferment other forms of hatred and oppression in societies. Consequently, antisemitism presents a threat to society and social justice.

The poem by Martin Niemoller, a Lutheran pastor who lived through the Holocaust in Germany, spending eight years in Nazi prisons and concentration camps, poignantly describes the impact of indifference (Hochenos, 2018):

First, they came for the socialists, and I did not speak out—because I was not a socialist.
Then they came for the trade unionists, and I did not speak out—because I was not a trade unionist.
Then they came for the Jews, and I did not speak out—because I was not a Jew.
Then they came for me—and there was no one left to speak for me.

We hope that this book encourages you to include antisemitism in your teaching and in practice. Social work can play a pivotal role in combating this insidious form of oppression and assuring the security and rights of all Jewish people, thus helping to confirm that dignity and justice for all are recognized and protected.

Main Points

- Human rights and social justice are foundational principles of the social work profession, emphasizing the importance of promoting security and support for all people to ensure their human rights and dignity are respected.
- Social work is responsible for challenging all forms of discrimination and oppression that obstruct the actualization of human rights and act as barriers to individual well-being.
- NASW is committed to social justice for all and ending racism, discrimination, and prejudice.
- The UDHR created in 1948 provides a global standard for human rights.
- The rights-based perspective contrasts with the needs-based perspective as it applies to everyone irrespective of their culture or society.
- Human rights practice involves all levels of social work.
- IFSW's principles include the recognition of the inherent dignity of humanity, promoting human rights and social justice, challenging discrimination and institutional oppression, and respecting diversity.
- CSWE specifies competencies for social work graduates including promoting human and community well-being, Competency 2 (ADEI) and Competency 3 (Advancing Human Rights and Social, Economic, and Environmental Justice).
- Social work recognizes the role of the environment in causing problems and conditions that impact individuals.
- Social work aims to promote change both at the individual and systemic levels, including efforts against antisemitism.
- Social work's unique approach integrates both individual and systemic interventions.

- Social workers have a responsibility to uphold the UDHR and its principles including fighting antisemitism.
- Social workers engage at micro, mezzo, and macro levels of practice addressing both individual and systemic issues.
- Social workers are expected to challenge biases, stereotypes, and oppressive practices.
- Despite the profession's commitment to combating all forms of oppression, social work has tended to ignore antisemitism in both curricula and practice.
- Social work must recognize and address antisemitism as a specific form of oppression that impedes the security and participation of Jewish people in society.

Discussion Questions and Short Assignments

The following suggested discussion questions can be done in class in small groups or by having students write their own short papers.

- Discuss why human rights and social justice are crucial for the well-being of individuals and communities.
- Describe how human rights practice may be involved in combating antisemitism.
- Give examples of how oppression impacts individuals and societies.
- Discuss how social work's broader focus on the individual within their environment differs from other helping professions and how this impacts social work interventions.
- Despite the profession's commitment to combating oppression, why do you think social work has ignored antisemitism?
- Why is the Universal Declaration of Human Rights (UDHR) important? Discuss key points that you find most critical for people and society.
- Think about your own biases and stereotypes of a group…how do those impact your interactions and behavior?
- What are the challenges and opportunities for the social work profession in addressing antisemitism, and how can social workers effectively combat this form of oppression at all levels of practice?
- Describe the roles that you think social work could take in combating antisemitism.
- Describe what you might see as barriers to including antisemitism in the social work curricula.

In-Class Exercises: Applying a Human Rights Framework to Antisemitism

Goal: To have students gain a deeper understanding of a human rights-based framework and how to apply the framework to antisemitism.

Phase I: Review the Universal Declaration of Human Rights (UDHR) articles (20–30 min)

As a class, review the UDHR articles. These can be distributed as a handout or put on a whiteboard. This review should be done after students have already learned about the articles through their readings and lectures.

Phase II: Apply the UDHR articles to antisemitism (20–30 min).

In a class discussion, have the class choose which articles are violated by acts of antisemitism.

Phase III: Examples (30 min)

Break the students up into groups of 4–5. Ask them to do the following:

(a) Use social media to find 4 incidents of antisemitism.
(b) Discuss which specific human rights are being violated by each incident.
(c) Discuss how these violations impact individuals and communities.
(d) From a human rights perspective, discuss how these violations can be addressed.

Phase IV: Debrief (20–30 min)

(a) Ask each group to report back on each point that was asked of them in Phase III.
(b) Ask the class what steps can be taken to fight antisemitism on a micro, mezzo, and macro level.
(c) Ask the class what they learned during this process.

References

Androff, D. (2015). *Practicing rights: Human-rights based approaches to social work practice.* Taylor and Francis.

Anti-Defamation League (ADL). *Antisemtic attitudes in America 2024.* Retrieved from https://www.adl.org/resources/report/antisemitic-attitudes-america-2024

Barker, R. (2003). *The social work dictionary* (5th ed.). NASW Press.

Contler-Walsh, M. (2023). *Combating antisemitism with human rights and international law.* Academic Engagement Network, Pamphlet Series No 9.

Conversation, Retrieved from https://theconversation.com/antisemitism-isnt-just-jew-hatred-its-anti-jewish-racism-193614

Council on Social Work Education (CSWE). (2022). *Educational policy and accreditation standards.* Retrieved from https://www.cswe.org/accreditation/policies-process/2022epas/

Cox, C. (2021). Addressing anti-semitism in social work education. *Journal of Religion & Spirituality in Social Work, 40*(2), 111–125. https://doi.org/10.1080/15426432.2020.1871155
Cox, C., & Marlowe, D. (2023). Antisemitism in social work: Findings from an exploratory national survey. *Journal of Religion and Spirituality in Social Work: Social Thought*, published online. https://doi.org/10.1080/15426432.2023.2289435
Cox, C., & Maschi, T. (2023). *Human rights and social justice; Key issues and vulnerable populations*. Routledge.
Gold, N. (1996). Putting antisemitism on the anti-racism agenda in north American schools of social work. *Social Work Education, 32*. https://www.jstor.org/stable/23042741
Hochenos, M. (2018). *Then they came for me: Martin Niemoller, the Pastor who defied the Nazis*. Basic Books.
Ife, J. (2012). *Human rights and social work*. Cambridge University Press.
IFSW. (2023). Freedom, equality and justice for all: The essential role of social work. In *Advancing human rights*. Retrieved from https://www.ifsw.org/freedom-equality-and-justice-for-all-the-essential-role-of-social-work-in-advancing-human-rights/#:~:text=IFSW%20envisions%20a%20holistic%20human,protect%20and%20advance%20these%20rights
Mapp, S., McPherson, J., Androff, D., & Gatenio Gabel, S. (2019). Social work as a human rights profession. *Social Work, 64*(3), 259–269. https://doi.org/10.1093/sw/swz023
Maschi, T. (2016). *Applying a human rights approach to social work research and evaluation*. Springer.
Maschi, T., & Leibowitz, G. (2017). *Forensic social work: Psychosocial and legal issues across diverse populations and settings*. Columbia University Press.
NASW. (2021). *NASW code of ethics*. Retrieved from https://www.socialworkers.org/About/Ethics/Code-of-Ethics/Code-of-Ethics-English
NASW. (2022). *Ethnicity & race*. Retrieved from https://www.socialworkers.org/Practice/Ethnicity-Race
National Association of Social Workers (NASW). (2015). *Standards and indicators for cultural competence in social work practice*. NASW. https://www.socialworkers.org/Practice/NASW-Practice-Standards-Guidelines/Standards-and-Indicators-for-Cultural-Competence-in-Social-Work-Practice
Prager, D., & Telushkin, J. (2016). *Why the Jews? The reason for Antisemitism, the most accurate predictor of human evil*. Touchstone.
Reisch, M. (2012). Defining social justice in a socially unjust world. *Families in Society: The Journal of Contemporary Social Services, 83*, 343–354. https://doi.org/10.1606/1044-3894.17
Soifer, S. (1991). Infusing content about Jews and about antisemitism into the curricula. *Journal of Social Work Education, 27*. https://www.jstor.org/stable/23042741
United Nations. (n.d.). *Universal declaration of human rights*. Retrieved from https://www.un.org/en/about-us/universal-declaration-of-human-rights
United Nations, Department of Economic and Social Affairs. (2015). *Global sustainable development report 2015* (Advance Unedited Version) (GSDR 2015). Retrieved from https://sustainabledevelopment.un.org/gsdr2015.html
US Department of Justice. (2023, Oct). *2022 FBI hate crimes statistics*.
US Embassy. (2024). *Fighting the surge in global Antisemitism*. Retrieved from https://de.usembassy.gov/fighting-the-surge-in-global-antisemitism/
Waxman, D. (2022). *Antisemitism isn't just Jew-Hatred' it's anti-Jewish racism*. Retrieved from https://www.justice.gov/crs/highlights/2022-hate-crime-statistics
Wronka, J. (2017). *Human rights and social justice: Social action and service for the helping and health professions*. Sage.

Chapter 2
Antisemitism: History and Social Work

Definition of Antisemitism

The following definition of antisemitism has been globally adopted by countries around the world as well as by corporations, professional sports organization, and the media. "Antisemitism is a certain perception which may be expressed as hatred towards Jews. Rhetorical and physical manifestations of antisemitism are directed toward Jewish or non-Jewish individuals and/or their property, toward Jewish community institutions and religious facilities" (International Holocaust Remembrance Alliance, 2016).

As such, antisemitism is expressed in speech, writing, visual forms and action, and sinister stereotypes and negative character traits (AJC, 2024a, b). Antisemitism, hatred that targets Jewish people and Jewish institutions, is a prejudice built on discrimination and oppression. It is an ancient form of oppression that has dramatically increased in recent years both in the United States and globally.

The following are examples of antisemitism (AJC, 2024a, b):

- Calling for, aiding, or justifying the killing or harming of Jews in the name of a radical ideology or an extremist view of religion.
- Making mendacious, dehumanizing, demonizing, or stereotypical allegations about Jews as such or the power of Jews as collective—such as the myth about a world Jewish conspiracy or of Jews controlling the media, economy, government, or other societal institutions.
- Accusing Jews as a people of being responsible for real or imagined wrongdoing committed by a single Jewish person or group, or even for acts committed by non-Jews.
- Denying the genocide of the Jewish people at the hands of National Socialist Germany and its supporters and accomplices during World War II (the Holocaust).
- Accusing the Jews as a people, or Israel as a state, of inventing or exaggerating the Holocaust.

C. B. Cox, D. B. Marlowe, *Social Work and Antisemitism*,
https://doi.org/10.1007/978-3-031-72771-9_2

- Accusing Jewish citizens of being more loyal to Israel.
- Denying the Jewish people their right to self-determination.
- Applying double standards by requiring a behavior not expected or demanded of any other democratic nation.
- Using the symbols and images associated with classic antisemitism to characterize Israel or Israelis.
- Holding Jews collectively responsible for actions of the state of Israel.

Data from the Anti-Defamation League (ADL, 2023) reports 3697 antisemitic incidents in 2022, an increase of 36% from the previous year and the highest number since 1979, the first year that data on incidents was collected. Globally, harassment of Jews has increased since 2020 in 94 countries with incidents ranging from verbal and physical assaults to vandalism of cemeteries and scapegoating of Jews as responsible for the COVID-19 pandemic. Following the terrorist attacks in Israel, October 7, 2023, antisemitic incidents showed a 400 percent increase in both the United States and abroad (ADL, 2024).

Brief History of Antisemitism

Antisemitism, hatred that targets Jewish people and Jewish institutions, is a prejudice built on discrimination and oppression which can be traced to biblical times. In the Old Testament, the Hebrews were often persecuted because they refused to worship idols. With Christianity and the subsequent conversion of the Roman Emperors, Jews were persecuted as being threats to society with the Church charging as responsible for the death of Jesus.

In the early Middle Ages, Jews were excluded from intermarriage with Christians, holding political positions, and appearing as witnesses in courts. In most European cities they were restricted to living in specific areas and in the thirteenth century, required to wear a distinctive symbol so that they could easily be recognized. As it was forbidden for them to own land, they often became money lenders, an occupation that Christians could not assume but one that also led to further bias and stereotyping. Beliefs and myths developed to substantiate their exclusion, such as "blood libel," which claimed that Jews ritually murdered Christian children and used their blood in making matza.

Ostracized from society, Jews became an easy scapegoat and were frequently viewed as the causes of disease, including the Black Death, which killed thousands throughout Europe in the Middle Ages. The accusation that Jews were responsible for the COVID-19 pandemic is reminiscent of this targeting in the fourteenth century. In the fifteenth century, Jews in Spain were forced to convert, leave the country, or be executed, leading to the forced emigration of many to Portugal and North Africa (Baron, 1952).

With the enlightenment of the eighteenth century, Jews were gradually accepted into Western European society while their activities continued to be restricted in

Eastern Europe. Fears that Jews were trying to take over the governments in Germany and Russia contributed to attacks and pogroms against Jewish communities. During the reign of Catherine II in Russia, Jewish people were restricted to living in the Pale of Settlement, a restriction that limited their rights and that also contributed to the emigration of many to America (Simon, 1997).

The Dreyfus Affair, the false accusation against a Jewish French lieutenant of spying for the Germans, divided France and was a vivid example of antisemitism in society (Lindemann, 1991). A captain in the French artillery, he was convicted of treason and sentenced to life on Devils' Island. New evidence in 1896 led to another trial in 1899 which found him not guilty, with his being eventually exonerated, returning to the Army as a major. The accusations and trial impacted and divided France and had lasting repercussions on French society (Lindemann, 1991).

In the early 1900s, *The Protocols of the Elders of Zion*, a hoax that was used to discredit revolutionary forces hostile to the Tsar, was published in Russia, and described a Jewish plan for global domination (Whitfield, 2020). The fact that several of the leaders of the revolution were Jewish gave support to the accusations. In the 1920s, the Dearborn Publishing Company, owned by Henry Ford, published *The International Jew*, a four-volume set of antisemitic booklets based on the *Protocols* which included "The American Jew: The World's Foremost Problem", which contributed to increases in antisemitism in the United States (Whitfield, 2020).

Although there is no evidence for any international conspiracy, the works were influential in supporting Hitler's belief that the Jews were dangerous and skilled at deception, seeking world domination. However, even with the absence of supporting evidence, the *Protocols* continue to be influential today. The Rothschilds, who played key roles in the development of finance capitalism in nineteenth century Europe and the success and influence of George Soros, an investor, who spends billions on progressive causes, are frequently referred to as examples of Jewish power and control (Whitfield, 2020).

Social Work and Antisemitism

As discussed in the previous chapter (Chap. 1), a key principle of the social work profession is to challenge social injustice while promoting sensitivity to and knowledge about oppression and cultural and ethnic diversity (NASW Code of Ethics, 2021). The profession's ethical responsibilities call upon social workers to be culturally aware and understanding of diversity and oppression as it occurs in many forms, including race, ethnicity, sex, sexual orientation, gender, status, ability, and religion. Cultural competency, the ability to understand the unique experiences of diverse groups with an awareness of one's own privilege and power is essential to combating oppression (NASW Standards and Indicators for Cultural Competence, 2015).

To date, education on antisemitism is seldom dealt with in schools, universities, or in Schools of Social work. The absence of the inclusion of antisemitism in social work education may be attributed to the belief that Jews do not suffer from inequality as they are seen as economically successful and thus fully integrated into society (Altman, 2011). In addition, as they compose only 2% of the population and are usually not people of color, they are overlooked as a group that needs special attention (Sales, 2019). However, ignoring antisemitism contributes to its proliferation, further undermining social justice and human rights. Moreover, as shown throughout history, antisemitism does not impact only Jewish people.

Antisemitism does not rest with just targeting Jewish people. Studies find that antisemites tend to target other groups, marginalized groups such as the LGBTQ community. In fostering hate and marginalization, they have spread rumors that Jews are promoting a LGBTQ agenda that includes pedophilia promoting transsexual and homosexual propaganda (ADL, 2023). Thus, antisemitism and other types of hate become intertwined, further attacking the freedoms and rights of others.

Oppression and Antisemitism

At the personal level, antisemitism can be traced to negative stereotypes and myths which continue to influence beliefs and behaviors. A recent poll (ADL, 2020) found the beliefs that Jews control business and financial institutions, are likely to use shady business practices, are responsible for killing Christ, and are more loyal to Israel are held by approximately 14% of all Americans with 61% agreeing with at least one antisemitic sentiment. Such perceptions have been voiced by persons in power, through antisemitic comments that reinforce historic stereotypes (Levin, 2019). Personal beliefs reflect cultural sentiments, influencing institutional beliefs and subsequent antisemitic acts.

Personal responses to antisemitism are often efforts to be "invisible" (Gold, 1996), as Jews seek to not identify as Jewish. In doing so, they are attempting to "pass" as "white." Passing behavior among oppressed groups remains a typical means of coping with discrimination and maintaining one's position and status. However, even when successful, it can negatively impact self-identity, as Jews, common to others who have "passed" frequently live in fear of being discovered and its results (Altman, 2011). Clinical work with Jewish clients should explore the issue of "passing" as it can also be conducive to self-hatred (Alperin, 2016).

Microaggressions that include verbal, nonverbal, and environmental slights, snubs, or insults, which convey hostile derogatory or negative messages toward Jewish people are powerful reflectors of antisemitism (Cox, 2021). Awareness of these microaggressions is essential for dealing with antisemitism at personal and cultural levels. Remarks such as "Jewing someone down," a phrase recently used by city council members in Trenton, New Jersey (Pugliese, 2019), statements such as, "You don't look Jewish," or "You must be rich since you are a Jew, I wouldn't want my daughter to marry a Jew," are examples of microaggressions. Slights such as giving exams on a Jewish holiday serve to marginalize Jewish students, and though often an unconscious act, can be experienced as micro-aggressive indicators of antisemitism (Cox, 2021).

The cultural level includes negative stereotypes and beliefs that characterize Jewish people as different and unworthy. They are accepted by the oppressors and are used to justify oppressive actions. At the institutional level, these cultural beliefs can influence policies such as quotas placed on Jewish students in universities. The German government institutionalized antisemitism with the Nuremberg Laws passed in 1935 which denied basic human and civil rights to all Jews. Recent antisemitic comments and attacks by the Labor Party in the United Kingdom have been viewed as dangerous indicators of institutional antisemitism by a political party that threatens the well-being of Jewish people (Soley, 2019). Quota systems that limited the immigration of Jews into the United States during World War II are a vivid example of institutional or structural oppression as are the quotas or restrictions on the entry of other migrants into the country.

Antisemitism in the United States

In the United States, antisemitism in the 1920s was common in elite universities with Harvard, Dartmouth, Yale, and Columbia among those with quotas on the number of Jewish students (Karabel, 2006). In the 1930s medical schools based their quotas on beliefs that Jewish students were too bookish, aggressive, and greedy and concerns that too many were applying for admission (Halperin, 2019). Illustrative of the attitudes at the time is the example of Percy Bridgman, a Nobel laureate in physics, who wrote to Ernest Rutherford in 1925 on behalf of his Harvard student, J. Robert Oppenheimer. He described him as "a Jew, but entirely without the usual qualifications of his race. He is a tall, well set-up young man, with a rather engaging diffidence of manner, and I think you need have no hesitation whatever for any reason of this sort in considering his application" (Freedman, 2000). Public figures such as Charles A. Lindbergh, reinforced such stereotypes, "A few Jews add strength and character to a country, but too many create chaos" (Freedman, 2000, p. 65).

During the Second World War, antisemitism in the United States had a major impact on immigration policy as it limited the number of Jewish immigrants that the country would accept from Germany (Welch, 2014). Even with knowledge of the genocide occurring in Europe, the American public overwhelmingly opposed accepting more Jewish refugees (Wyman, 2018) resulting in strict quotas that limited Jewish immigration (Constitutional Rights Foundation, 2000).

The rising visibility of the White Nationalist movement in the United States continues to empower antisemites (Cox, 2023). Classifying Jews as a race that threatens American society and building on stereotypes empowers these extremists. In addition, the COVID-19 pandemic as it has isolated people at home has increased the groups' antisemitic expressions online, raising concerns about more antisemitic attacks (Kampeas, 2020). The virulence of these attacks was found in an FBI report documenting neo-Nazis and white nationalists' intent to infect Jews and policemen with the Coronavirus by spitting in their faces (Folley, 2020). The virus has also accentuated antisemitic stereotypes and myths that contribute to violence by fueling beliefs, spread through social media, that Jews are responsible for the virus and using it to make money (Greenblatt, 2020).

Factors Contributing to Antisemitism

Antisemitism is based on biases and stereotypes that depict Jews as an inferior and malicious race or a group who seeks to dominate societies. However, there is no such entity as a Jewish race, "Jewishness" is a religion or culture and not a distinct racial group. In fact, the concept of Jewishness itself is debatable due to the diversity of the Jewish population. In addition, the concept of race itself has been disputed as race is viewed as a social construct used to distinguish people and social hierarchy and not a biological classification (National Institute of Health [NIH], 2023). Thus, Jews may be considered an ethnic group or cultural group that shares and maintains specific cultural traditions and ties.

Moreover, it is impossible to use race as a discriminating variable in describing Jewish people. The Jewish population in the United States is composed of 12%–15% of people who describe themselves as nonwhite or "Jews of Color" (Stovall, 2022). This group is primarily composed of younger people and continues to increase. Subsequently, classifying Jews as white and privileged is not accurate and certainly overlooks the specific experiences that these nonwhite Jews may encounter.

When societies are threatened or those in power perceive themselves to be threatened, history shows that antisemitism tends to reveal itself. It reflects broad social and political issues and regressive, dangerous tendencies in the fabric of society (United Nations Educational, Scientific and Cultural Organization [UNESCO], 2017). These tendencies are reflected in the October 7th attack by Hamas on Israel as the attacks occurred soon after Israel's dialogues to normalize relations with Saudi Arabia, a coalition which could undermine the political power of Hamas (Sofaer, 2023).

Antisemitic tropes and beliefs continue to be powerful conduits of antisemitism as Jews remain a traditional target on which to place all the ills and problems in a society. For example, "The Great Replacement Theory" sees people of color, immigrants and Jews, as specific groups that threaten to pollute the white race (Clark, 2020). Stereotypic tropes based on claims that Jews caused the COVID-19 pandemic and that Jewish bankers are using lasers to start forest fires to finance railroads reflect these historical stereotypes (Zipperstein, 2020).

Findings from a National Survey of Social Workers

An exploratory survey of social workers that included 510 responses from students, practitioners, and educators was conducted in 2022 (Cox & Marlowe, 2023). The survey was distributed through newsletters and social media and focused on experiences with antisemitism. The surveys were anonymous and included both quantitative and qualitative data. The focus of the research was to understand social worker experiences and perceptions of antisemitism.

The majority of the respondents, 66%, were Jewish with the remainder, 34%, identifying as another religion. In comparison to the non-Jewish respondents, the Jewish group were more aware of antisemitic incidents in their schools and communities and less likely to report that their schools of social work included content on antisemitism in any of the classes. But, given these significant differences, it is important that both Jewish and non-Jewish respondents believed that antisemitism was a critical problem in the community and that social work should be doing something about it.

Particularly important were the qualitative responses where respondents were asked to elaborate on their answers. Among the student respondents, many responded that they were considered by social work faculty to be white and privileged and thus not compatible with those experiencing oppression. One student stated she was told that Jews are white and wealthy and have too much privilege to ask for affinity groups and that it was an insult to other oppressed groups to focus on antisemitism. The prevailing sentiment was that as Jews were white, they were not oppressed and therefore had no right to express such feelings.

In addition, students also commented on pervasive stereotypes held by faculty.

> Students took over the class with anti-Semitic and anti-Zionist rhetoric. They shut down anyone who tried to raise another opinion, and the teacher did not try to stop them.

> Was referred to as a "loud Bossy Jewish woman" by a professor; was frequently told by classmates that I was racist simply because I identified as Jewish.

> Mostly in my social work program—all Jews were considered "white" and therefore "oppressors". That was the general vibe.

Practitioners also commented on their experiences, reporting that they felt vulnerable in agencies, often subjected to antisemitic comments from other staff and peers. Among the comments were:

> There was antisemitism at my agency where there were "tremendous microaggressions, an employee made a Heil Hitler salute and people laughed, knowing I was Jewish…frequently heard, "Jewed him down…"

> Problems with taking off for religious holidays, comments 'Jew it down' from colleagues Israel bashing with a concomitant blaming of American Jews.

> I have been in practice for 40 years and there has never been an agency where I did not experience antisemitism.

> When I speak with others about my social work experiences, I encourage them to run far away, because until there is real change, social work is not a safe place for Jewish people.

Although these findings may be biased in that those responding to the survey are likely to be concerned about antisemitism, the study is the first and only research that has explored antisemitism among Jewish social work students and practitioners. These data suggest that antisemitism is a major issue in the profession that continues to oppress students and practitioners. Without dealing with it in the profession, it is difficult to challenge and counter it in the greater society.

Hamas Attacks on October 7, 2023

The attacks by Hamas on Israel on October 7th have been described as the largest mass killing of Jewish people since the Holocaust. Over 1300 people were murdered and 240 kidnapped and taken hostage. The attack also included atrocities, beheadings and the maiming, torture, and rape of children and women, not differentiating between Jewish and non-Jewish victims (Vinograd & Kershner, 2023).

People became afraid to wear Jewish symbols and anxious about attending Jewish meetings as well as synagogues. Families became concerned about sending their children to Jewish day schools and other activities. Concerns that schools were not supportive of Jewish children and that the atmosphere was hostile led to tensions and the resulting transfers of children due to fears for their safety (Toms, 2024). Many parents in London, England transferred their children out of Jewish schools due to fears of terrorism and threats to the Jewish community. In many London areas, schools were surrounded by police while they also carried out drills with children practicing how to use safe rooms (Stavrou, 2023).

Globally, all Jews have been perceived as responsible for Israeli policies and actions with phrases such as "Kill the Jews" and the chant from the "River to the Sea," heard in pro-Palestinian groups suggesting the elimination of Israel and the erasure of all Jewish people. Such perspectives not only foster antisemitism but also ignore the debates in Israel itself about government policies and actions in Gaza.

The attacks have made survivors of the Holocaust particularly anxious as they view the new threats as reminiscent of those associated with the Nazis (Gradstein, 2024). Many experience a new sense of trauma as the attacks are a reminder of attacks that happened years earlier and could be happening again. Consequently, social work with this group demands the clinical skills essential for working with those suffering from trauma and its consequences.

In discussing the recent wave of antisemitism and the role of "misinformation" in shaping views and attitudes that contribute to it, Hillary Clinton, former U.S. Secretary of State, had these comments at the Munich Security Conference in February 2024.

> What is so frustrating is that people have little to no information about all the efforts that were made, literally starting in 1948, but certainly moving most dramatically to the year 2000, to actually create a state for the Palestinian people. I say that because even when I'm teaching with very smart students and the students are from all over the world at the School of International and Public Affairs, Columbia University, they have no idea about any of

> this. They have no idea about the collapse of the peace process, or the rise of an intifada. They have no idea about then–prime minister Ariel Sharon, a man noted for his military experience, withdrawing from Gaza. They have no idea of Hamas' takeover of Gaza. They have no idea that another Israeli prime minister back when I was secretary of state, namely [Benjamin] Netanyahu, was willing at least to keep talking about some kind of two-state solution process. (Former U.S. Secretary of State Hillary Clinton, Munich Security Conference, 2024).

Interventions

Educating About Antisemitism

Educating about antisemitism should begin with a study of the Holocaust, the factors contributing to it and its impact, even in today's society. A national survey of persons aged 19–39 by the Claims Conference (2020) found that nearly 20 percent of Millennials and Generation Z believed the Jews caused the Holocaust. Moreover, approximately 49% had seen Nazi symbols on social media platforms. In addition, 64% of respondents felt that Holocaust education should be included in schools and 80% felt such teaching was essential to prevent it from happening again.

Consequently, it can be assumed that many students in social work programs have little knowledge or understanding of antisemitism and the extent to which it can threaten and harm Jewish people and societies (Cox, 2023). Educating students about the impact that antisemitism had on a whole population, how stereotypes and biases contribute to oppression, and how such oppression can be institutionalized is a foundation for understanding both antisemitism and the nefarious outcome that stereotyping and marginalization can have on individuals and groups.

The trauma and mental health problems experienced by victims of the Holocaust and even their relatives can be related to the trauma experienced by migrants and refugees who are forced to flee their native countries and seek refuge in another country. Migrants and refugees face many stressors associated with their relocation which can lead to mental health problems, particularly depression, often intensified by a lack of supports and feelings of alienation (WHO, 2022). Studying the experiences of Holocaust survivors and the trauma sometimes felt by their children can provide important insight into the experiences of those forced to migrate in today's world.

Anti-oppressive Practice

As discussed earlier, Social Work Competencies 2 and 3 (CSWE, 2022), which apply to the ability of being able to work with diverse groups and advancing the rights of all individuals and groups, directly pertain to the need for teaching about antisemitism. The precipitous rise in antisemitism, both in the United States and globally, demands that social workers understand the nature of this specific oppression and its impact on individuals and communities. Similar to educating about the oppression of any specific group, teaching about the experiences of Jewish people and how antisemitism impacts them is a critical part of the education program.

Anti-oppressive practice begins with understanding one's own biases and stereotypes. Reflecting on one's own beliefs and thoughts is essential for developing new ways of understanding and acting. Critical reflection helps to bring out unconscious thoughts and feelings which contribute to oppression and injustice. It is important that faculty themselves reflect on their own biases and stereotypes of Jewish people and how they may affect their own behavior and interactions (Cox, 2020).

Self-reflective exercises can also be helpful for Jewish students. Students who are not orthodox and assimilated may be helped to realize how being Jewish impacts their interactions with others. Orthodox students, who may be more accustomed to antisemitic actions, may be helped to develop effective responses to victimization rather than coping by normalizing it (Flax, 2021).

It is important to recognize that individuals respond in varying ways to antisemitism. Some may simply be annoyed or shocked while others are deeply troubled. Holocaust survivors and their descendants often experience mental health disorders related to the trauma they experienced and maybe particularly vulnerable to antisemitic rhetoric and the threats they pose (Flasch & Fulton, 2019). Students who have been harassed and intimidated may feel unsafe, while statements such as "You're Jewish, show me your horns" can make people anxious, dazed, and angry.

An innovative way to teach about antisemitism and racism focuses on the cases of Anne Frank and Emmett Till. Both were 15-year-old children murdered because of social hatred based on stereotypes and oppression. The comparison of the two cases vividly illustrates the similarities that hatred and social injustice can have on innocent people (Meyer, 2022). The class stimulates students to explore their own assumptions and confront their biases and could be adapted into social work education.

Teaching about antisemitism must include education about specific Jewish affiliations (Cox, 2020). The practices and beliefs of ultraorthodox communities, whose lives are often secluded from society and are dictated by Jewish law, are very different from that of the larger more secular Jewish community. Working with orthodox clients demands a knowledge of their beliefs and values and their influences on identity and relationships (Price & Silverstein, 2019).

At the same time, it is the Orthodox, who due to their seclusion and visibility, are most likely to be targeted. As an example, the upsurge in the Coronavirus among ultraorthodox communities in New York resulted in new restrictions on them aimed at containing the virus. The outcome was that the communities felt targeted and oppressed. Concomitantly, there was an increase in antisemitic acts toward all

Jews who were blamed for being responsible for and spreading the infection (Kushner, 2020).

Educating about antisemitism must include educating about advocacy. As it is a social issue, policies and institutions that ignore or condone it must be confronted. Administrators and educators in schools and universities must be made cognizant of the affront to Jewish students when exams or important meetings are scheduled on Jewish holidays. Recognizing statements made by faculty that are perceived as antisemitic and how these can impact Jewish students is important. The increase in antisemitism on college campuses that has threatened the security of Jewish students is a vivid example of the impact that it can have on their sense of security and even their ability to learn. In this regard, it is important to note that it was the advocacy of the students, their parents, and other community groups that contributed to giving greater recognition to the role of college administrators in condoning or ignoring antisemitism and its impact.

With the upsurge of antisemitism spread on social media sites, students can be encouraged to view these sites for noxious posts and quotes and to respond. Such efforts are ways to encourage them as change agents that are working against oppression and social injustice. Students may be encouraged to join with other marginalized groups who continue to be targeted and oppressed. Such efforts can bring more awareness and attention to the broad extent and propagation of hate in our society and the need for all to combat it.

The important role of social work in confronting antisemitism is underscored in the federal government's hearing on Confronting the Rise in Anti-Semitic Domestic Terrorism which expresses the need for social workers to join with community advocates and law enforcement in efforts to heal and work for justice in combatting antisemitism (Allen, 2020).

Equally important, incorporating antisemitism into the curriculum can be an important tool for educating students about the extremes that hate, prejudice, and oppression can reach. In our diverse society, there are continual threats to marginalized groups that deprive people off their human rights and security. Learning about the impact of antisemitism can be a platform for understanding the substance and potential harm that threats have to other marginalized groups. As antisemites tend to transfer their hatred to include other marginalized groups, its impact can be experienced by any that those in power see as undesirable or threats.

Conclusion

Antisemitism is one of the oldest forms of oppression and unfortunately one that shows no sign of abating. Whenever there are challenges to society or to those in control feel threatened, antisemitism begins to thrive. For over 2000 years, Jews have been the target for those who are dissatisfied with their lives or their societies. To permit this to continue deprives Jewish people of their rights to security and safety in the community. Many become fearful of even expressing Jewishness as it can be a trigger to harassment or even violence.

Social work is the one profession that focuses on overcoming oppression and developing societies where all feel safe and equal and can participate. Consequently, the profession cannot ignore antisemitism but must take an active stance in combatting it. Incorporating antisemitism into the curriculum is an initial and important step in the quest for a just society.

Social work interventions are necessary at all levels to ensure that antisemitism is confronted. At the micro level, this involves responding to antisemitic comments and microaggressions, working with both those who do the harassing as well as those who are the victims. At the mezzo level, social workers must ensure that institutions are respectful of Jewish persons so that they feel safe and secure in their environments. The structural level demands that policies and programs that ignore or target Jewish people are confronted and eradicated.

Rather than being reactive, the challenge for social work is to be proactive in the advancement of policies that assure the security and rights of Jewish people. The profession must commit to its mandate to fight oppression in all its forms, including antisemitism. Whereas it has been a leader in confronting racism, the same attention has not been given to antisemitism. Injustice in all its forms, which impedes the rights and freedoms of any group, including Jews, must be opposed. A rights-based profession must encompass the rights of all people and the eradication of all forms of group hatred. Ignoring antisemitism is condoning it, an action that directly undermines the goals of the profession.

Main Points

- The definition of antisemitism made by the International Holocaust Remembrance Alliance has been globally accepted by many countries.
- Incidents of antisemitism continue to increase.
- Antisemitism can be traced to the Old Testament.
- Throughout history Jews have been oppressed and excluded from society.
- Myths and stereotypes continue to fuel antisemitism.
- *The Protocols of the Elders of Zion* is a book used for centuries that describes a Jewish plan for world domination.
- Antisemitism feeds discrimination and targeting of other groups.
- Oppression of Jews appears at multi-levels including microaggressions and the cultural level.
- Conspiracy theories are powerful conduits of antisemitism.
- Both Jewish social work students and practitioners are subjects of antisemitism.
- The October 7, 2023, attacks on Israel by Hamas is the largest mass killing of Jewish people since the Holocaust.
- The October 7, 2023, attacks fueled dramatic increases in antisemitism globally.
- There is a need for more education in schools of social work on antisemitism.

- Misinformation contributes to antisemitism and other forms of oppression.
- Anti-oppressive practice begins with an understanding of one's own biases and stereotypes.
- Social work interventions are needed at all levels of practice to combat antisemitism.
- Incorporating antisemitism into the curriculum can be important in understanding the impact and nature of other forms of oppression.

Discussion Questions and Short Assignments

The following suggested discussion questions can be done in class in small groups or by having students write their own short papers.

- Discuss the definition of antisemitism and how it might apply to the students' work on oppression.
- Describe why Jews have been persecuted throughout history.
- Describe any stereotypes the students may have of Jewish people and where they learned these stereotypes.
- Research a recent conspiracy theory and discuss who it targets and the reasons for the targeting.
- Describe any incidents you may have encountered that are related to antisemitism.
- Discuss how antisemitism feeds the oppression of other specific groups.
- Provide examples of micro-aggressions that social workers may need to confront.
- Discuss why certain groups of Jewish people are most likely to be targeted.
- Discuss the types of advocacy a social worker can engage in to combat antisemitism.
- Why do you think social work has tended to ignore antisemitism?

In-Class Exercises: Understanding and Fighting Antisemitism

Goal: To deepen student's understanding of antisemitism and to learn strategies to fight antisemitism.

Phase I: Understanding antisemitism (20 min)

(a) Ask students to share what they believe antisemitism is.
(b) Provide a definition of antisemitism. The definition from the International Holocaust Remembrance Alliance (IHRA) can be used or one from another reliable source. Explain the different aspects of antisemitism, such as stereotypes, Holocaust denial, and demonization of Jews.
(c) Explain antisemitism and intersectionality.

Phase II: Examples of antisemitism (15–20 min)

Break the class up into groups of 3–4 students. Ask each group to do the following:

(a) Use the Anti-Defamation League (ADL) website (adl.org) to review antisemitic incidents and review the audit of antisemitic incidents.
(b) Reflect in their groups about the feelings that are evoked when discussing these.
(c) Report back about three recent incidents and their emotions related to them.

Phase III: Fighting antisemitism (15–20 min)

Following the completion of the exercises, students should return to their groups. Ask each group to do the following:

(a) Come up with three strategies to fight antisemitism. These strategies should address antisemitism in different areas, such as the workplace, the social work profession, social media, schools, etc.
(b) Share these ideas on a whiteboard for the entire class to see.
(c) Review all of the strategies with the class, encouraging each group to share their ideas. Focus on the implementation of these strategies and how they fit into social work.

Phase IV: Debrief and reflection (20 min)

(a) As a class, discuss how learning about antisemitism, antisemitic incidents, and ways to fight antisemitism have impacted them.
(b) Highlight the importance of human rights and social work's obligation to fight for social justice and an equitable and inclusive society.

References

Allen, J. (2020). *Confronting the rise in anti-semitic domestic terrorism*. Brookings Institute. https://www.brookings.edu/president/confronting-the-rise-in-anti-semitic-domestic-terrorism/

Alperin, R. (2016). Jewish self-hatred; the internalization of prejudice. *Clinical Social Work Journal, 44*(3), 221–230. https://doi.org/10.1007/s10615-016-0577-2

Altman, A. (2011). Exploration of Jewish ethnic identity. *Journal of Counseling and Development, 88*(4), 165–180. https://doi.org/10.1002/j.1556-6678.2010.tb00005.x

American Jewish Committee. (2024a). *The working definition of anti-Semitism: What does it mean, why is it important and what should we do with it*. https://www.ajc.org/the-working-definition-of-antisemitism

American Jewish Committee. (2024b). *The state of antisemitism in America 2023: AJC's survey of American Jews*. https://www.ajc.org/AntisemitismReport2023/AmericanJews

Anti-Defamation League. (2023). *Antisemitism & anti-LGBTQ+ hate converges in extremist and conspiratorial beliefs*. https://www.adl.org/resources/blog/antisemitism-anti-lgbtq-hate-converge-extremist-and-conspiratorial-beliefs

Anti-Defamation League. (2024). *U.S. Antisemitic incidents soared 140 percent in 2023-breaking all previous records*. https://www.adl.org/resources/press-release/us-antisemitic-incidents-soared-140-percent-2023-breaking-all-previous

Baron, S. (1952). *A social and religious history of the Jews: Christian Spain*. Columbia University Press.

Claims Conference. (2020). *First ever 50 state survey on holocaust knowledge among millennials and Gen Z reveals shocking results*. Claims Conference. http://www.claimscon.org/millennial-study/.

Clark, S. (2020). *How white supremacy returned to mainstream politics*. Center for American Progress. https://www.americanprogress.org/article/white-supremacy-returned-mainstream-politics/

Constitutional Rights Foundation. (2000). *United States immigration policy and Hitler's Holocaust*. Constitutional Rights Foundation. https://www.crf-usa.org/bill-of-rights-in-action/bria-10-2-a-united-states-immigration-policy-and-hitler-s-

Council on Social Work Education (CSWE). (2022). *Educational policy and accreditation standards*. https://www.cswe.org/accreditation/policies-process/2022epas/

Cox, C. (2021). Addressing antisemitism in social work education. *Journal of Religion & Spirituality in Social Work: Social Thought, 40*, 111–125.

Cox, C. (2023). Conspiracy theory: The demand for social work interventions. *Families in Society: The Journal of Contemporary Social Services, 0*. https://doi.org/10.1177/104438942311740

Cox, C., & Marlowe, D. (2023). Antisemitism in social work: Findings from an exploratory national survey. *Journal of Religion & Spirituality in Social Work: Social Thought*. https://doi.org/10.1080/15426432.2023.2289435

Flasch, P., & Fulton, C. L. (2019). Counseling Jewish Americans: Considerations for practice. *Counseling and Values, 64*(1), 2–19. https://doi.org/10.1002/cvj.12091

Flax, M. (2021). Antisemitism is just part of my day-to-day life: Coping mechanisms adopted by orthodox Jews in North London. *International Review of Victimology, 27*, 295–310. https://doi.org/10.1177/02697580211006663

Folley, A. (2020). FBI warns white supremacists encourage members to spread coronavirus to law enforcement Jews report. Retrieved from *The Hill*. https://thehill.com/blogs/blog-briefing-room/news/488919-fbi-white-supremacists-encouraging-members-to-spread

Freedman, J. (2000). *The temple of culture: Assimilation and anti-semitism in literary Anglo-America*. Oxford University Press.

Gold, N. (1996). Putting anti-semitism on the anti-racism agenda of North American schoolsof social work. *Journal of Social Work Education, 32*(1), 77–89. https://doi.org/10.1080/10437797.1996.10672286

Gradstein, L. (2024). *For holocaust survivors, October 7 Massacre Revived Grim Memories*. Retrieved from Voice of America https://www.voanews.com/a/for-holocaust-survivors-october-7-massacre-revived-grim-memories/7458077.html

Greenblatt, J. (2020). *Blaming jews for the spread of the coronavirus is anti-semitism pure and-simple*. NY Daily News. https://www.nydailynews.com/opinion/ny-oped-jews-coronavirus-antisemitism-20200408-4arvpei6wvd4td7eyqxpjfhaka-story.html

Halperin, E. (2019). Why did United States medical school admissions quota for Jewish students end. *The American Journal of the Medical Sciences, 358*(5), 317–325. https://doi.org/10.1016/j.amjms.2019.08.005

Kampeas, R. (2020, April 23). *With white supremacists driven online by the pandemic, anti- semitism trackers watch for new threats*. Jewish Telegraphic Agency.

Karabel, J. (2006). *The chosen: The hidden history of admission and exclusion at Harvard, Yale, and Princeton*. Mariner Books.

Kushner, A. (2020). *Pandemics have always incited anti-Semitism: Here's the history you need to know*. Forward, May 4, 2020. https://forward.com/culture/445419/pandemic-anti-semitism-coronavirus-black-death-typhus-cholera-immigrants/

Levin, B. (2019). *Trump goes full anti-semite in room full of Jewish people*. Vanity Fair. https://www.vanityfair.com/news/2019/12/donald-trump-anti-semitic-remarks

Lindemann, A. (1991). *The Jew accused: Three Antisemitic affairs (Dreyfus, Beilis, Frank (1894–1915))*. Cambridge University Press.

Meyer, M. (2022). Anne and Emmett, university education students' reactions to a course in countering racism and antisemitism in the classroom. *Journal of Curriculum and Pedagogy*. https://doi.org/10.1080/15505170.2022.2098209
Munich Security Conference. (2024). Retrieved from https://securityconference.org/en/msc-2024
National Association of Social Workers. (2015). *Standards and indicators for cultural competence in social work practice*. NASW. https://www.socialworkers.org/Practice/NASW-Practice-Standards-Guidelines/Standards-and-Indicators-for-Cultural-Competence-in-Social-Work-Practice.
National Association of Social Workers. (2021). *NASW code of ethics*. NASW. https://www.socialworkers.org/About/Ethics/Code-of-Ethics/Code-of-Ethics-English.
NIH (National Human Genome Research Institute). (2023). *Race*. https://www.genome.gov/genetics-glossary/Race
Price, J. and Silverstein, E. (2019). *Combating antisemitism in the classroom should not fall to Jews*. https://forward.com/opinion/426018/combatting-anti-semitism-in-the-classroom-should-not-fall-to-jews/
Pugliese, N. (2019). *Under pressure, Trenton officials apologize for antioSemitic remarks*. WHYY, Public Broadcasting Service. https://whyy.org/articles/some-trenton-officials-apologize-for-jew-her-down-remarks/
Sales, B. (2019). *America's 7.5 million Jews are older and more liberal than the country as whole*. Retrieved from https://www.jta.org/2019/10/07/united-states/americas-7-5-million-jews-are-older-whiter-and-more-liberal-than-the-country-as-awhole
Simon, R. (1997). *In the Golden land: A century of Russian and soviet Jewish immigration in America*. Praeger.
Sofaer, A. (2023). Don't let Hamas derail Saudi-Israeli Normalization. *The Hill*. Retrieved from https://thehill.com/opinion/international/4279356-dont-let-hamas-derail-saudi-israeli-normalization/
Soley, C. (2019). *Labour's institutional racism must be tackled before it destroys the party*. The New Statesman. https://www.newstatesman.com/politics/uk/2019/07/laboursinstitutional-racism-must-be-tackled-it-destroys-party
Stavrou, R. (2023). *Fear grips Jewish schools amid closures over safety concerns: Parents are not sleeping*. https://www.aol.com/fear-grips-jewish-schools-amid-144829023.html
Toms, L. (2024). *Jewish parents transfer children out of Oakland unified over antisemitism concerns*. https://www.cbsnews.com/sanfrancisco/news/jewish-parents-transfer-children-out-of-oakland-unified-over-antisemitism-concerns/
United Nations Educational, Scientific and Cultural Organization (UNESCO). (2017). *Addressing antisemitism through education*. UNESCO. https://www.unesco.org/en/education-addressing-antisemitism
Vinograd, C., & Kershner, I. (2023). *Israels attackers took about 240 hostages; here's what to know about them*. https://www.nytimes.com/article/israel-hostages-hamas-explained.html
Welch, S. (2014). American opinion toward Jews during the Nazi era: Results from quota sample polling during the 1930s and 1940s. *Social Science Quarterly, 95*, 615–635.
Whitfield, S. (2020). *"The protocols" why the protocols of the elders of Zion is still used by anti-Semites*. https://www.brandeis.edu/now/2020/september/whitfield-conversation.html
World Health Organization. (2022). *Refugee and migrant health*. https://www.who.int/news-room/fact-sheets/detail/refugee-and-migrant-health
Wyman, D. (2018). *The abandonment of the Jews. America and the holocaust, 1941–1945*. The New Press.
Zipperstein, S. (2020). *The conspiracy theory to rule them all, what explains the strange long life of the protocols of the elders of Zion*. https://www.theatlantic.com/politics/archive/2020/08/conspiracy-theory-rule-them-all/615550/

Chapter 3
The Holocaust and Its Impact

The Holocaust, the Nazi's war against and almost total destruction of the Jewish population of Europe, has been labeled the greatest genocide in history. The term Holocaust, derived from the Greek "a burnt offering," was first used in the 1960s to describe the murder of almost 6,000,000 Jews by the Nazis and their collaborators during World War II (Bergen, 2009). However, approximately 50 percent of the world's population does not know about the Holocaust or that it targeted Jewish people (World Jewish Congress and UNESCO, 2022). Understanding the Holocaust and its beginnings is critical for understanding the impact of antisemitism today.

Stages of the Holocaust

Laws

Germany began its persecution of the Jews in 1933 with the rise to power of the Nazi party. The Nazis divided people into two racial groups, Aryans who they considered superior to all, and those who were inferior, Jews, Slavs, Romas, and Blacks. The inferior groups, particularly the Jews, were seen as poignant threats to the Aryan race which needed to be controlled and eliminated. The restrictions on the Jews went through steps that continued to limit and ostracize them from German society.

Between 1933 and 1939, a series of laws and restrictions were introduced in Germany that were directed at Jewish people, which composed less than 1% of its population (Montreal Holocaust Museum, 2018). The restrictions on the Jewish population began with a German boycott of all Jewish business in April 1933, followed quickly by the removal of Jews from all civil service professions and the banning of Jewish teachers from public schools. Within the same month, Jews were forbidden from taking the bar for the legal profession, and universities and schools

C. B. Cox, D. B. Marlowe, *Social Work and Antisemitism*,
https://doi.org/10.1007/978-3-031-72771-9_3

limited the enrollment of Jewish students to 1.5% of the total student body. Other laws passed in 1933 banned Jews from influential positions in the arts and from owning farms. More anti-Jewish laws followed, including in 1935, the Nuremberg Laws, that forbade marriage and sexual relationships between Jews and Germans with the ruling that only persons of German or related blood could be citizens.

On November 9 and 10, 1938, the Nazis orchestrated the burning and destruction of synagogues and Jewish-owned businesses in Germany, Austria, and parts of occupied Czechoslovakia with instructions that fire marshals could not intervene to stop the fires. The night, known as Kristallnacht or "Night of the Broken Glass," refers to the thousands of windows and synagogues that were shattered. The event, carefully planned and organized by the Nazi party, marks the escalation of civic persecution of the Jews with thousands of Jewish businesses looted and properties destroyed. The government declared that the Jews themselves were responsible for the violence and were fined one billion Reichsmarks with their insurance confiscated. Approximately 30,000 Jewish men were arrested and sent to concentration camps (Montreal Holocaust Museum, 2018).

In the following years, Jews were restricted from most professions, including ownership of businesses. Identity cards were issued to Jewish people and passports also identified them as Jews. Jewish people were prohibited from owning cars or attending cultural events. All Jewish children were expelled from public schools. The movement of Jews throughout the country was strictly curtailed.

Shocking to many German Jews was the complicity of the non-Jewish Germans who watched the vicious attacks, arrests, and destruction and did not intervene (Bergen, 2009). In fact, many of the non-Jewish population benefited from the losses of their Jewish neighbors. Not surprisingly, this confiscation and redistribution of Jewish property and valuables was a key element in the Holocaust.

Given the knowledge that the world had of the actions occurring in Germany, there was little global response. In the United States, Jewish leaders were indecisive in how to respond and were reluctant to admit more Jewish refugees during a period when work was scarce. This reluctance influenced later refugee policy toward Jews trying to escape Europe (Lebovic, 2018).

Ghettos

Ghettos were places within cities and towns where Jews were forced to live with many having walls around them so that it was difficult to leave. They were first created in Poland in 1939–1940 in Lodz and Warsaw and after 1941, created in parts of Eastern Europe, including Hungary, where they were used as temporary holding places until deportation to concentration camps could occur. Guards prevented Jews from leaving the ghettos.

In some ghettos, residents became forced laborers assigned to factories that contributed to the war effort. Food and medical supplies were scarce in the ghettos with thousands dying from starvation, disease, and exhaustion from the labor. The

Germans also frequently assaulted the Jews submitting them to beatings, torture, and arbitrary shootings (U.S. Holocaust Memorial Museum, n.d.-a). Beginning in 1941–1942, as a part of the Final Solution, the Germans began conducting mass murders in the ghettos.

Resistance movements occurred in many ghettos. The Warsaw ghetto uprising in 1943 was the most famous and perhaps most "successful." It began in April 1943 when Germans entered the ghetto to remove people for deportation to Treblinka. The deportations had begun in July 1942 and by September, more than 200,000 inhabitants had been deported from the ghetto to extermination camps.

The uprising began in April 1943. Initially, the fighters took control of the ghetto away from the Germans, barricading themselves in bunkers and continuing to attack. On the eve of Passover, 1943, the Germans who had been surprised by the resistance, attacked with several thousand troops, burning and blowing up buildings, as well as the Great Synagogue of Warsaw (Edelman, 1990). On May 8, 1943, the Germans captured the resistance headquarters and declared victory over the Jewish resistance. More than 13,000 Jews were killed during the uprising with the remaining 50,000 sent to Majdanek and Treblinka (Moshe, 2011). The ghetto uprising was the first urban uprising against the Germans and was the inspiration for further smaller uprisings in other ghettos (Lichten & Segel, 1963).

The Final Solution

The Final Solution to the Jewish Problem was instituted in 1941 and lasted through 1945. The ultimate goal was the murder through mass extermination of all of the Jews of Europe. It was the outcome of the early beliefs and writings of Adolf Hitler. In 1919, Hitler stated that the Jews were an alien race and not a religion and were a threat to Germany as they dominated societies through the power of money (Browning, 2007). In contrast to Aryans, who saw work as a moral duty and virtue, Jews were viewed as nomadic people who abhorred work, lived as parasites, and were incapable of culture. In addition, Hitler saw them as a Bolshevik threat focused on spreading Marxism in order to dominate states by destroying existing races and economies (Browning, 2007).

In the early years of Hitler's reign, deporting Jews from Europe to Africa or another colony was considered a way of solving the Jewish problem. A plan to ship all European Jews to Madagascar using British ships was formulated in 1940. The plan would resettle a million Jews a year for 4 years with Jewish assets paying for the resettlement. However, as the Nazis did not defeat Britain, the plan could not be carried out. Subsequently, plans to move the Jewish populations to the Soviet Union were formulated, but with the prolonged war and eventual defeat by the Soviets, this plan was also abandoned.

The "Final Solution," the plan for the extermination of all of the Jews of Europe, was formulated in January 1942, by a group of German leaders meeting in Wannsee, a suburb of Berlin (Yad Vashem, n.d.-c). The extermination began in the Soviet

Union with the army, police, and local collaborators systematically murdering local Jews. They first targeted men of military age and proceeded to entire Jewish communities. Often, the killings were committed in daylight so they could be easily seen by others.

Spreading from the Soviet Union, these mass killings were conducted in more than 1500 cities and communities throughout Eastern Europe (U.S. Holocaust Memorial Museum Encyclopedia, n.d.-a). They tended to follow a specific pattern beginning with the roundup of Jewish people, taking them outside of the town where they were forced to dig large pits into which their bodies were thrown. In addition to shooting, mobile vans were used to suffocate people, with the bodies also disposed of in the mass graves. Although the murders were orchestrated and led by the SS and the special forces, they were frequently joined by local collaborators.

In July 1942, extermination camps were created in Poland and Germany to which Polish Jews were deported and murdered. Extermination centers, Sobibor, Belzac, Chelmo, Treblinka, and Auschwitz, were created in the Spring of 1942 (Yad Vashem, n.d.-c). Jews were transported across Europe to these killing centers, usually by train and in freight cars, under the guise of being resettled. The cars were overcrowded, often forcing people to stand for days without food. The cars lacked bathrooms or heat, with many dead, before reaching the camps. Upon reaching the camps, those who looked able were often selected for labor, while the majority were immediately gassed. Jews were also forced to assist with the killings by removing bodies from the gas chambers, sorting through belongings, and burning the bodies in specially designed ovens.

Collaborators

Although the Nazis were responsible for the development and implementation of the Holocaust, German citizens and those of other occupied and annexed countries participated. The SS, Gestapo, and the police were actively involved in the arrests and murders of Jews but other German institutions, civil service, banks, railroads, industries, and medical, joined by locating and informing on Jewish people. Many collaborated with the government by reporting on people who they suspected were Jewish. Reasons for informing included antisemitism, a strong belief in Nazi doctrine, fear, personal gain, and personal dislike of the person (The Weiner Holocaust Library, n.d.). Teachers collaborated through their teaching of antisemitic beliefs and propaganda, while many in business profited from the liquidation of Jewish companies and banks.

Collaborators were also other governments who passed antisemitic regulations and cooperated with the Germans, such as Vichy France which assisted by locating and arresting Jews. The Netherlands, following their occupation by Germany, banned Jews from civil service and forced Jews to register their assets. Dutch Jews were segregated and 15,000 were sent to forced labor camps and Auschwitz and Sobibor. Less than 25 percent of Dutch Jewry survived the Holocaust (U.S. Holocaust Memorial Museum, n.d.-a).

Given the collaboration of European countries with Germany, it is important to recognize that Denmark, occupied by the Germans in 1940, was unique in its treatment of its Jewish population. The Danish government claimed there was no Jewish problem as Jews were like all other citizens. Consequently, they were not forced to wear identifying stars, and were not isolated or barred in the community or from employment (Yad Vashem, n.d.-d). The Danish Lutheran Church was a major force in saving and protecting the Danish Jews. The Church acted on its sacred belief that all human beings were linked to each other. In total, approximately 120 Danish Jews died during the Holocaust, and within 1 week of the end of the German occupation, the government established a system for any property restitution required by Jewish people (U.S. Holocaust Memorial Museum, n.d.-b).

The Holocaust ended in 1945 with the surrender of Germany. In addition to the near extermination of the Jews of Europe, millions of others were murdered, including over three million Soviet prisoners of war, more than 250,000 Romani (gypsies), approximately 300,000 people with disabilities, thousands of homosexual men, Black people, and Jehovah's witnesses (Centre for Holocaust Education, 2016). All of these groups were viewed as threats to Germany and the purity of the Aryan race, they had to be exterminated.

Questions remain regarding who knew about the Holocaust and the fate of the Jews. The Germans kept the extent of the murders from the public, but rumors spread along with letters and photographs. People knew about the deportations of the Jews, but less was known about the extermination camps. In 1942, the Allies were informed about the murders, but as there was little evidence, the stories were generally perceived as inconceivable. The United States refused to expand its immigration quotas to permit the entry of more Jews either before or during the War. Between 1941 and 1945, the Final Solution killed two out of every three European Jews living in Germany and in the countries it annexed or occupied (U.S. Holocaust Memorial Museum, n.d.-a).

After the Holocaust

Prior to the Holocaust, the Jewish population in all of Europe approximated 9.3 million persons. In May 1945, the Jewish population in all of Europe was approximately 1,500,000, and the Jewish population of Germany was 60,000 persons (U.S. Holocaust Memorial Museum, n.d.-a). Most of these survivors were liberated from concentration camps, while a minority had hidden during the war and others had survived using false identity papers.

Survivors were physically, mentally, and emotionally exhausted as they comprehended the losses they experienced as well as the terror they had endured. Many realized that they had lost entire families and felt despair and emptiness. The original plan of the Allies was to repatriate survivors to their home countries, but this became infeasible as local populations were often hostile and antisemitic. Following liberation, there were more than 250,000 Jewish displaced persons in Europe

(U.S. Holocaust Memorial Museum, n.d.-a). These were people who no longer had homes to return to or were unwilling or unable to return as they were anxious about their safety. In a poll taken in 1946 of over 9000 displaced persons, only one was interested in returning to his country (Yad Vashem, n.d.-e).

Many who returned home had found intense antisemitism and hostility from their neighbors. Pogroms in Poland against Jewish survivors contributed to fear about their future in the country. In Poland, more than 1000 Jews were killed in the first year after liberation (Warhaftig, 1946). The United Nations Relief and Rehabilitation Administration (UNRRA) administered Displaced Persons (DP) camps in Germany, Austria, and Italy where people could stay. The immediate concern for many was to find relatives who may have survived the war and the camps. The UNRRA formed a Central Tracing Bureau to help people locate relatives as well as publish lists of survivors. The camps developed schools and social centers with many volunteer agencies assisting. The camps were noted for being harsh and often lacking sufficient food and shelter, with Jewish people often living in the same camps as Nazi collaborators. The Harrison Report of July 1945 documented the conditions leading to the United States responding with efforts to improve conditions (Penkower, 2016). Almost all DP camps were closed by 1952.

Concomitantly, the United Nations pressured Britain who controlled the Palestinian territory, to permit the settling of more Jews. Britain had resisted this immigration but in 1947, the UN Special Committee on Palestine recommended that the region be portioned into an Arab and Jewish state. In May 1948, the state of Israel was created leading to the almost immediate immigration of 250,000 Jewish survivors from Europe (U.S. Department of State, Office of the Historian, 2018).

Impact of the Holocaust

The United Nations (UN) was created shortly after the ending of World War II, in October 1945, with 29 nations ratifying its Charter. The UN's objectives include maintaining international peace and security, protecting human rights, delivering humanitarian aid, promoting sustainable development, and upholding international law (UN, 2018).

In December 1948, the Universal Declaration of Human Rights was passed by the United Nations, affirming the faith in the dignity and worth of the human person. Although the Declaration does not mention the Holocaust, it declares the importance of forbidding discrimination based on race or religion with the declarations that all are equal before the law and all have the right to seek asylum from prosecution. The Nuremberg Trials which held individual Nazis responsible for the prosecution and treatment of Jews led to the formation of the term, "Crimes Against Humanity," consequently holding all countries responsible for the treatment of their own citizens.

Genocide

The term "genocide" was coined by a Polish Jewish scholar who emigrated to the United States having lost his whole family in the Holocaust. He felt that the terms barbarity and vandalism did not convey the extent of the atrocities, destruction, and murder committed by the Nazis of a particular racial or ethnic group (Gigliotti & Earl, 2020).

The Genocide Convention was the first human rights treaty adopted by the United Nations in 1948 (UN Office on Genocide Prevention, n.d.). The treaty criminalizes genocide and obligates states to pursue the enforcement of its prohibition. It was a direct response to the Holocaust and its atrocities, placing the crime under international law. The Convention compels member states to prevent and/or punish any attempt to destroy a group. In 1997, the International Tribunal for Rwanda applied genocide law to the country, the first case under the Convention and one in which rape during war was declared a specific crime.

The Convention, created after the Holocaust, gives substance to the importance of human rights and the consequences, which can occur when a society ignores and flagrantly dismisses them. The laws are significant in that they recognize that people can be deprived of their humanity even before their death (Gigliotti & Earl, 2020). Accordingly, the Holocaust played a key role in setting an agenda for human rights law.

Impact on Survivors and Their Children

Much has been written about the impact of the Holocaust on survivors and societies (Levi, 1993). Primo Levi, a survivor and psychologist, expresses the extent to which the Holocaust and the camp deprived people of their basic humanity and human rights. Upon arrival in Auschwitz, a person was deprived of everything they loved and everything that was associated with identity and dignity. In addition, the laws of the camps, as they stripped people of their identity, defied and deprived people of all human rights.

Studies of the impact of the Holocaust on survivors, particularly on those who were prisoners of the death camps, detail the struggles they endured just to survive. As stated by Elie Wiesel, "never shall I forget that night, the first night in camp which has turned my life into one long night" (Wiesel, 2006). For many, the shock of the terror was followed by apathy and emotional hibernation (Chodoff, 1997). Many engaged in regressive behavior, becoming dependent on the SS guards, while others lived in denial and isolation often suppressing all emotions.

With liberation, personality disorders and psychiatric problems were common. The Concentration Camp Syndrome (Chodoff, 1997), marked by hypervigilance, sleep disturbances, night terrors, and often anxiety and fatigue caused difficulty in concentrating. During interviews, these symptoms could become intense as survivors became preoccupied with experiences in the camps. Many also experienced deep feelings of guilt and loss. "Survivor guilt" was a response to having survived while others did not or feelings that they may have endangered the lives of others (Chodoff, 1963). For some the guilt and shame made them envy the dead for their peace (Schneider, 1975).

Post-traumatic stress disorder (PTSD) has been applied to their symptoms due to the presence of unrelenting anxiety as well as the trauma that survivors experienced. Living with the guilt and the anxiety kept many survivors from forgetting and often resulted in their reliving experiences in the camp. According to Schnieder (1975), it was the ability to come to terms with the guilt and loss which determined whether they could be reintegrated into society.

For survivors, children were critically important as they represented their success in defeating the plans for genocide. However, the traumas experienced by parents were often transferred to their children. The "child of the survivor" syndrome refers to the family that overprotects the child from its environment to the degree that the child becomes overly fearful and reacts to strangers and new situations with distrust and suspicion with paranoia about external forces (Plunka, 2018).

Children often felt guilt as they might experience happiness that was denied to their parents. If they made their parents unhappy, they frequently felt guilty for their actions (Kestenberg, 1980). In addition, children frequently became overachievers as they felt they must fulfill their parents' hopes. Research has also found that children whose parents have PTSD have a greater sense of filial obligation than other children and thus greater filial anxiety with regard to obligations to their parents and the need to protect them from further pain (Shira et al., 2019). Such feelings can cause additional stress if they have difficulty in meeting their parents' needs.

Interventions

Clinical Interventions

In working with survivors and their children, clinicians must be trained in working with post-traumatic syndromes and their often-long-lasting effects. They must be knowledgeable about the Holocaust and the experiences of Jewish people both during and after the War. They must also be knowledgeable about how these experiences may have impacted their children. Chapters in this book discuss these interventions in depth as well as offer case studies that help to illustrate the conditions and issues faced by these groups.

Teaching About the Holocaust

"Never Again" is a phrase often used in referring to the Holocaust. It was first used by liberated prisoners of Buchenwald concentration camp and since then has been used at Holocaust memorials and remembrance days and continues to be evoked in documentaries and stories about the Holocaust. Recently, German Chancellor Olaf Scholz, in a memorial for the Holocaust, stated "Never again is every day as people must continue to fight against antisemitism, racism, and hatred for our democracy" (Grieshaber, 2024).

Educating people about the Holocaust is important as it identifies the factors that can result in genocide. The Holocaust did not just happen. It began with small steps focused on individuals that became major steps encompassing an entire population. It progressed from restrictions to policies of extermination. Warning signs were ignored as people did not believe their significance or even that such intolerance could be a reality. Jewish people themselves, having been acculturated into so many societies, could not believe that they could be so hated or that such unified efforts to destroy them could actually exist.

Knowledge of the Holocaust highlights the value of promoting human rights while it also illustrates the dangers of unchecked prejudice, discrimination, antisemitism, and dehumanization (UNESCO, 2023). It is important for understanding the motivations and beliefs that lead people to participate in the hatred or ignore it. It is important not simply as a historical event, but for becoming aware of warning signs and acts based on prejudice and discrimination that can lead to mass persecution. Consequently, Holocaust education is critical for assuring that it does not happen again.

As discussed by UNESCO (n.d.), *Teaching about the Holocaust and Genocide*:

- Demonstrates the fragility of all societies and of the institutions that are supposed to protect the security and rights of all and how institutions can be turned against.
- Highlights aspects of human behavior that affect all societies, such as the susceptibility to scapegoating and the desire for simple answers to complex problems; the potential for extreme violence and the abuse of power; and the roles that fear, peer pressure, indifference, greed, and resentment can play in social and political relations.
- Demonstrates the dangers of prejudice, discrimination, and dehumanization.
- Deepens reflection about contemporary issues that affect societies around the world, such as the power of extremist ideologies.
- Teaches about human possibilities in extreme and desperate situations, by considering the actions of perpetrators and victims as well as other people who, due to various motivations, may tolerate, ignore, or act against hatred and violence.
- Draws attention to the international institutions and norms developed in reaction to the Second World War and the Holocaust.
- Highlights the efforts of the international community in responding to modern genocide.

Holocaust Denial

Holocaust denial is any attempt to negate the established facts of the Nazi genocide of European Jews (U.S. Holocaust Memorial Museum, 2021). Holocaust denial and distortion are particularly dangerous as they distort the course of the Holocaust and its toll. Denial and distortion are specific forms of antisemitism that claim that the Holocaust was invented or exaggerated with Jews as the instigators in efforts to advance their self-interests.

Hate speech and oppression that separates and targets any group must be recognized as they are potential triggers for attacks on basic human rights and atrocities. Following are examples of Holocaust denial (U.S. Holocaust Memorial Museum, 2021):

- Public statements denying or minimizing national and societal responsibility for crimes against Jews or collaboration with Nazi Germany.
- Attempts to limit academic and public discourse on Holocaust history by means of legislation and penalties.
- Political interference with the accurate representation of history in museums and exhibitions and at historical sites.
- The rejection of the importance of Holocaust remembrance and memorials by political and societal leaders.
- Efforts to glorify horror, exonerate, or otherwise rehabilitate Holocaust-era historical figures or entities despite their association with crimes against humanity, collaboration with Nazi Germany, or direct involvement in the persecution and murder of Jews.

Following the War, many European countries responded with doubts about atrocities (Lipstadt, 1993). In response, 17 European countries, as well as Israel and Canada, instituted laws that view Holocaust denial as a punishable offense. Concomitantly, holocaust denial continues to increase in parts of Europe and Eastern Europe and in the United States (Lipstadt, 1993).

The Institute for Historical Review (IHR), created in 1978, is a network of deniers that spreads publications and videos through its website that denies the Holocaust. Although the materials have been discredited by both academics and the courts, they continue to be viewed and are influential in supporting antisemitism (Against Holocaust Distortion, 2024).

On January 20, 2022, the United Nations approved a resolution condemning Holocaust denial and distortion and urged all nations and social media companies to take active measures to combat antisemitism and Holocaust denial or distortion (UN, 2022). The resolution was put forth by Israel and approved by consensus of the General Assembly with only Iran objecting. The resolution was declared as a warning to all people of the dangers of hatred, bigotry, racism, and prejudice.

The Lessons of the Holocaust

As denial and antisemitism continue to spread, it is critical that attention be given to the strong role of social media in fostering misinformation and lies and spreading theories and accusations (Prince, 2024). The ignorance as well as the false beliefs enable the spread and acceptance of antisemitism. Challenging these myths and responding with facts can be critical in halting the spread of antisemitism. Closing accounts of those spreading antisemitic posts as well as posting counter-narratives can be effective but demand to be done on a large scale and really call for the involvement of both government and non-government organizations (Indiana University Institute for the Study of Contemporary Antisemitism, 2017).

Conclusion

The Holocaust continues to play a significant role in understanding antisemitism and its impact. The genocide by the Nazis that killed over six million Jewish people as well as other "undesirable" groups offers an indelible imprint of what can happen when hate and oppression are permitted to flourish. The saying "Never Again," needs little interpretation or explanation. At the same, without understanding the horrors and genocide that were committed, the statement makes little sense. Consequently, learning about the Holocaust is a foundation for comprehending the impact that antisemitism may have on Jewish people. The Holocaust began with small steps and restrictions and culminated in concentration and death camps. However, there are many who deny its existence or its magnitude.

The trauma experienced by survivors and often passed on to their children cannot easily be overcome while many are burdened by feelings of "survivor guilt." Clinical interventions can be important in reducing the stress and psychological issues of both generations. At the same time, clinicians must be specifically trained in working with survivors as antisemitism itself can trigger memories of the Holocaust and new worries that it is beginning again.

Consequently, social workers can play significant roles working at the micro level to provide counseling and services to survivors and their families. At the same time, they can use their macro skills to advocate for the censure of hate and antisemitic tropes and myths on social media and elsewhere. Particularly important are the roles they can assume in advocating for policies that challenge antisemitism as well as assuring that persons are educated about it. Advocating for education about the Holocaust with its inclusion in school curricula can help to ensure "Never Again" is truly never again.

Main Points

- The Holocaust, derived from the Greek term meaning "a burnt offering," refers to the genocide of approximately six million Jews by the Nazis during World War II.
- The persecution of Jews began in 1933 with the rise of the Nazi Party in Germany, starting through small steps followed by further laws and prohibitions.
- Jews were increasingly confined to ghettos, walled areas in cities which they were prevented from leaving.
- The Final Solution, the plan for the extermination of all the Jews in Europe, was written by the Nazis in 1942, with Jews transported from across Europe to the killing centers.
- The War ended in 1945, resulting in the near extermination of the entire Jewish population of Europe as well as the mass murder of other groups seen as threats to society.
- In May 1948, Israel was created resulting in the mass immigration of over 250,000 persons.
- Holocaust survivors faced extreme trauma, including psychological disorders and "survivor guilt," which often impacted their children as well.
- The first human rights treaty adopted by the UN in 1948 was the Genocide Convention, created in direct response to the Holocaust that criminalized genocide.
- The Holocaust had an immense impact on survivors, including trauma and a sense of dehumanization.
- Holocaust denial continues and contributes to antisemitism.
- Holocaust education is considered crucial in preventing future genocides and combating antisemitism.
- Social media plays a significant role in spreading Holocaust denial and antisemitism.
- *"Never Again":* The phrase underscores the importance of Holocaust education and remembrance to prevent future genocides and combat ongoing antisemitism.

Discussion Questions and Short Assignments

The following suggested discussion questions can be done in class in small groups or by having students write their own short papers:

- Define the term "Holocaust" and explain its origins.
- Describe the initial steps taken by the Nazis to isolate and persecute Jewish people.
- Kristallnacht is an important event in the history of the Holocaust. Explain what occurred and its significance.

- What was the Final Solution and what was its impact?
- Discuss the situation of the survivors of the Holocaust including the role of Displaced Persons Camps.
- What are some of the psychological and emotional impacts of the Holocaust on survivors?
- Describe what is meant by Holocaust denial and why it is significant.
- Discuss the importance of being educated about the Holocaust.
- Describe how the Holocaust influenced the creation of the United Nations and several of its important documents.
- Discuss the roles that social work can play at both the micro and macro levels in working with individuals affected by the Holocaust and in ensuring that it does not happen again.

In-Class Exercises

Goal: To have social work students gain a deeper understanding of the Holocaust and its impact on Jewish people today.

Phase I: Beginning discussion (20–30 min).

After teaching about the Holocaust, ask students to share their thoughts and feelings about it. Ask students why understanding the Holocaust is crucial for social workers.

Phase II: Survivor testimonies (30–60 min).

Use reliable resources (One Survivor Remembers, USC Shoah Foundation, United States Holocaust Memorial Museum) to show Holocaust survivors' testimonies to the class.

Phase III: Debrief (15–20 min).

After viewing the testimonies with the class, process what they saw and use discussion questions.

(a) What stood out to them?
(b) How were these atrocities allowed to happen?
(c) What was most upsetting about the testimonies?
(d) Was there something new that they learned? And what was it?

Phase IV: Impact of the Holocaust today (20 minutes).

Continue the discussion with the students and then move to the current impact of the Holocaust.

(a) What is the impact of the Holocaust on Jewish people today?
(b) Why is "Never Again" a phrase that is used by Jewish people?
(c) What is the impact of Holocaust denial on Jewish people?

Emphasize to students that the creation of the United Nations, the Universal Declaration of Human Rights (UDHR), and the Genocide Convention are direct responses to the Holocaust.

References

Against Holocaust Distortion. (2024). A brief history of Holocaust denial and distortion. *Protect the facts*. https://www.againstholocaustdistortion.org/news/a-brief-history-of-holocaust-denial-and-distortion

Arens, M. (2011). *Flags over the Warsaw Ghetto*. Gefen Publishing House.

Bergen, D. (2009). *War and genocide: A concise history of the Holocaust*. Rowman and Littlefield.

Bergmann, M., & Jucovy, M. (1982). *Generations of the Holocaust* (p. 100). Columbia University Press.

Browning, C. (2007). *The origins of the final solution*. The Evolution of Nazi Jewish Policy, September 1939-March, 1942, Bison Books.

Centre for Holocaust Education. (2016). *Non-Jewish victims of Nazi persecution and murder*. https://holocausteducation.org.uk/wp-content/uploads/1.-Non-JewishVictimsOfNaziPersecutionMurder-Digital.pdf

Chodoff, P. (1963). Late effects of the concentration camp syndrome. *Archives of General Psychiatry, 8*, 323–333.

Chodoff, P. (1997). The Holocaust and its effects on survivors, an overview. *Political Psychology, 18*, 147–157. https://www.jstor.org/stable/379198-

Deutsche Welle. (2024, January 27). *Never again: Holocaust remembered in Germany*. https://www.dw.com/en/never-again-holocaust-remembered-in-germany/a-68100050

Edelman, M. (1990). The ghetto fights, Warsaw, 1941–43. Bookmarks.

Gigliotti, S., & Earl, H. (2020). *A companion to the Holocaust*. Wiley-Blackwell.

Grieshaber, K. (2024). *Never again is every day: Scholz's Antisemitism warning on holocaust remembrance day*. Retrieved from https://www.timesofisrael.com/never-again-is-every-day-scholzs-antisemitism-warning-on-holocaust-remembrance-day/

Indiana University, Institute for the Study of Contemporary Antisemitism. (2017). *Best Practices to Combat Antisemitism on Social Media,* https://isca.indiana.edu/documents/Report-to-State-Department-on-Best-Practices.pdf

Kellner, H. (1994). Never again is now. *History and theory, 33*, 127–128. https://doi.org/10.2307/2505381

Kestenberg, J. (1980). Psychoanalyses of children of survivors from the Holocaust: Case presentations and assessment. *Journal of the American Psychoanalytic Association, 28*.

Lebovic, M. (2018). *How to explain the timid reaction of American Jewish leaders to Kristallnacht*. https://www.timesofisrael.com/how-to-explain-the-timid reaction-of-american-jewish-leaders-to-kristallnacht/

Levi, P., 1919–1987. (1993). *Survival in Auschwitz: the Nazi assault on humanity*. New York: Toronto: Collier Books; Maxwell Macmillan Canada.

Lichten, J. L., & Segel, H. B. (1963). The Warsaw ghetto uprising: Legend and reality. *The Polish Review, 8*(3), 61–69. http://www.jstor.org/stable/25776492

Lipstadt, D. (1993). *Denying the Holocaust: The growing assault on truth and memory*. Penguin.

Montreal Holocaust Museum. (2018). *A brief history of the Holocaust, a reference tool*.

Penkower, M. (2016). The Earl Harrison Report: Its genesis and its significance. *American Jewish Archives Journal, 68*(1), 1–75.

Phillipps, R. (1978). Impact of Nazi holocaust on children of survivors. *American Journal of Psychotherapy, 32*, 370–378. https://doi.org/10.1176/appi.psychotherapy.1978.32.3.370

Plunka, G. A. (2018). Symptoms of psychological problems among children of Holocaust survivors: Faye Sholiton's the interview. *Journal of Literature and Trauma Studies, 7*(1), 1–22. https://doi.org/10.1353/jlt.2018.0000

Prince, C. (2024). *Are conspiracy theories about Oct 7 a form of Holocaust denial? Experts weigh.* https://www.timesofisrael.com/are-conspiracy-theories-about-oct-7-a-new-form-of-holocaust-denial-experts-weigh-in

Schneider, G. (1975). Survivor and guilt feelings of Jewish concentration camp victims. *Jewish Social Studies, 37*, 74–83. https://www.jstor.org/stable/4466862

Shira, A., Menashe, R., & Bensimon, M. (2019). Filial anxiety and sense of obligation among offspring of Holocaust survivors. *Aging and Mental Health, 23*, 752–761. https://doi.org/10.1080/13607863.2018.1448970

The Weiner Holocaust Library. (n.d.). German collaboration and complicity. *The Holocaust explained*, Retrieved from https://www.theholocaustexplained.org/resistance-responses-collaboration/german-collaboration-and-complicity/

U.S. Department of State, Office of the Historian. (2018). *Creation of Israel, 1948*. Retrieved from https://history.state.gov/milestones/1945-1952/creation-israel

U.S. Holocaust Memorial Museum. (2021). *Holocaust memory at risk*. Holocaust Museum.

U.S. Holocaust Memorial Museum. (n.d.-a). *Holocaust encyclopedia*. Retrieved from https://encyclopedia.ushmm.org/

U.S. Holocaust Memorial Museum. (n.d.-b). Denmark. *Holocaust Encyclopedia*. Retrieved from https://encyclopedia.ushmm.org/content/en/article/denmark

UNESCO. (2023). *What you need to know on education about the Holocaust and Genocide*. Retrieved from https://www.unesco.org/en/teaching-holocaust-genocide/need-know?hub=84617

UNESCO. (n.d.). *Teaching about the Holocaust and Genocide*. Retrieved from https://www.unesco.org/en/teaching-holocaust-genocide

United Nations. (2018). *What we do*. https://web.archive.org/web/20181122092127/http://www.un.org/en/sections/what-we-do/index.html

United Nations. (2022). *UN general assembly approves resolution condemning Holocaust Denial.* https://www.un.org/en/outreach-programme-holocaust/un-general-assembly-approves-resolution-condemning-holocaust-denial

United Nations. (Office on Genocide Prevention). (n.d.). *Genocide*. https://www.un.org/en/genocideprevention/genocide.shtml

Warhaftig, Z. (1946). *Uprooted* (p. 135). Institute of Jewish Affairs of the American Jewish Congress and World Jewish Congress.

Wiesel, E. (2006). *Night*.MacMillan https://us.macmillan.com/books/9780374500016/night

World Jewish Congress and UNESCO. (2022). *Facts about the Holocaust*. https://aboutholocaust.org/en/

Yad Vashem. (n.d.-a). *The Wannsee conference*. Retrieved from https://www.yadvashem.org/holocaust/about/final-solution-beginning/wannsee-conference.html

Yad Vashem. (n.d.-b). *About the Holocaust*. Retrieved from https://www.yadvashem.org/holocaust.html

Yad Vashem. (n.d.-c). *The implementation of the final solution*. Retrieved from https://www.yadvashem.org/holocaust/about/final-solution.html

Yad Vashem. (n.d.-d). *The uniqueness of the Rescue of Danish Jewry*. Retrieved from https://www.yadvashem.org/righteous/resources/uniqueness-of-rescue-of-danish-jewry.html

Yad Vashem. (n.d.-e). *Liberation and the return to life: The first moments of liberation*. Retrieved from https://www.yadvashem.org/articles/general/liberation-and-the-return-to-life.html

Chapter 4
Palestine, Israel, and Zionism

Palestine and Israel

To understand antisemitism, it is important to be knowledgeable about the history of Palestine and Israel. This is particularly true as presently antisemitism, which focuses on Jewish people and institutions, and anti-Zionism, which focuses on the state of Israel, are viewed as converging into only antisemitism. Consequently, Jewish people are frequently subject to harassment and even violence as they are considered responsible for Israel's actions and policies.

Israel has been called a colonizing country. This term implies that Israel took control of an existing country, overpowering the residents, and claiming the land for itself.

However, Jews have been in the land of Israel for over 3000 years, always maintaining a presence and self-governing. In the period of King David in the Old Testament, Jerusalem was the capital of the Jewish state. They were conquered by the Babylonians and exiled but returned to conquer the Maccabees and build the Second Temple and Kingdom of Judea, an event celebrated on the holiday of Chanukah.

The country was conquered in 70 AD by the Romans who changed the name from Judea to Palestina. Subsequently, it was conquered by the Byzantines, Crusaders, the Ottomans, and finally became part of the British Empire in 1917. Until 1922, Palestine was a part of the Ottoman territories. In 1922, when Palestine was given by the League of Nations to the British for administration, the land included the region between the Mediterranean Sea and the Jordan River. Palestine itself was never an autonomous country.

Following World War II, Jewish emigration to the Palestinian territory drastically increased. In 1947, the British recommended that the British Mandate Palestine be divided into two parts, Arab and Jewish states, with Jerusalem placed under international control. In 1948, the United Nations recognized Israel as a country also

C. B. Cox, D. B. Marlowe, *Social Work and Antisemitism*,
https://doi.org/10.1007/978-3-031-72771-9_4

giving it membership in the UN. The Israeli Declaration of Independence was passed, with David Ben Gurion, becoming the first prime minister, declaring the State open for all Jewish immigration and with complete equality of social and political rights to all its inhabitants regardless of religion, race, or sex (The Declaration of the Establishment of the State of Israel, Jewish Virtual Library, n.d.).

Shortly after Israel was proclaimed a state, it was invaded by troops from Jordan, Egypt, Syria, Lebanon, Iraq, and Saudi Arabia leading to a civil war that continued until 1949. Following the cease-fire, the West Bank became part of Jordan and Egypt assumed control of Gaza. Subsequently, the Arab populations began emigrating to the West Bank, Gaza, Jordan, Lebanon, and Syria. Jordan annexed the West Bank and East Jerusalem in 1950, with all emigrants granted Jordanian citizenship (Kenyon et al., 2021).

In 1967, rumors and concerns of an imminent Arab invasion resulted in Israel launching strikes against Egypt, Jordan, and Syria. At the end of the Six-Day War, June 5–10, 1967, Israel controlled the Sinai, Golan Heights, Gaza Strip, West Bank, as well as Jerusalem. In November 1967, The United Nations Security Council passed Resolution 242 (1967) which outlined principles for a lasting peace, including Israeli withdrawal from the occupied territories, a just settlement of the refugee problem, and the termination of all claims or states of belligerency. The aim was to achieve a lasting settlement among all countries, an aim that has yet to be realized.

The 4th Arab-Israeli War, known as the Yom Kippur War, occurred in October, 1973, with Egypt and Syria attacking Israel. The outcome of the War was a series of peace treaties between Israel and Egypt which negotiated Israel's withdrawal of troops from the Sinai and Egypt and reducing its forces on the east bank of the Suez Canal. At the same time, the United Nations established a peacekeeping buffer zone between Israel and Egypt. In March 1979, Egypt and Israel signed a permanent peace agreement that normalized relations between the two countries with Israel withdrawing completely from the Sinai Peninsula.

In 1988, the Palestine Liberation Organization (PLO) declared the establishment of the state of Palestine claiming the West Bank, Jerusalem, and the Gaza Strip. Palestine was given observer status at the United Nations. Under President Bill Clinton, in 1993, the Oslo Accords, a declaration of principles on interim self-government, was signed at the White House by the Israeli Prime Minister, Yitzhak Rabin, and the head of the Palestinian Liberation Organization, Yasser Arafat, The Plan called for the countries to work together toward a solution that would be enacted in 10 years. The PLO agreed to renounce terrorism and recognize Israel's right to exist in peace. A Palestinian authority would assume governing the West Bank and Gaza Strip for 5 years followed by permanent talks on borders, refugees, and the status of Jerusalem (US Department of State, Office of the Historian, 2018).

The promises of the Accords were broken with the November 1995 assassination of Prime Minister Rabin by an Israeli who opposed the Accords on religious grounds. Following his murder, Hamas made several terrorist attacks which further undermined the peace process and the support for Israel's ruling party (US Department of State, Office of the Historian, 2018). To date, through a series of Israeli governments, no agreements have been made. Reasons for the continual failure include a lack of shared vision among the participants and differences on issues, such as borders and the status of Jerusalem, as well as a lack of faith in any outcome (Miller, 2023).

There are nearly two million Arab Israelis, composing about 20 percent of the Israeli population (Carnegie Endowment, 2024). Except for those living in East Jerusalem, all are Israeli citizens. Data indicate that they have much higher poverty rates than the Jewish population and this was severely impacted by the COVID-19 pandemic due to a loss of employment (Council on Foreign Relations, 2022). They live in five main areas of Israel with nearly half living in cities and towns with lower standards of living and less service access than the Jewish population (The Israel Democracy Institute, 2021). In 2021, the government created a $9 billion, five-year plan to overcome the disparities facing the Arab population by boosting employment, improving healthcare services and housing, and developing a new infrastructure (CFR, 2022).

Most Arab Israelis are permitted to vote except those living in East Jerusalem where the majority identify as Palestinian. As such, they have permanent resident status but not citizenship. The status permits them to live, work, and travel within Israel as well as having access to health insurance and social services. However, they do not have Israeli passports.

Although Israeli laws state that Arab Israelis have equal rights with Jewish Israelis, these rights are limited by the Law of Return, which permits all Jews to move to Israel and immediately have citizenship while this is denied to Arab citizens. In 2018 Israel passed the nation-state law that removed Arabic as an official language, but gave it special status, while declaring that the Jewish people have a unique right to national self-determination (CFR, 2022). Concomitantly, Arab citizens have served on the Supreme Court and have their own political party, United Arab List (UAL). The Party has members in the Knesset (Parliament) and is part of the Israeli coalition government.

The Palestinian Authority, Hamas, and Israel govern Palestine. The Palestinian Authority is responsible for governing the West Bank and Gaza while the PLO represents Palestine at international meetings. Gaza is controlled by Hamas, which opposes the existence of Israel and has vowed to seek its destruction (Robinson, 2024). In 1997 Hamas was designated a foreign terrorist organization by the U.S. State Department (Counter Terrorism Guide, 2022). In its control of Gaza, Hamas has evoked strict Islamic laws that repress the rights of women, the LGBTQ+ community, and other marginalized groups (Robinson, 2024).

West Bank Settlements

An important issue of dissension is the West Bank settlements inhabited by Jews in land that was acquired in the 1967 Six-Day War. This is disputed territory as Israel does not have sovereignty over the area but has settled it for security. Initially, civilian communities were not permitted but the Religious Zionist ideology deemed it imperative for Jews to settle the entire land of Israel and thus the population increased (Israel policy, 2024). The control of the territories has meant the expansion of settlements on the West Bank, often with Israelis taking the land of Palestinians. Israel gave up control of Gaza to the Palestinian Authority in 2005 but views any restrictions in the area of the settlements as needed for security (Bell, 2008). However, the settlements and their expansion remain a major international concern.

Forty percent of the West Bank is under the control of Israeli settlers, a move that is deplored by the United Nations as it contributes to oppression, violence, and discrimination against Palestinians (UN, 2024). The United Nations argues that human rights are being ignored and that Israel acts as an apartheid state, an accusation that Israel and the United States claim is biased (Robinson, 2024). In February 2024, the International Court of Justice of the United Nations began deliberations on the legality of Israel's occupation of Palestinian lands, focusing on its violations of rights to self-determination, racial discrimination, and apartheid, claims denied by Israel (Euronews, 2024).

The settlements continue to erode Palestinian trust in Israel and contribute to doubts that a just two-state solution can be reached. At the same time, frequent settler violence against Palestinians further jeopardizes any hope of peace agreements. The settlements and their expansion are major obstacles to Israeli-Palestinian peace while also contributing to anti-Zionism (J Street, December 2022).

This perceived occupation and right of return and the status of the Arab population in Israel underlies much of the present anti-Zionist sentiments. Although Israel's Declaration of Independence declares no discrimination among the citizens with all having equal rights and integration into society, concerns about the Arab population remain and fuel much of the anti-Zionist sentiments (Karsh, 2000).

A Two-State Solution

A two-state solution in which Israel and Palestine live peacefully and securely is favored by the United States, the European Union, and most of the world's democracies (Abrams, 2024). In September 2022, the question of the two-state solution was addressed by the United Nations (UN, 2022). According to a Gallup Survey, 2024, the two state solution is not supported by the majority of Israelis, 64%, or the majority, 64%, of the residents of the West Bank and East Jerusalem (Vigers, 2024).

The USA and the European Union continue to press for a two-state solution while the Israelis and Palestinians are unable to reach any agreement (Abrams, 2024). Among the concerns are who would govern the Palestinians and the realization of human rights and democracy in both Israel and any new Palestinian state. Moreover, the rising popularity of Hamas among Palestinians which has vowed to erase Israel brings doubts as to whether a two-state solution is even possible.

Since the October 7 war in Gaza, Arabs have faced increasing discrimination in Israel (Carnegie Endowment, 2024). People are anxious about sharing opinions of the war on media as it can lead to repercussions against them. There have been increased incidents of violence and racism and many feel targeted and uncomfortable. Consequently, their ties and feelings of integration into society are strained.

Presently, given the status and concerns of Arabs and the anxiety and distrust of the Israelis, efforts to achieve a two-state solution are in limbo. The comments by Mahmoud Abbas, President of the Palestinian Authority, shed doubt on the possibilities of any imminent solution. In his speech to members of the Fatah movement in October 2023, he claimed that European Jews were persecuted by the Nazis due to their predatory lending practices, rather than their religion, and that Hitler killed the Jews because they were Jews and that Europe hated the Jews because they were Jews (European Union, 2023). The statements were refuted as trivializing the Holocaust and fueling antisemitism further, supporting the views of those opposing a two-state solution (European Union, 2023).

The war in Gaza has compounded antisemitism and anti-Zionism. Israel has been accused of genocide, a charge taken to the International Court on Human Rights and one that Israel refutes. The impact of the war on the civilians in Gaza, the bombing, and the near starvation of the population has caused worldwide censure. At the same time, Hamas's vow to destroy Israel and replace it with an Islamic Palestinian State cannot be ignored. Israel claims that its actions in Gaza are essential to combat and defeat Hamas, an organization focused on its complete destruction.

Zionism

Zionism, Jewish national movement, was founded by Theodore Herzel, a Viennese Jew, in 1897. The goal was the creation and support of a Jewish national state in Palestine, the historical home of the Jewish people. The broadest definition of Zionism is that Zion refers to the biblical land of Israel. The Old Testament refers to Zion as Jerusalem and refers to both the city of Jerusalem and the nation of Israel and is first mentioned in the Book of Samuel 5:7. The concept of Zion was substantiated by David when he became king of Israel and made Jerusalem the capital. Further references to Zion occur in the Psalms, Psalms 78:68, "He chose the tribe of Judah, Mount Zion, which He loved," and again in Psalms 87:2, "The Lord loves the gates of Zion more than all the dwellings of Jacob." The Five Books of Moses, the Torah, reference Jerusalem and elaborate on its significance to the Jewish people.

Zionism is a term meaning the national movement for the return of the Jewish people to their homeland and their sovereignty in the Land of Israel (Jewish Virtual Library, n.d.). Zionism is derived from the word Zion, referring to the Biblical Land of Israel. The term was developed in the late 1800s as a response to antisemitism in Central and Eastern Europe (Gans, 2008). The founders of the Zionist movement were secular non-religious Jews responding to increasing anti-Jewish pogroms and violence.

For the Zionists, Palestine was considered the natural historical homeland for the Jews and the main goal of the movement was to establish a homeland for Jewish people in Palestine. Following the first Zionist Congress in late 1888, increasing numbers of Jews began immigrating to Palestine, a territory under the control of the Ottoman empire. Zionism is defined as the movement for the return of the Jewish people to—and their sovereignty in portions of—what they consider the historic and religious Land of Israel while anti-Zionism is opposition to the existence of a Jewish state in that territory.

Palestine was a territory of the Ottoman Empire until 1922 when the League of Nations Mandate gave responsibility for Palestine to Britain. The Mandate incorporated Britain's Balfour Declaration of 1917 that declared "the establishment in Palestine of a national home for Jewish people" making Palestine a distinct political country. Under the British mandate, between the years 1922 and 1947, due to intense antisemitism in Eastern Europe including pogroms, focused on murdering whole communities, Jews began immigrating to Palestine.

With the rise of Nazism, Jewish immigration to Palestine increased although Britain maintained strict quotas on immigration (UN, 2023). Concomitantly, the Arab communities opposed immigration and demanded even stricter restrictions on immigration. In 1937, the Arab population rebelled with claims that their historical connection to the land was ignored and that their rights were being violated.

Following World War II, the need for a Jewish national home was made even clearer by the mass immigration of European Jews. Although limits on Jewish immigration remained, immigrants continued to come and in 1946 a plan for provincial autonomy for Arabs and Jews was developed. In 1947, the United Nations formed the Special Committee on Palestine and recommended the partitioning of the country into three zones, a Jewish state, an Arab state, and a UN-controlled territory. While the Zionists welcomed the partition, the Arab population rejected the partition, leading to outbursts of violence among the Arab communities and the Jewish settlers.

Anti-Zionism and Antisemitism

Anti-Zionism, as distinct from antisemitism, opposes the existence and sovereignty of the state of Israel in the territory that it assumed. According to anti-Zionism, Israel is the product of an imperialist and/or racist movement that is illegitimately occupying land that rightfully should either be a secular state or under Arab control (Hey Alma, 2023). Anti-Zionists include Palestinian nationalists who seek self-determination and sovereignty over Palestine as well as members of the Arab League, Russia, and even many Orthodox Jews who believe that

Israel can only be regained by God and therefore cannot be a secular state (Joffe, 2017; Poupko, 2021).

The terrorist attacks of October 7, 2023, blurred the distinction between antisemitism and anti-Zionism as all Jews, regardless of who they are or where they live, became targets of hate. As noted previously in this book, targeting of Jews has occurred throughout history. Whenever societies are threatened or those in power perceive themselves to be threatened, history shows that antisemitism tends to reveal itself. Consequently, antisemitism reflects broad social and political issues and regressive, dangerous tendencies in the fabric of society (United Nations Educational, Scientific and Cultural Organization [UNESCO], 2017).

In December 2023, following the Hamas attacks, the US House of Representatives resolved that anti-Zionism is antisemitism with a vote of 311 to 14, giving a consensus that the two are the same (H.Res.894-118th Congress). However, reflective of the concerns of conflating the two, 92 Democrats voted present, not taking a position while 95 supported it. Consequently, there was concern that those who love and support Israel but are critical of some of its policies were de facto antisemites (Demirjian, 2023).

Distinguishing Anti-Zionism and Antisemitism

Anti-Zionism is antisemitism when the word "Jews" substitutes for Israel or Israelis. It places all Jews as responsible for Israeli policy or actions. It is used as a tool to ignore or condone Jew-hatred (WJC, 2023). Calling for the destruction of Israel and challenging its right to exist is antisemitic while criticizing its policies is not (Weisman, 2023).

It is important to recognize that many Israelis, both Jewish and Arab, do not support the government's policy but are still supportive of Israel as a country. Jewish Israelis have demonstrated against the policies of their government and its leaders, including policies toward the Palestinians, a two-state solution, and efforts to alter the Israeli Supreme Court (Hasnas, 2023). Unfortunately, antisemitism, prejudice against Jewish people, has been broadened to include not only those who oppose Israel's policies but also those who question its right to exist as a state.

Advocating for a two-state solution that includes a Palestinian nation-state, criticizing policies of the Israeli government, and speaking up in support of Palestinian rights is not anti-Zionist nor is it antisemitic. Opposition to all forms of nationalism or borders, including Jewish nationalism, is not antisemitism. However, the belief that the Jews, alone among the people of the world, do not have a right to self-determination—or that the Jewish people have no religious and historical connection to Israel—singles out and discriminates against Jews, which is the very definition of antisemitism. When Jews around the world are verbally or physically harassed or Jewish institutions are vandalized in response to actions of the State of Israel, that is antisemitism (AJC, 2022). As defined by the International Holocaust Remembrance Alliance (2016), antisemitism is:

- Applying double standards by requiring of Israel a behavior not expected or demanded of any other democratic nation.
- Drawing comparisons of contemporary Israeli policy to that of the Nazis.
- Holding Jews collectively responsible for actions of the state of Israel.

Using antisemitic tropes or stereotypes when referring to Israeli policies or actions is antisemitism. Describing Israel's actions and policies as greedy or power-seeking is antisemitic when they categorize all Jewish people rather than the government as responsible. Thus, opposing Israel's policies, demanding reforms, and changes, including its treatment of Palestinians, is not in itself antisemitism nor anti-Zionism. However, challenging the right of Israel to exist while not questioning the legitimacy of other nations is antisemitic. It is asking that this right of self-determination, which many in the anti-Zionist camp want for Palestinians, be denied to Jewish state (Greenblatt, 2023).

When Jews are verbally or physically harassed or Jewish institutions and houses of worship are vandalized in response to actions of the State of Israel, it is antisemitism. When criticisms of Israel use antisemitic ideas about Jewish power or greed, utilize Holocaust denial or inversion (i.e., claims that Israelis are the "new Nazis"), or dabble in age-old xenophobic suspicion of the Jewish religion, otherwise legitimate critiques cross the line into antisemitism. Calling for a Palestinian nation-state, while simultaneously advocating for an end to the Jewish, as it applies a double standard, can be viewed as antisemitic (AJC, 2020).

Woke Antisemitism

Woke antisemitism, which is spreading across the globe (Koleib, 2022), is a by-product of critical race theory. It views Jews as white and privileged, wealthy, and in control of the media and government. It is applied to both Jewish people and Israel by perceiving the Jews as the oppressors and the Palestinians as the oppressed, making it into a racial conflict between the powerful and the less powerful (Koleib, 2022). Woke ideology, in its dichotomy of oppression, causes many Jews to question their support for Israel while also silencing any debate. As noted by Bernstein (2022), Jews have become alienated from each other as they abandon their Jewish identity.

Neither Israelis nor Palestinians are a race; they are ethnic groups, with both having indigenous ties to the land (Koleib, 2022). Accordingly, American Jews are placed in a strange situation as societies are divided between oppressors and the oppressed with Jews defined as the oppressors (Bernstein, 2022). This has been very noticeable on college campuses where Jewish students are often on the defensive as activist groups focus on support for Palestinians and opposition to Israel and/or Zionism (ADL, 2024). Simultaneously, far-left Jewish students supporting Palestinians often find themselves in ambiguous positions.

While criticism of Israeli policy regarding its equal treatment of all its citizens is valid, the fact that Israel alone becomes the most villainized nation with regard to human rights and social justice can be perceived as antisemitism. Moreover, holding Israel to standards not demanded of other countries can be defined as antisemitic.

Group Differences in Antisemitism

In comparison to the progressive left, the far right is more likely to hold and dispel traditional antisemitic tropes and stereotypes, such as Jews having too much power, seeking world control, and being privileged. A survey of antisemitic attitudes in 3500 young adults in the United States found overt antisemitic attitudes to be rare on the left but to be common among those on the right (Hersh & Royden, 2023). Most respondents on the left did not believe that Jews had too much power or that Israel should be boycotted while they were voiced by a majority of those with right-wing views.

Antisemitism is particularly high among younger people. A survey by the Anti-Defamation League (ADL) (2024) of 4143 Americans in January 2024 found 24% believing anti-Jewish tropes, an increase from 20% in 2022 with younger persons likely to view Jews as oppressors. Over 40% of the respondents felt that Israelis intended to cause maximal suffering for the Palestinians while, at the same time, almost 90% were supportive of a separate Jewish state (ADL, 2024).

Prospect for Peace

Given the long history of hostilities between Israel and Palestinians, several organizations composed of members of both populations, focus on reconciliation, environmental issues, and joint economic development and cooperation. Within Israel, groups continue to work for reconciliation and understanding between the populations, including youth organizations that bring together Israeli and Arab children and organizations for Arab and Jewish parents who have lost children due to violence. The groups work for greater understanding and the lasting peace for both communities. A 2020 survey of citizens of Israel, the West Bank, and the Gaza Strip, found that each group wanted peace but underestimated the wishes of the others, which influenced their own interest in peace-building and each seeking a peaceful coexistence (Leshem & Halperin, 2020). A 2023 study of Arabs living in Gaza and the West Bank (Jamal & Robbins, 2023) found Hamas and Gaza leaders very unpopular. However, chances for peace remain slight as long as the hostages are held, a cease fire is not reached, and the suffering continues.

Social Work Interventions

Social work interventions that support these efforts can be important in easing the suffering of all involved and, hopefully, in securing peace. At the micro level, social workers can use their counseling skills to work with Arab clients in Israel, by listening to their concerns and issues and empowering them to work for change. Their skills are also essential in working with Israelis to help them deal with the multitude of feelings they may have experienced after the October 7 attacks. At the macro level, social workers can play key roles in advocating for policy changes that address the needs of both Arab and Jewish Israelis.

Working together, Jewish social workers and Arab social workers may become a force that can stimulate understanding and communication critical for the country and peace. Several organizations in Israel that include both Jewish and Arab people work to increase cooperation and communication between the populations, some working specifically with children and others working with entire communities. Social work involvement in these groups can be an important asset for ensuring policy changes that contribute to both populations and help to ensure a thriving united country is established.

Conclusion

The history of Israel and the Palestinians is fraught with distrust and violence on both sides. The creation of the state of Israel in 1948 continues to be a source of tension that has lately been heightened by the Hamas attack on Israel in October 2023 and Israel's invasion of Gaza. As discussed in this chapter, one outcome has been that antisemitism is conflated with anti-Zionism, causing further dissension. Such dissension is not limited to Jews or non-Jews but has also divided the Jewish community.

Particularly troubling is how anti-Zionism has become synonymous with antisemitism. The outcome has been the immense increase in antisemitic acts around the globe. The failure to distinguish Jewish people and institutions from Israeli policy is frightening and does not show any abatement. This is a subject of grave concern that warrants much attention, including that of the social work profession, as it fosters oppression and violence.

The Doctrine of Hamas views Israel as a racist, anti-human, and colonial project with Hamas having the goal of liberating the Palestinian people (Wilson Center, 2023). Israel sees the destruction of Hamas as essential for its continued existence while Hamas rejects any prospect of peace or coexistence, demanding the entire country under its rule.

Given the history of the area and the diverse perspectives of the people living there, the prospect of a lasting peace is questionable without sensitive interventions and policies that recognize and support the rights of all groups. The war with Gaza, the humanitarian crisis it inflicts, Hezbollah, the conflict with Lebanon, the release of the remaining hostages, and the role of Iran in the region, continue to undermine all ceasefire efforts. However, the existence of many organizations working to promote peace and establish ties offers a measure of hope for the region. Social workers can use their macro skills in working for policy and social changes by engaging with the many organizations in Israel that focus on Arab and Jewish issues, needs, and concerns critical for the establishment of a just, peaceful, and cohesive society.

Main Points

- In order to understand antisemitism, it is necessary to be knowledgeable about the history of the Jewish people, Palestine, Zionism, and Israel.
- Zionism refers to the biblical land of Israel and also refers to the national movement of the Jewish people to their homeland and their sovereignty in the land of Israel.
- Jewish people have maintained a continual presence in Israel for more than 3000 years since the time of King David having been controlled by the Romans, Byzantines, Ottomans, and British.
- After World War I, the League of Nations assigned the British administration over Palestine, which included land between the Mediterranean Sea and the Jordan River.
- The British Mandate on Palestine terminated at the end of World War II with the British proposing the division of the territory into Arab and Jewish states. In 1948, the United Nations recognized Israel as a country giving it full membership in the UN.
- It was subsequently invaded by several neighboring Arab countries. Following the cease-fire in 1949, the West Bank became part of Jordan and Egypt assumed control of Gaza.
- The Six-Day War in 1967 evolved due to rumors that Arab countries were going to invade Israel. At the end of the war, Israel had extended its territorial control including the control of Jerusalem. This was followed by the Yom Kipper War of 1973, and a series of peace treaties between Egypt and Israel.
- **The Palestinian Authority,** established in 1988 by the Palestine Liberation Organization (PLO), governs the West Bank and Gaza. In 1988, the PLO declared the establishment of the state of Palestine claiming the West Bank, Jerusalem, and the Gaza Strip with Palestine given observer status at the United Nations.
- The Oslo Accords in 1993 aimed at a two-state solution, but the assassination of Israeli Prime Minister Yitzhak Rabin and subsequent terrorist attacks by Hamas undermined these efforts. Continuous failures are attributed to differing visions and a lack of faith in outcomes by Arabs and Israelis.
- The Arab population of Israel is poorer with a lower standard of living and fewer services. In 2021, the government committed to a $9 billion five-year plan to overcome disparities. The Israeli parliament has Arab representatives in parliament and in the coalition government and Arab citizens have also served on the Supreme Court.

- West Bank Settlements are Jewish settlements in the West Bank acquired in the 1967 War. They are a major point of contention with the Arab residents contributing to accusations of occupation and apartheid.
- A two-state solution is widely supported by the international community but remains elusive due to governance issues, distrust, and support for Hamas among Palestinians. The war in Gaza has intensified antisemitism and anti-Zionism, further deterring peace efforts.
- Zionism is the Jewish national movement for establishing and supporting a Jewish state in Palestine. It is based on historical, religious, and cultural ties of Jews to the land of Israel.
- **Anti-Zionism** opposes the existence and policies of the state of Israel but has blurred with antisemitism.
- **US House Resolution**: In December 2023, the US House of Representatives resolved that anti-Zionism equates to antisemitism, sparking debate about criticism of Israel's policies versus outright antisemitism.
- Social work skills in counseling are important to both Jewish and Arab Israelis as they deal with the aftermath of the October 7 attacks.
- At the macro level, social workers can advocate for policies that benefit both populations and the country.

Discussion Questions and Short Assignments

The following suggested discussion questions can be done in class in small groups or by having students write their own short papers:

- Discuss the difference between antisemitism and anti-Zionism and how the terms impact Jewish people.
- Given the history of Israel, discuss your views on whether it is an occupying country.
- Describe the Oslo Accords and some of the reasons for their failure.
- Discuss the status of the Arabs in Israel and the efforts made by the government to address the problems.
- Discuss the issue of the West Bank settlements from the perspective of the Israelis and the global community. How do the settlements impact any potential peace efforts.
- Describe why Hamas has been termed a terrorist organization and why this may hamper any lasting peace.
- Do you consider advocating for a two-state solution and criticizing Israeli policies to be antisemitic? Explain your views.
- Explain what is meant by woke ideology and how it impacts Jewish people.
- Discuss what is meant by holding Israel to standards not demanded of other countries and why you think this may happen.
- Discuss the roles that social work could assume in efforts to reach peace and stability in the region.

In-Class Exercises

Goal: To deepen students' understanding of the role that social media is playing in increasing antisemitism and anti-Zionism.

Phase I: Social media survey (20–30 min).

Break the class into groups of 3–4 students. Ask each group to do the following:

(a) Conduct a survey of social media. This survey consists of looking at posts on different platforms and reviewing the posts and comments that are related to Israel and to Palestine.
(b) Find common themes in these posts.
(c) Discuss the effects these posts would have on society's general beliefs.
(d) Discuss the effects these posts would have on mental health.

Phase II: Documenting themes and effects (15–20 min).

Using an online whiteboard, a whiteboard in a face-to-face classroom, or a file-sharing program (i.e., Google docs), ask each group to do the following:

(a) Write the common themes they found.
(b) Write a minimum of five effects.
(c) Write the impact on mental health.

Phase III: Reviewing the impact (15–20 min).

Have each group present on the findings of their social media survey, including the themes and effects.

Phase IV: Debrief (20 min).

(a) Discuss the common themes that each group had and the themes that were less common in the groups.
(b) Summarize the effects that social media has on one's beliefs. Discuss the validity of the posts.
(c) Summarize their responses and possible effects on mental health. Discuss how students would address this in their practice.

References

Abrams, E. (2024). *Democracy and the two-state solution. Council on foreign relations.* https://www.cfr.org/article/democracy-and-two-state-solution

ADL. (2024). *Antisemitic attitudes in America 2024.* https://www.adl.org/resources/report/antisemitic-attitudes-america-2024

AJC (American Jewish Committee). (2020). *Anti-zionism and Antisemitism.* https://www.ajc.org/sites/default/files/pdf/2020-10/AntiZionism%20and%20Antisemitism.pdf

AJC (American Jewish Committee). (2022). *10 Tough questions on Antisemitism explained.* https://www.ajc.org/news/10-tough-questions-on-antisemitism-explained

Anti-Defamation League. (2024). *N Nearly 40% of Respondents in J7 Countries Endorse Antisemitic Tropes*. ADL Survey Finds Retrieved from https://www.adl.org/resources/press-release/nearly-40-respondents-j7-countries-endorse-antisemitic-tropes-adl-survey

Bell, A. (2008). *International law and Gaza: The assault on Israel's right to self defense*. https://archive.ph/20130415040103/http://www.jcpa.org/JCPA/Templates/ShowPage.asp?DRIT=1&DBID=1&LNGID=1&TMID=111&FID=443&PID=0&IID=2021&TTL=International_Law_and_Gaza:_The_Assault_on_Israel%27s_Right_to_Self-Defense

Bernstein, D. (2022). *Woke antisemitism: How a progressive ideology harms jews*.

Carnegie Endowment for International Peace. (2024). *The many civil and human rights challenges facing Israel's Palestinian citizens*. https://carnegieendowment.org/posts/2024/02/the-many-civil-and-human-rights-challenges-facing-israels-palestinian-citizens?lang=en

Council on Foreign Relations. (2022). *What to know about the Arab citizens of Israel*. Retrieved from https://www.cfr.org/backgrounder/what-know-about-arab-citizens-israel

Counter Terrorism Guide. (2022, September). *Overview*. HAMAS. https://www.dni.gov/nctc/ftos/hamas_fto.html#:~:text=HAMAS%20emerged%20in%201987%20during,Palestinian%20state%20in%20Israel's%20place

Demirjian, K. (2023). *House declares Anti-Zionism is Antisemitism, dividing democrats*. https://www.nytimes.com/2023/12/05/world/middleeast/house-anti-zionism-antisemitism.html

Euronews. (2024). *UN court begins hearing on Israeli 'occupation' of Palestinian land*. https://www.euronews.com/2024/02/19/un-court-begins-hearing-on-israeli-occupation-of-palestinian-land

European Union. (2023). *Palestine: Statement by the Spokesperson on President Abbas' remarks on Jews and anti-Semitism*. https://www.eeas.europa.eu/eeas/palestine-statement-spokesperson-president-abbas-remarks-jews-and-anti-semitism_en?channel=eeas_press_alerts&date=2023-09-07&newsid=0&langid=en&source=mail

Gans, C. (2008). *A just Zionism: On the morality of the Jewish state*. Oxford University Press. https://doi.org/10.1093/acprof:oso/9780195340686.001.0001

Greenblatt, J. (2023). *Is Anti-Zionism Anti-Semitism*. Retrieved from https://americeltic.net/2023/12/11/is-anti-zionism-anti-semitism/

Hasnas, A. (2023, March 24). Anti-Zionism and antisemitism are not the same. Equating them harms all Jews. *The Georgetown Voice*. https://georgetownvoice.com/2023/03/24/anti-zionism-and-antisemitism-are-not-the-same/

Hey Alma. (2023). *What is Zionism*. https://www.heyalma.com/israel-guide/what-is-zionism/

Hersh, E., & Royden, L. (2023). Antisemitic attitudes across the ideological spectrum. *Political Research Quarterly, 76*, 697–711. https://doi.org/10.1177/10659129221111081

International Holocaust Remembrance Alliance. (2016). *Working Definition of Antisemitism*. https://holocaustremembrance.com/resources/working-definition-antisemitism

Israel Policy Forum. (2024). *West Bank Settlements* https://israelpolicyforum.org/west-bank-settlements-

Jamal, A., & Robbins, M. (2023). *What Palestinians really think of Hamas*. https://www.foreignaffairs.com/israel/what-palestinians-really-think-hamas

Jewish Virtual Library. (n.d.). *Zionism: A definition of Zionism*. https://www.jewishvirtuallibrary.org/a-definition-of-zionism

J Street. (2022). *Occupation, annexation & settlements*. https://jstreet.org/policy/settlements/

Joffe, A. (2017). *Palestinians and internationalization: Means and ends*. Begin–Sadat Center for Strategic Studies. 26 November 2017.

Karsh, E. (2000). *Fabricating Israeli history* (p. 55). Frank Cass.

Kenyon, K. M., Albright, W. F., Brice, W. C., et al. (2021). Palestine. *Encyclopaedia Britannica*. Retrieved from https://www.britannica.com/place/Palestine

Koleib, S. (2022). *Is Woke antisemitism becoming mainstream*. https://www.australianjewishnews.com/is-woke-antisemitism-becoming-mainsstream

Leshem, O., & Halperin, E. (2020). Hoping for peace during protracted conflict: Citizens' Hope is based on inaccurate appraisals of their Adversary's Hope for peace. *Journal of Conflict Resolution, 64*(7–8), 1390–1417. https://doi.org/10.1177/0022002719896406

Miller, A. (2023). *Why the Oslo peace process failed, Foreign policy*. https://foreignpolicy.com/2023/09/13/oslo-accords-1993-anniversary-israel-palestine-peace-process-lessons/
Poupko, E. (2021). *We cannot ignore anti-Zionist Jews anymore*. https://www.jpost.com/opinion/we-can-no-longer-ignore-anti-zionist-jews-opinion-676881
Robinson, K. (2024). *Who governs the Palestinians*. https://www.cfr.org/backgrounder/who-governs-palestinians
The Declaration of the Establishment of the State of Israel (n.d.), retrieved from https://www.jewishvirtuallibrary.org/the-declaration-of-the-establishment-of-the-state-of-israel
The Israel Democracy Institute. (2021). *Statistical report on Arab society in Israel 2021*. https://en.idi.org.il/publications/39557
UNESCO. (2017). *Addressing Antisemitism through education*. Retrieved from https://www.unesco.org/en/education-addressing-antisemitism
United Nations. (2022). *Israeli, Palestinian leaders' statements on two-state solution positive sign, but words must be turned into action, speakers tell security council*. Press Release (SC/15042). https://www.un.org/unispal/document/israeli-palestinian-leaders-statements-on-two-state-solution-positive-sign-but-words-must-be-turned-into-action-speakers-tell-security-council-press-release-sc-15042/
United Nations. (2023). *The question of Palestine*. https://www.un.org/unispal/history/
United Nations. (2024, March). *UN high commissioner of human rights, human rights council, state of Palestine: Israeli settlement in the occupied Palestinian Territory*. UN Office of the High Commissioner. https://www.ohchr.org/en/countries/palestine
U. S. Congress H. Res 894 *Strongly condemning and denouncing the drastic rise of antisemitism in the United States and around the world*. https://www.congress.gov/bill/118th-congress/house-resolution/894
U. S. Department of State, Office of the Historian. (2018). *The Oslo Accords and the Arab-Israeli peace process*. Retrieved from https://history.state.gov/milestones/1993-2000/oslo
Vigers, B. (2024). *Dim outlook for peace in the middle east*. Retrieved from https://news.gallup.com/poll/650636/dim-outlook-peace-middle-east.aspx).
Weisman, J. (2023). Is anti-Zionism always antisemitic? A fraught question for the moment. *The New York Times*. https://www.nytimes.com/2023/12/10/us/politics/anti-zionism-antisemitism.html
Wilson Center. (2023). *Doctrine of Hamas*. https://www.wilsoncenter.org/article/doctrine-hamas#:~:text=Hamas%20also%20rejected%20any%20prospect,rights%20and%20fate%20toyed%20with.%E2%80%9D
World Jewish Congress, WJC. (2023). *Defining antisemitism: Why anti-Zionism is a form of antisemitism*. Retrieved from https://www.worldjewishcongress.org/en/anti-zionism

Chapter 5
Contemporary Antisemitism

Contemporary antisemitism is more difficult to recognize than historical versions as it is not clothed in a Nazi uniform and does not openly claim hatred of Jews (Hirsh, 2018). It has reversed the perspective of Jews as the oppressed to their being the oppressor with those they are acting against, the oppressed (Hirsh, 2018). Two of the terms, genocide and apartheid, have been used to describe and characterize Israel and its actions, continuing to fuel antisemitism.

Genocide

The term genocide was coined after the Holocaust and refers to the deliberately planned murder of people from a particular nation or group with the aim of destruction. Israel's actions in Gaza are frequently described as acts of genocide against the people of Gaza. However, the use of this term is also challenged as supporters of Israel claim that it is not seeking to murder citizens, but is really working to eliminate Hamas whose intention is to destroy Israel (Hroub, 2017). When pro-Palestinian protesters carry signs "Gas the Jews" and "From the River to the Sea," they are calling for the deaths of and total eradication of millions of people, acts that have been interpreted as genocidal (Curtis, 2024). The October 7 attacks by Hamas, which killed over 1200 civilians and the taking of more than 240 hostages, and the rape and sexual assault of women, are representative of a genocidal intent (Curtis, 2024) that has not been condemned by international law (Cotler-Wunsch, 2024).

In December 2023, South Africa took Israel to the International Court of Justice with the charge that it was committing genocide against Palestinians in Gaza, contravening the Genocide Convention (International Court of Justice, 2024). Israel refuted the charges in that it was conducting a war of self-defense against Hamas, a group focused on destroying Israel. In January 2024, the Court requested that Israel take all steps to prevent any actions that could be considered genocide but did not ask Israel to stop its actions (International Court of Justice, 2024).

C. B. Cox, D. B. Marlowe, *Social Work and Antisemitism*,
https://doi.org/10.1007/978-3-031-72771-9_5

Moreover, the charge itself is considered controversial as it ignores countries such as Syria, North Korea, and China which have gassed and imprisoned citizens but have never been charged with genocide (Stephens, 2024). The charges ignore the intent of Hamas to eradicate Jews both in Israel and worldwide and are an example of "Holocaust Inversion" or modern-day antisemitism (Parsons, 2024).

Apartheid

Israel has been called an apartheid state that institutionalizes oppression and dominance against Palestinians (Amnesty International, 2022). An apartheid state is one in which minority populations are segregated and oppressed by law with the intention of maintaining a system of control. Apartheid was the South African system that denied certain racial groups access to the political and judicial systems in the country, relegated them to inferior living spaces and educational opportunities and controlled every aspect of their lives (Sekulow & Ash, 2023).

Arab-Israelis compose over 20% of Israelis and they receive the same benefits and services as all other citizens. They are represented in the Knesset (Parliament) and have the same rights as others. Israeli health services are available to them, including the medical care of persons in Gaza. Any restrictions experienced by Palestinians are those on persons living outside of Israel's established borders, the West Bank and Gaza.

Many, including Israeli's, consider Israel's policies as being apartheid (Pogrund, 2023). In reviewing Israel's actions against Palestinians in the West Bank, two Israeli human rights NGOs agreed that the occupation of the West Bank, which included Israel's illegal construction on Palestinian land and the expansion of settlements, was apartheid (Sfard, 2020). The claim has been supported by Amnesty International and Human Rights Watch (2022). The charges are refuted by those who claim that the measures were taken to increase the security of Israel, and not racist and that a double standard applies to Israel which promotes antisemitism (Carey, 2022).

Boycott Campaign Against Israel

The 2001 United Nations Conference Against Racism and Discrimination, held in Durban, South Africa, was partially in response to the growing problem of antisemitism in the world. According to Hirsh and Miller (2022), the Conference, as it initiated global efforts to deal with antisemitism, marks the beginning of contemporary antisemitism.

However, there was much anti-Israel and anti-Jewish rhetoric and political agendas at the Conference causing Israel and the United States to withdraw their delegations. Copies of the Protocols of the Elders of Zion were sold at the Conference amid chants that "Zionism equals Racism." The final resolution of the Conference called Israel a racist apartheid state guilty of racist crimes, genocide, and ethnic cleansing. The Conference was viewed as laying the foundation for the undermining of Israel and the beginning of the BDS (boycott, divestment, and sanctions) campaign against it (Baker, 2021). Antisemitic rallies and statements were seen as efforts to attack and delegitimize Israel (Lantos, 2001). Although criticized by many human rights groups, the Resolution was adopted.

The Boycott campaign against Israel began in 2003 with British antizionists asking for the boycott of Israeli academics. It spread into Boycott, Divestment and Sanctions (BDS) against Israel as an apartheid state grounded in antisemitic tropes and stereotypes (Hirsh & Miller, 2022). The BDS Movement believes that pressure on Israel by ceasing economic investment in the country could force it to end its occupation of Arab countries (BDS, 2024).

Universities have been the primary focus of BDS activities as faculty and students are the most likely to become concerned about social justice without necessarily knowing all the facts (Nelson & Brahm, 2015). Its efforts to get divestment from Israel urge banks, churches, pension funds, as well as universities to withdraw investments. The sanctions movement asks businesses to ban all activities that support settlements, end free-trade agreements with Israel, and suspend Israel's membership in United Nations bodies (BDS, 2023). BDS asks for an end to Israel's occupation of the West Bank, Gaza Strip, and the Golan Heights and the denying of Palestinians the right to return to their homes (BDS, 2023).

Opposition to BDS comes from many diverse sectors including all state governors in the United States, four of the former British Prime Ministers, and the Arab Council for Regional Integration in 2019. The latter viewed the BDS as increasing the suffering of the Palestinian people and weakening the chances for peace (Frazer, 2019).

Many, including Israelis, view it as a modern form of antisemitism while the movement sees itself as a human rights movement (Feldman, 2018). The request that there is a boycott of Israeli goods has been perceived as reminiscent of the Nazi boycott of Jewish goods and businesses (Nasr & Alkousas, 2019). The fact that such actions have not been taken against other countries where there are concerns about their policies and actions suggests a double standard being applied to Israel.

Conspiracy Theories

Conspiracy theories are responsible for the spread of much contemporary antisemitism. The beliefs that they rest on drive behaviors that can impact relationships and society, frequently resulting in violence ((Bartlett & Miller, 2010; van Prooijen & Douglas, 2018). The theories contain justice judgments as they involve moral responsibility, blame, and accusations of unethical conduct, placing the blame for specific events on the actions of groups who are viewed as working secretly together for some perceived malevolent goals (van Proojen, 2022).

Among the many factors contributing to adherence to the theories are feelings of uncertainty, a need for control and security, and a need to maintain a positive self or group image (Douglas et al., 2017). Although the assumptions that the theories are based upon are unsupported by evidence, the beliefs in the theories meet many psychological needs, including the need for relationships, as persons unite with others who share the same experiences and anxieties.

Susceptibility to these theories is heightened by fear, insecurity, and a longing to belong and feel good about oneself and one's social status (Jolley et al., 2020). The theories give those who feel isolated, powerless, and alienated, proof that their shortcomings are not the result of individual failure but are the result of external forces beyond their control. In addition, as the theories help the powerless to feel stronger and more engaged, they are particularly attractive to those who feel vulnerable and insecure in society. The ties they offer to others through the shared messages and beliefs further reinforce adherence (Jolley et al., 2020). Sharing the same beliefs and concerns about threats further justifies adherents' concerns (Imhoff & Lamberty, 2018).

Other psychological factors conducive to believing in conspiracy theories indicate that feelings of uncertainty and narcissism are important (Dagnall et al., 2017). For these persons, scientific data may be disregarded in favor of more easily explained causes. Particularly susceptible to believing in these theories are those with less education and little understanding of science and the need for empirical evidence to support such claims (Boberg et al., 2020).

Great Replacement Theory

Great Replacement Theory is a vivid example of a widespread conspiracy theory that continues to be influential and widely spread. The Theory, which originated in France in 2012, claimed that the Muslims posed a threat to French culture and civilization (Bergmann, 2021). Since then, it has transmitted to other countries, including the United States, where it is tied to White Nationalism, racism, antisemitism, and anti-immigrant views. The chants of the 2017 demonstrators in Charlottesville, Virginia, "Jews will not replace us," reflect fears of the dangers that Jews pose to society while numerous racial attacks against Blacks and other persons of color demonstrate the violence that the theory can incite.

Conspiracy theories have a long connection with antisemitism with Jews historically having been viewed as seeking to dominate the world (Byford, 2011). As discussed earlier, *The Protocols of the Elders of Zion* that appeared in a Russian newspaper in 1903 and was adapted by Henry Ford into a newspaper series, *The International Jew*, in the 1920s (Baldwin, 2002), remains a stunning symbol of the basis for conspiracy theories that target Jews. Although a fabrication based on ancient stereotypes and attitudes, the book continues to stir antisemitic acts and violence. Among the more recent claims are that Jews caused the COVID-19 pandemic (Zipperstein, 2020) and that Jewish bankers are using lasers to start forest fires to finance railroads (Chaitt, 2021). Jews remain a threat to society not because they are inferior but because they are too powerful and have too much control of the media and other institutions.

The far right continues to use conspiracy theories that spread and normalize anti-Jewish bigotry and actions (Human Rights Watch, 2023). Extremists portray Jews as intent on subverting the government or enslaving white Christians, encouraging violence against Jewish people. The Great Replacement Theory is a primary example of this as is the description of George Soros as an all-powerful force who is controlling government policies and world events. The far-right has also promoted that a Jewish cabal is working with the LGBTQ community to create pedophile rings that target Christian children, thus fusing antisemitism with anti-gay sentiments (Logan, 2023). The impact of the conspiracy theories is increased antisemitism as they are accepted without discourse. Conspiracy theories contribute to antisemitic attacks as believers target Jews who are perceived as a pervasive threat to society and its institutions, and they undermine democracy itself. A poll made by the Southern Poverty Law Center (2022) found that those holding extremist far-right beliefs are also likely to mistrust the government and its policies. White supremacist theories contributed to the attacks on Jews in Poway, California in 2018 and Pittsburg, Pennsylvania in 2019 (Human Rights First, 2023).

Antisemitism and the Progressive Left

At the same time, there has been an upsurge in antisemitism by progressive lefts. As noted by Greenblatt (2023), inflammatory rhetoric about Israel and the Jews has become popular and even trendy. Describing Zionism as a form of oppression and Israel as an apartheid country or singling it out for condemnation while ignoring countries such as China, which continues to subjugate Tibet with its efforts of cultural destruction and persecution of the Uyghur Muslims, can be interpreted as antisemitism.

The Israeli-Hamas war, October 2023, incited the most antisemitic attacks since the Holocaust with a 400% increase in the 10 days following the Hamas attack on October 7 on Israel (ADL, 2023). Liberal progressive Jews struggled as they contemplated the murder and abductions of Israelis by Hamas and Israel's military response (Zeitz, 2023). The basic question was whether the Israelis, as occupiers, deserved the attack and whether or not it was a genocidal state that deserved the violence (Tishby, 2023).

Following the attacks, there was an unprecedented rise in antisemitic attacks in the United States with false slogans and antisemitic tropes frequently appearing in Pro-Palestinian protests and on college campuses (Huffnagle, 2023):

1. Dirty/filthy Jews—seen in signs during pro-Palestine protests which is a term traced to the spreading of the bubonic plague in fourteenth Century Europe.
2. Dual Loyalty, which accuses Jews of having allegiance to Israel or other Jews and therefore cannot be trusted.
3. Justifying Hamas, which excuses them for the attacks and violence on October 7, 2023.
4. "From the River to the Sea, Palestine will be Free," a pro-Palestinian phrase that implies the eradication of Israel and all Jews residing there.

5. Deicide—Blaming Jews for the crucifixion of Christ carried with signs saying Jesus was a Palestinian and you killed him too.
6. Blood Libel—contributing to antisemitic trope that Jews are bloodthirsty and intentionally killed Palestinian civilians.
7. Holocaust denial or distortion—claims that Israel is perpetuating a second Holocaust by trying to annihilate Palestinians.
8. Holding Jews collectively responsible—associating all Jews with the policies of Israel, collectively sees them of seeking secret Jewish control.

The progressive left blamed Israel for the Hamas attacks on October 7, justifying the murders, attacks, and taking of hostages as revenge for Israeli policies. For the progressive Jewish left, speaking of Jewish suffering means ignoring Palestinian suffering (Abidor, 2023). According to Harsanyi (2023), liberal Jews should not be surprised by progressive antisemitism. The Women's March in March 2018 was led by a progressive group that spread blood libel and conspiracy theories while the original Black Lives Matter Movement accused Israel of being complicit in oppressing the Palestinian people which had nothing to do with civil rights (Harsanyi, 2023).

Progressives, which include Jews, who view Israel as an occupying state, contribute to increased antisemitism. Such views impact politics as found in the Democratic party which has itself become divided in its support of Israel. The dissension among progressives impacts the Jewish community in the United States. Many liberal Jews who opposed the occupation of the West Bank and the blockade of Gaza as well as the Netanyahu government were devastated by the October 7 attacks by Hamas. Concomitantly, many on the Left were dismayed by Democrats who focused on and supported the Palestinian cause. The sentiments are reflected in the censure of the one Palestinian representative, a Democrat, by the House of Representatives, for her remarks against Israel.

Groups such as "If Not Now" and the "Jewish Voice for Peace," composed of Jewish people who are fighting for the rights and freedom of Palestinians, are often viewed negatively by the greater Jewish community. However, they also are important as they underscore the fact that antisemitism is distinct from Israeli policy. These activists, mostly young people, are supporting the freedom of people which transcends ethnic and religious groups. They represent a struggle for principles that attempts to transcend antisemitism by viewing the Hamas attacks as justified. However, the perspective, as it views Israel as the oppressor, borders on antisemitism.

Antisemitism on College Campuses

Contemporary antisemitism, rather than seeing Jews as an inferior race, now sees them as oppressors. Rage at Israel has become rage against all Jewish people with attacks against Jewish students on college campuses rising sharply. Even liberal Jews were stunned by the threats and violence associated with these attacks and dismayed by the slow and moderate responses by the administration. In response to the increasing incidence of antisemitism and violence on college campuses, the federal government passed resolutions in both the House and Senate condemning the support of terrorist organizations and antisemitism on college campuses. As noted by Weiss (2019), anti-Zionism on elite college campuses has become a plank for progressivism, along with abortion rights, racial justice, and the legalization of drugs. As such, Israel is viewed as an oppressor and its very right to exist is challenged. Consequently, Zionism is viewed as racism and all Jews are perceived as Zionist, justifying antisemitism. Jews become whatever society hates the most and for the progressive left, that is whiteness (Weiss, 2019).

Many view college administrators concerned about the right for free speech as hesitant and frequently silent in their responses to student protests (Toure & Cordero, 2023). A contributing factor in their reluctance may be funding, as American universities received $8.5 billion from Arab sources between the years 1986 and 2021 (Biagini, 2023). Even when protestors chanted "From the river to the sea, Palestine will be free," a phrase commonly used to call for the eradication of Israel, there was hesitancy regarding their roles in intervening (Canahan, 2023).

The AMCHA Initiative (AMCHA Initiative, 2024) was created to combat antisemitism on college campuses and has documented antisemitic incidents on campuses across the United States since 2014. The intent is to conduct research that can document and inform college administrators about antisemitic activity. Not surprisingly, incidents have risen significantly with increases in anti-Zionist activity on many campuses that fuel antisemitism. Among its findings are:

- Swastikas and other antisemitic graffiti on campus.
- Physical aggression, harassment, and intimidation.
- Speakers, films, and exhibits that engage in antisemitic discourse.
- Descriptions of Israel as a racist, apartheid, or Nazi state.
- Holocaust was exaggerated.
- Suppression of free speech that presents Israel's viewpoints.

In November 2023, the Ways and Means Committee of the US House of Representatives hearing on campus unrest found the underlying concern was universities' shift from free speech to preferred speech creating a double standard that results in Jewish students fearing for their safety from threats of violence and intimidation (Ways and Means Committee, 2023). Significant in reaching their decision were chants at Cornell University such as *"If I see another Jew on campus, I will stab you and slit your throat. If I see another pig female Jew, I will drag you away, rape you and throw you off a cliff. Jews are human animals and deserve pigs' death. Liberation by any means 'from the River to the Sea, Palestine will be free' and Gonna shoot up 104 West, the Kosher dining hall. Glory to Hamas, liberation by any means necessary"* (Ways and Means, 2023).

Subsequently, the United States Department of Education began investigating complaints as colleges receiving federal funding must bar discrimination based on ancestry, ethnicity, or national origin (Saric, 2023). The Brandeis Center, a Jewish civil rights legal organization, filed complaints against Wellesley College and the

University of Pennsylvania for failing to respond to the harassment of Jewish students while a student at Cornell was charged with online posts threatening to kill or harm Jewish students. As Colleges are required to provide a safe and inclusive environment for all students, violating these requirements can result in a loss of federal funding. Following the hearings, the presidents of the University of Pennsylvania, Harvard University and Columbia University resigned.

Impact on College Students

In 2023 nearly 70% of Jewish college students reported encountering antisemitism with incidents ranging from vandalism to violence and assault often making many fearful to continue with their studies. Some reported having to have security guards accompany them from their dorms to classrooms (ADL, 2023). However, there is variation among the campuses with regard to the tensions and protests. A survey of approximately 2000 Jewish students in colleges across the country found that 83% of students in top quartile colleges and universities were concerned about antisemitism in comparison to only 55% in the lowest quartile (Blake, 2023). Concomitantly, the survey found a majority of all students, 63%, felt a sense of anti-Israel hostility.

The campus pro-Palestinian protests proliferated in April 2024, in response to Israel's war with Gaza. Students demanded schools cut financial ties to Israel and divest from companies believed to be supporting Israel. The first large demonstration at Columbia University in New York led to similar protests at other universities, often with students camping out on campuses. While many of the protests were peaceful, some included harassment of students and faculty, endangering the rights to both academic freedom and free speech as well as threatening physical violence (Kim, 2024).

The protests blurred the fine line between anti-Zionism and antisemitism with harassment and personal attacks on Jewish students leading to anxiety and fear (Meckler & Boorstein, 2024). In response to the protests, more than 500 Columbia University students circulated a letter defending their support for Israel and attacking the university's reaction which was viewed as pro-Palestinian and anti-Israel (Osterman, 2024). They called for peace stating that Judaism cannot be separated from Israel and that they themselves were subjected to threats of violence and harassment.

The spread and intensity of the campus protests prompted a response from the President of the United States. On May 3, 2024, President Joe Biden issued a statement that peaceful college protest is protected but vandalism, disrupting classes, trespassing, breaking, and entering is not, adding that there should be no place in America, including college campuses, for antisemitism or threats of violence against Jewish people (The White House, 2024).

Social Media and the Spread of Antisemitism

Conspiracy theories with antisemitic roots continue to be prevalent on social media. QAnon's obsession with George Soros has been viewed as reminiscent of earlier theories of Jewish power and financing that targeted the Rothschilds (Langer, 2022). Accordingly, the idea of a Jewish state within a state references a secret Jewish world with its own rules inside the greater society is reminiscent of the views of an eighteenth century Prussian pastor who saw Jews as walling themselves off (Langer, 2022).

In recent years, social media have been active sources in the spread of antisemitic tropes and stereotypes. Disseminating is simplified through comments, sharing, and liking, common features in social media platforms. The platforms and the hate they disperse can provoke violence as illustrated by the shooting in Pittsburg's Tree of Life synagogue in 2019, where the shooter, a follower of social media, killed 11 worshipers (Pegus, 2018).

Technology has a history in spreading hate. The Nazis used radio and newspapers to spread antisemitic propaganda at the beginning of the Holocaust. The growth of technology has enabled much greater dissemination of materials that foster hate and contribute to oppression. A striking example is given by Facebook, which according to the United Nations fostered violence in Myanmar against the Muslim Rohingya community (UN Human Rights Council, 2018).

Social media which is widely available and accessible is now a key instrument in the spread of antisemitism. It thrives on polarization as it encourages followers to respond. It is found in memes, gifs, videos, blogs, and comments where people and institutions are attacked because they are Jewish or have some affiliation with Jews (Hubscherm & von Mering, 2022). A study based on findings from 10,000 Jews in 13 countries found 89% responding that social media was more problematic with regard to antisemitism than any other public sources (FRA, 2018). According to UNESCO (2022), social media has provided unprecedented visibility and availability to antisemitic ideas and has contributed to the growth of antisemitism as followers are able to network and learn from each other. During the COVID-19 pandemic, Jews were targeted via social media, with conspiracy theories spreading stories that Jews were responsible for the virus (Global Network on Extremism & Technology, 2020).

Following the October 7 Hamas attacks on Israel, there was a 50-fold increase in the absolute volume of antisemitic comments on YouTube videos as well as significant increases on other social media platforms (Rose et al., 2023). Many of the messages called for direct violence against Jewish people with some sharing tactics for attacks. A common thread to these messages is that all Jews are responsible for all wars and that they are oppressors who must be stopped, reflecting ancient tropes that the Jews are seeking to control the world. The specific frames for antisemitism may be new, but they are ultimately repackaged versions of the myth that Jews control major political and societal dynamics for nefarious purposes (UNESCO, 2022).

Tik Tok, created in 2016, is one of the most widely used social media sites. In 2020, it showed a video of an antisemitic song about Jewish people being killed in Auschwitz (Weimann & Masri, 2021). The video was accessed six million times worldwide with over a hundred users adding graphics to the song. The site is particularly popular with children and teenagers. Posts regarding Holocaust denial and featuring cartoon images of Jewish people are common with a range of antisemitic comments, statements, taunts, and references to the Holocaust. Between February and May of 2020, TikTok had a 41% increase in antisemitic posts, a 912% increase in antisemitic comments, and a 1375% increase in antisemitic usernames. Given the large user base, over one billion, these tropes were accessed by millions of people around the world (Weimann & Masri, 2021).

The October 7 attacks also led to new concerns that TikTok was being pro-Palestinian, a claim that it denied, although a study of hashtags related to Palestine and Israel found those that were pro-Palestinian had 3.4 billion views worldwide in comparison to 313.6 million views for those that were pro-Israel (Ingram & Tenbarge, 2023). Overall, online platforms surged with antisemitic and anti-Israel posts, many voicing support for more violence and justifying the attacks with threats of violence against Jews in America (ADL, 2023).

In response to social media involvement in spreading antisemitism, the ADL (2023) offers these suggestions for actions that companies should take to assure that they are not contributing to antisemitism:

- Monitoring content to assure that it does not contribute to or incite violence.
- Platforms need to label unverified of misleading stories with companies ensuring they prioritize fact-based reports.
- Use emergency measures to prevent any increase of misinformation and violent content.
- Coordinate and share information across platforms to identify and take down nefarious content.
- Add warning labels to content that might incite violence or be traumatizing.
- Ensure that neither people nor platforms profit from posting violence.

European Commission

The European Commission, in response to increases in antisemitism, composed a strategy intending to combat it and foster Jewish life (European Union, 2021). The Document was created in response to an increase in European countries. Antisemitism is discussed as incompatible with the core values of respect for human dignity, freedom, democracy, equality, the rule of law, and respect for human rights, including the rights of persons belonging to minorities (p. 1). It is a threat to not only Jewish people but to democracy and Jewish life. The Strategy was developed to fight antisemitism and work toward creating an inclusive society. The three pillars are:

- Preventing and combating all forms of antisemitism.
- Protecting and fostering Jewish life in the EU.
- Education, research, and Holocaust remembrance.

To achieve these aims, the Commission organizes an annual forum that brings together various stakeholders to create links and joint actions. The Commission also offers funding and technical support. Countries were to develop national plans and strategies. However, the success of the plans is a concern as antisemitism, particularly since October 7, 2023, increased across Europe, with the rise in Spain, France, and the UK over 1000% (Margolin, 2024). Consequently, even with the concern and involvement that the Strategy engendered, governments appear unprepared or unwilling to actually take actions to combat antisemitism.

Social Work Interventions

Social work can assume several roles in dealing with contemporary antisemitism. On the micro level, workers must be able to offer counseling and support to those who have experienced antisemitic harassment or actions. They must be sensitive to the feelings, fears, and anxieties that these clients may experience. Particularly important is giving support to Jewish students and their families whose encounters with antisemitism may be terrifying.

The macro level of practice is particularly important in dealing with antisemitism. With social media a primary instrument in its spread, social workers must use their research and advocacy skills in challenging false statements and accusations that falsely target Jewish people and Israel. They can become active in refuting incorrect information and helping people to discern what is true and what is false. Through lobbying and other political actions, they can become involved in curtailing propaganda. Joining with other groups concerned about social media platforms, they can press for urgent reforms.

Social work research is critical for collecting evidence of the statements proliferated on these sites and their impact. Additionally, bringing these sites to the awareness of agencies responsible for monitoring them and offering testimony as to the hate and antisemitic beliefs they are spreading can be an important factor in containing and regulating their content.

Conclusion

Conspiracy theories have assumed a major role in the spread of antisemitism as they are easily spread through social media often including historical myths and stereotypes of Jewish people. Thus, as well as using their clinical skills to counsel and support victims of antisemitism, social workers can play a major role in halting the spread of hate on these platforms. Using both research and advocacy skills, they can challenge social media platforms and their monitoring, lobbying for more controls on hate speech that fosters antisemitism.

At the same time, contemporary antisemitism is often difficult to identify as it blurs with anti-Zionism with many politically progressive groups opposed to Israeli policy but supportive of Jewish people. Recognizing the distinction between Israeli policies and the rights of Jewish people and their safety is often difficult to discern. Moreover, with many progressives and liberals critical of Israel policy in Gaza, the separation of antisemitism from anti-Zionism is complicated. But, statements that call on the murder of all Jewish people, viewing them all as oppressors seeking control, singling them out among all groups, are antisemitic.

Particularly troubling is the finding that strategies to counter and prevent antisemitism, such as the ones recently made in the United States (The White House, 2023) and the European Commission (European Union, 2021), seem to be failing. Antisemitism continues to rise, and the broad strategies are basically ineffective in countering it.

Social work involvement must include counseling and support of those who are the victims of antisemitism, particularly students who encounter it on college campuses. At the macro level, they must become involved in sanctioning and controlling social media platforms that spread antisemitic tropes and propaganda.

Contemporary antisemitism, which thrives on division and hate, demands the attention, commitment, and consistent vigilance of all stakeholders if it is to be stopped. Ignoring it is not an option as it threatens not only the Jewish community but also societies themselves.

Main Points

- Contemporary antisemitism is difficult to recognize as it is frequently disguised as anti-Zionism.
- Genocide has been applied to Israel's actions in Gaza, a term that Israel refutes as it claims it is seeking to eliminate Hamas and is not targeting civilians.
- Apartheid has been used to describe Israel due to its treatment of Arab-Israelis and the fact that they do not have equal rights. However, Israel refutes these claims as Arab-Israelis have access to all services and benefits, are represented in the government, and have had places on the Supreme Court.
- In contrast to historical antisemitism, contemporary antisemitism sees Jews as the oppressors rather than the oppressed.
- The BDS movement calls for boycotts, divestments, and sanctions against Israel and remains controversial and often viewed as a form of contemporary antisemitism.
- The application of the BDS movement only to Israel and not to other countries suggests a double standard is being applied.

- Conspiracy theories continue to play a major role in spreading antisemitism with The Great Replacement Theory a vivid example as it is connected to White Nationalism, racism, and antisemitism.
- There has been an upsurge in antisemitism in the Progressive Left which tends to view Israel as an occupying state and an oppressor.
- Protests on college campuses have surged with rage against Israel impacting Jewish students.
- Progressive Jewish groups that advocate for Palestinian rights blur the lines between antisemitism and anti-Zionism.
- Support for Israel has impacted political parties in the United States.
- Free speech has included threats and chants against Jewish students suggesting a shift from free speech to preferred speech.
- Jewish students report feeling insecure and even terrified on campuses.
- Social media plays a major role in spreading conspiracy theories and antisemitism.
- Social media uses traditional stereotypes and tropes to foster hate and provoke violence, thriving on polarization.
- Following the October 7 attacks, there was a 50% upsurge in antisemitic comments on social media.
- The effectiveness of the strategies developed by the United States to combat antisemitism is in doubt as antisemitism continues to spread.
- Social work interventions at the micro level with those targeted by antisemitism must involve counseling and support and is particularly important for college students.
- At the macro level, social workers can use their research skills in reviewing social media for antisemitic content.
- At the macro level, social workers can use their advocacy skills in lobbying for reforms that control the spread of antisemitism.

Discussion Questions and Short Assignments

The following suggested discussion questions can be done in class in small groups or by having students write their own short papers.

- Discuss what is meant by genocide and apartheid and why Israel objects to the terms being applied to its actions.
- Describe some of the factors that can make people susceptible to conspiracy theories.
- Discuss how conspiracy theory relates to antisemitism and how it has been used historically.
- The Progressive Left has been viewed as anti-Israel. Discuss the reasons for this and its impact on antisemitism.

- Discuss the meaning behind the phrase "From the River to the Sea, Palestine will be Free."
- There is much discussion about Free Speech on college campuses and when it becomes threatening or "preferred speech." Discuss your responses and thoughts about this distinction.
- Describe what is meant by the lines between antisemitism and anti-Zionism have become blurred and how that has impacted college students.
- Social media plays a major role in transmitting antisemitism. Describe important measures for dealing with this spread.
- How has support for Israel impacted politics in the United States?
- Describe some of the macro interventions that social workers can do to combat the spread of antisemitism.

In-Class Exercises

Goal: To have students have a deeper understanding of how to address antisemitism and related political issues.

Phase I: Introduction (15 min)

With the students, review the importance of understanding antisemitism, related issues, and ways to address it.

Phase II: Group assignments and discussion (20–30 min)

(a) Break the students into groups of 3–4.
(b) Assign each group one of the discussion questions listed above.
(c) Ask each group to do the following:

    1. Discuss the question assigned to them.
    2. Include current events and real examples in their discussion.

Phase III: Presentations (20–30 min)

(a) Each group should present the main points of their discussion to the class.
(b) Ask the students to ask questions and provide feedback to each presentation.
(c) After the group presentations, have a class discussion on what was presented.

Phase IV: Debrief (15 minutes).

(a) Students summarize the presentations and discussions.
(b) Students discuss the role of a social worker in the fight for social justice and fighting against antisemitism.

References

Abidor, M. (2023). *About the reaction of the American left.* https://k-larevue.com/en/about-the-reaction-of-the-american-left/?utm_campaign=K.%20La%20Revue%20%23138EN&utm_medium=email&utm_source=Mailjet

ADL. (2023). *Hamas attack draws cheers from extremists, spurs antisemitism and conspiracies on line.* Retrieved from https://www.adl.org/resources/blog/hamas-attack-draws-cheers-extremists-spurs-antisemitism-and-conspiracies-online

AMCHA Initiative. (2024). *Setudent voices.* Retrieved from https://amchainitiative.org/student-voices-being-jewish-on-campus/#student-voices2/display-by-date4/?view_169_page=2

Amnesty International. (2022). *Israel's Apartheid against Palestinians.* Retrieved from https://www.amnesty.org/en/latest/campaigns/2022/02/israels-system-of-apartheid/

Baker, A. (2021). *Cancel the Durban IV review conference.* Retrieved from https://jcpa.org/article/cancel-the-durban-iv-review-conference/

Baldwin, N. (2002). *Henry Ford and the Jews: The Mass Production of Hate.* Public Affairs.

Bartlett, J., & Miller, C. (2010). *The power of unreason: Conspiracy theories, extremism and counter-terrorism.* Demos.

BDS movement. (2023). *What is BDS?* Retrieved from https://bdsmovement.net/what-is-bds

Bergmann, E. (2021). *The Eurabia conspiracy theory, in Europe: Continent of Conspiracies.* Routledge.

Biagini, W. (2023). *Ivy league among top recipients of $8.5 billion Arab funding.* https://www.campusreform.org/article/ivy-league-among-top-recipients-of-85-billion-arab-funding/24195

Blake, J. (2023). *New study highlights campus Antisemitism 'Hot Spots' inside higher education.* https://www.insidehighered.com/news/students/free-speech/2023/12/15/new-study-highlights-campus-antisemitism-hot-spots

Boberg, S., Quandt, T., Schatto-Eckrodt, T., & Frischlich, L. (2020). *Pandemic populism: Facebook pages of alternative news media and the corona crisis—A computational content analysis.* https://arxiv.org/abs/2004.02566

Boycott, Divestment, Sanctions (BDS). (2024). *History and indicators of the BDS.* https://bdsmovement.net/

Byford, J. (2011). *Conspiracy Theories: A Critical Introduction.* Palgrave Macmillian.

Canahan, A. (2023). *Funding from Arab countries to US universities raises questions: "Almost always come with strings attached".* https://www.foxbusiness.com/media/funding-from-arab-countries-us-universities-raises-questions-almost-always-come-strings-attached

Carey, A. (2022). *Amnesty accuses Israel of apartheid over treatment of Palestinians, prompting angry response.* CNN. https://www.cnn.com/2022/02/01/middleeast/israel-apartheid-amnesty-intl/index.html

Chaitt, J. (2021). Marjorie Taylor Greene blamed wildfires on secret Jewish space laser, New York Magazine, January 28. https://nymag.com/intelligencer/article/marjorie-taylorgreene-qanon-wildfires-space-laser-rothschildexecute.html

Cotler-Wunsch, M. (2024). https://twitter.com/CotlerWunsh/status/1745811666694967547.

Dagnall, N., Denovan, A., Drinkwater, K., Parker,A., & Clough, P. (2017). Statistical bias and endorsement of conspiracy theories. Applied Cognitive Psychology, 31(4), 368–378. https://doi.org/10.1002/acp.3331

Douglas, K., Sutton, R., & Cichocka, A. (2017). The psychology of conspiracy theories. *Current Directions in Psychological Science, 26*(6), 538–542.

European Union. (2021). *EU strategy on combating antisemitism and fostering Jewish life (2021–2030).* https://eur-lex.europa.eu/legal-content/EN/ALL/?uri=COM:2021:615:FIN&pk_campaign=doc&pk_source=EUR-Lex&pk_medium=tw&pk_keyword=No2Antisemitism

Feldman, D. (2018). Boycotts: From the American revolution to BDS. In D. Feldman (Ed.), *Boycotts past and present: From the American revolution to the campaign to Boycott Israel* (pp. 1–19). Springer. https://doi.org/10.1007/978-3-319-94872-0_1

Frazer, J. (2019). *A groundbreaking Arab initiative to repudiate BDS.* https://jewishjournal.com/news/worldwide/307371/a-groundbreaking-arab-initiative-to-repudiate-bds/

Global Network on Extremism and Technology (GNET). (2020). *Antisemitism Research Initiative.* Retrieved from https://extremism.gwu.edu/antisemitism-research-initiative

Greenblatt, J. (2023). Antisemitism on the left is subtler than the right. *But it's getting worse.* https://www.washingtonpost.com/outlook/2021/10/27/antisemitism-left-rising/

Harsanyi, D. (2023). *Liberal Jews Have no reason to be surprised by progressive Antisemitism.* https://thefederalist.com/2023/10/30/liberal-jews-have-no-reason-to-be-surprised-by-progressive-antisemitism/

Hirsh, D. (2018). *Contemporary left antisemitism.* Routledge.

Hirsh, D., & Miller, H. (2022). Durban antizionism: Its sources, its impact and its relation to older anti-Jewish sentiment. *Journal of Contemporary Antisemitism, 5*(1), 35–42.

Hroub, K. (2017). A Newer Hamas? The Revised Charter. *Journal of Palestine Studies, 46*(4) (184), 100–111.

Hubscherm, M., & von Mering, S. (2022). *Antisemitism on social media.* Routledge.

Huffnagle, H. (2023). *There are not two sides to antisemitism: These are signs of Jew Hatred.* https://www.ajc.org/news/there-are-not-two-sides-to-antisemitism-these-are-signs-of-jew-hatred?ms=EL_EML_20231121_Israel2023-11.21.2023&p2asource=Israel2023-11.21.23&utm_campaign=Israel2023&utm_source=LuminateEmail&utm_medium=Email&utm_content=Israel-11.21.2023-2L1

Human Rights Watch. (2023). *Extremist fact sheet, recycled Bigoty: Antisemitic conspiracy theories go mainstream.* https://humanrightsfirst.org/wp-content/uploads/2023/06/HRF-Fact-Sheet-Antisemitic-Conspiracy-Theories_6.29.23.pdf

Imhoff, R., & Lamberty, P. (2018). How paranoid are conspiracy believers? Toward a more refined understanding of the connect and disconnect between paranoia and belief in conspiracy theories. *European Journal of Social Psychology, 48*, 909–926. https://doi.org/10.1002/ejsp.2494

Ingram, D., & Tenbarge, K. (2023). Critics renew calls for a Tik Tok ban, claiming platform has an anti-Israel bias. *NBC News.* https://www.nbcnews.com/tech/social-media/tiktok-ban-israel-gaza-palestine-hamas-account-creator-video-rcna122849

International Court of Justice. (2024, January 12). *Application of the Convention on the Prevention and Punishment of the Crime of Genocide in the Gaza Strip* (South Africa v Israel). https://www.icj-cij.org/sites/default/files/case-related/192/192-20240112-pre-01-00-en.pdf

Kim, C. (2024). What's really happening on college campuses according to student journalists. *Politico.* Retrieved from https://www.politico.com/news/magazine/2024/05/03/college-campus-protests-israel-gaza-student-journalists-00155672

Langer, A. (2022). Dog-Whistle politics as a strategy of American nationalists and populists: Soros, the Rothschilds and other conspiracy theories. In F. Jacob & C. Schapkow (Eds.), *Nationalism and populism: Expressions of fear or political strategies?* (pp. 157–187). De Gruyter.

Lantos, T. (2001). *Antisemitic circus.* Retrieved from https://www.washingtonpost.com/archive/opinions/2001/12/15/anti-semitic-circus/715f7129-c2a7-4a4a-9d81-9260b36ab7f1/

Logan, N. (2023). *How antisemitic tropes are being used to target the LGBTQ community.* https://www.cbc.ca/news/world/antisemitism-transphobia-lgbtq-hate-1.6729223

Margolin, M. (2024). Europe's policies to combat antisemitism have failed the "real world test". https://www.politico.eu/article/europe-antisemitism-failed-policies/

Meckler, L., & Boorstein, M. (2024). *For Jewish students, protests stir fear, anger, hope and questions.* https://www.washingtonpost.com/education/2024/04/28/jewish-students-campus-protests-israel-gaza/

Nelson, C., & Brahm, G. (2015). *The case against academic boycotts of Israel* (MLA members for scholars rights, 2015), 13. Qtd. in Pessin, Introduction, Anti-Zionism on Campus, 6.

Osterman, C. (2024). Hundreds of Columbia Jewish students sign pro-Israel letter. Not all Jewish students agree. *USA Today.* Retrieved from https://www.usatoday.com/story/news/nation/2024/05/09/columbia-jewish-students-campus-protests-letter/73615496007/

Parsons, D. (2024). International Christian Embassy Jerusalem. *Justice inverted in Genocide Petition Against Israel.* Retrieved from https://www.icej.org/blog/justice-inverted-in-genocide-petition-against-israel/

Pegus, J. (2018). *Pittsburgh shooting suspect wrote anti-semitic posts on social media*. CBS Evening News. [online] Available at: https://www.cbsnews.com/news/robert-bowers-pittsburgh-shooting-suspect-anti-semitic-posts-social-media-ga

Pogrund, B. (2023). *For Decades, I defended Israel from claims of Apartheid. I no longer can*. https://www.haaretz.com/israel-news/2023-08-10/ty-article-opinion/.highlight/for-decades-i-defended-israel-from-claims-of-apartheid-i-no-longer-can/00000189-d4ac-d821-afdd-dfacb4060000

Rose, H., Guhl, J., & Cornerford, M. (2023) *Rise in antisemitism on both mainstream and fringe social media platforms following Hamas" terrorist attack*. Institute for Strategic Dialogue. https://www.isdglobal.org/digital_dispatches/rise-in-antisemitism-on-both-mainstream-and-fringe-social-media-platforms-following-hamas-terrorist-attack/

Saric, I. (2023). Education Dept. investigating alleged antisemitism and islamophobia at 6 colleges. *Axios*. https://www.axios.com/2023/11/17/biden-department-of-education-colleges-antisemitism-islamophobia

Sekulow, J., & Ash, R. (2023). *Why allegations that Israel is an 'apartheid' state are false under international law*. American Center for Law & Justice. Available at SSRN: doi:https://doi.org/10.2139/ssrn.4343950.

Sfard, M. (2020). *The Israeli occupation of the West Bank and the crime of Apartheid*. Retrieved from https://s3-eu-west-1.amazonaws.com/files.yesh-din.org/Apartheid+2020/Apartheid+ENG.pdf

SPLC. (2022). *Anti-government beliefs and faith in institutions*. https://www.splcenter.org/news/2022/06/01/poll-finds-support-great-replacement-hard-right-ideas#replacement

Stephens, B. (2024). The genocide charge against Israel is a moral obscenity. *The New York Times*. https://www.nytimes.com/2024/01/16/opinion/israel-hamas-war-genocide.html

The White House. (2023). *The U.S. national strategy to counter Antisemitism: Key actions by Pillar.* Retrieved from https://www.whitehouse.gov/briefing-room/statements-releases/2023/06/02/the-u-s-national-strategy-to-counter-antisemitism-key-actions-by-pillar-2/

The White House. (2024). *Remarks by president Biden on recent events on college campuses*. https://www.whitehouse.gov/briefing-room/speeches-remarks/2024/05/02/remarks-by-president-biden-on-recent-events-on-college-campuses/

Tishby, N. (2023). A member of the squad is slandering the Jewish state-again. *New York Post*. https://nypost.com/2021/04/28/a-member-of-the-squad-is-slandering-the-jewish-state-again/

Toure, M., & Cordero, K. (2023). Colleges are struggling with their response to the Israel-Hamas war. *Politico*. https://www.politico.com/news/2023/10/21/colleges-israel-hamas-war-00122845

UN Human Rights Council. (2018). *Report of the independent international fact-finding mission*.

UNESCO. (2022). *Online Antisemitism: A toolkit for civil society*. https://unesdoc.unesco.org/ark:/48223/pf0000381856

van Prooijen, J., & Douglas, K. (2018). Belief in conspiracty theories: Basic principles ofan emerging research domain. *European Journal of Social Psychology, 48*, 897–908.

Ways and Means Committee. (2023, November 17). *Seven key moments on Nexus between Antisemitism, tax-exempt universities and terror financing*. https://waysandmeans.house.gov/seven-key-moments-from-ways-means-hearing-on-nexus-between-antisemitism-tax-exempt-universities-and-terror-financing/

Weimann, G., & Masri, N. (2021). TikTok's spiral of antisemitism. *Journalism and Media, 2*, 697–708. https://doi.org/10.3390/journalmedia2040041

Weiss, B. (2019). *How to Fight Antisemitism*. Crown.

Zeitz, J. (2023). *Anti-Israel proressives are handing liberal Jews an impossible decision, just like in 1967*. Retrieved from https://www.politico.com/news/magazine/2023/10/23/anti-israel-left-jewish-politics-00122848

Zipperstein, S. (2020). *The conspiracy theory to rule them all*. The Atlantic, August 25. https://www.theatlantic.com/politics/archive/2020/08/conspiracy-theory-rule-themall/615550/

Chapter 6
Antisemitism and Mental Health

Antisemitism, hatred of Jews, as discussed in this book, is one of the oldest forms of oppression and one that continues to increase and to harm Jewish people (Lipstadt, 2019). There is hardly an evil that has not been attributed to the Jewish people with hatred acted out in numerous ways (Brenner, 2007). However, when Jews are categorized as White, the history of marginalization, ethnic identity, and discrimination are easily ignored and even erased (Rubin, 2017). Consequently, it may not be surprising that in comparison to other targeted populations, very little research exists on the impact of antisemitism on Jewish people or that Jewish people tend to be ignored by many DEI programs.

This absence is noted in The American Psychological Association's (APA) strategic plan to eliminate racism in all of its forms and promote equity and diversity, which fails to include antisemitism, its nature, and the psychological and social harm that it causes (Walker et al., 2024). This absence is particularly disturbing as findings from a 2023 survey show that 63% of American Jews felt less secure in society in 2023 than in the previous year with 46% reporting that they altered their behaviors out of fear of antisemitism (AJC, 2024).

Oppression

Oppression is based on differences with the more dominant group subjugating the less powerful. People are oppressed as members of a category that are labeled inferior or less valued in society. The oppressed are commonly used as scapegoats for the problems faced by society. Thus, as discussed earlier in this book, Jews have often been used as scapegoats for plagues, and economic and social disasters. Chants by White Supremacists, "Jews will not Replace Us," reflect the fears of the more powerful and the ease with which Jewish people today can be targeted. Research on the impact of oppression indicates that it can lead to fear, stress, poor

C. B. Cox, D. B. Marlowe, *Social Work and Antisemitism*,
https://doi.org/10.1007/978-3-031-72771-9_6

mental health, and potentially negative self-perceptions (Williams et al., 2023). However, given these findings, there is a notable absence of its specific effect on Jewish people.

Most oppression is covert or hidden, with both oppressors and victims unaware of its dynamics (Mallaly & West, 2018). It can become so common in society that it is accepted as natural, with the oppressed group accepting the role. Gender discrimination is an example of how discrimination, as reflected in salary differences between men and women, and the harassment of those who identify as transgender or non-binary, have almost become commonplace in society. However, such acceptance does not reflect the inequality and potential harm experienced by those who are victimized.

Oppression occurs at several levels of society: personal, cultural, and structural (Mallaly & West, 2018). The personal level involves thoughts, attitudes, and negative judgments about a specific group. Micro-aggressions such as all Jews are rich, Jews are sneaky, and Jews can't be trusted are examples of antisemitism on a personal level. The cultural level entails values and norms that are accepted and passed down and shared, such as never go to a Jewish banker, Jewish success is due to their dishonest practices, and Jews are working to control the world. Structural oppression codifies institutional beliefs into laws and policies, such as school quotas on Jewish admissions and housing and social club restrictions that deny or limit access to Jewish people.

Oppression at all these levels must be addressed as those who are victimized internalize the narratives of the dominant group leading to fear and problem-based forms of thinking (Mallaly and West, 2018). According to Mallaly and West (2018), such ways of thinking are characterized by survival mode with outcomes marked by a mental contraction in which individuals tend to see each other as separate. Consequently, Jewish people may feel insecure or even anxious about voicing their concerns or feelings as they feel different and alienated from the majority.

White privilege is an important component in oppression as it acts as the norm by which non-white groups are judged and is an important component in determining their places and resources in society. Those who are not White are vulnerable in society, often living on marginal incomes with scant resources or as in the case of Asian Americans, subjected to hate crimes based on myths and stereotypes. Other characteristics, such as heterosexual privilege, which marginalizes those who declare themselves as gay, lesbian, bi-sexual, or transgender, can subject people to harassment, bullying, and other forms of violence, with laws and policies limiting their full participation in society.

Intersectionality describes how many factors can interact to oppress, determine, and influence one's place in society. The term was created to show how black women were impacted by the intersection of race and sex (Crenshaw, 1989). It has expanded to include the multiple identities that a person holds and the challenges they may present as they intersect and affect a person's life. Consequently, Jewish people may be privileged by income and education, but oppressed by their religion, which limits their full participation in society. Jews have been oppressed as a race, an ethnic group, a religion, and a culture (Hollinger, 2006). Myths and stereotypes continue to underlie this oppression.

Judaism is a religion, but many who identify as Jews are not religious. They are not a distinct ethnic group as Jewish people are from different cultures and societies, including Ashkenazi Jews, Sephardic Jews, Ethiopian Jews, Moroccan Jews, and Syrian Jews. These groups differ in their norms and customs, including their foods and languages, and thus do not meet the criteria for a specific ethnic group. Jews are not a distinct race or a nationality as most Jewish people do not live in Israel. Jews have been accused of having White Privilege and thus not vulnerable to oppression, while they have also been murdered due to being a threatening and undesirable race.

Impact of Oppression

The majority of research on the impact of oppression has focused on race with a growing body of work focusing on sexuality, particularly those who do not identify as heterosexual. Given the history of antisemitism and its increase across the globe, the scant attention to its impact on Jewish people is in itself troubling. The absence is glaring in social work and also notable in psychology. Being devalued and abused results in psychological scars, but the psychodynamics of antisemitism have been ignored.

The absence of attention paid to oppression and Jews in comparison to other minority groups has been attributed to the fact that much of the research has been conducted by Jewish psychoanalysts who may have been reluctant to discuss Jewishness (Ostow, 1997). Moreover, as they are White, they tend to be ignored as an invisible minority as they are seen as very assimilated (Schlosser, 2006). Regardless of the reasons, antisemitism persists, and the impact on Jewish people should be addressed.

Jewish Self-hatred

The term Jewish self-hatred refers to Jewish people disliking anything that is Jewish as it will separate them from the majority to which they want to belong and turn away from those who are outwardly Jewish (Lewin, 1948). As Jews have historically been subjected to oppression and discrimination, they have also experienced insecurity and fear, and trauma. Such trauma experienced in the hate of the persecutors can result in identification with the aggressor (Frankel, 2004) and in self-hatred (Volkan, 2014). The defense mechanism of self-hatred is a means of coping with prolonged feelings of rage and humiliation. Presently, the term is often used against Jewish people who criticize Israeli policy and frequently used by the Jewish right against the more liberal and left-leaning groups such as Jews for Palestine.

Concealing Identity

There is a lack of information on the current psychological impact of antisemitism on Jewish people. Frequently, they are discouraged from expressing their experiences of being targets of discrimination. During the Holocaust, many Jews hid their Jewish identity for survival. The hidden Jews assumed the names of non-Jews and even obtained papers and documents showing these false identities (Yad Vashem, n.d.). For many, this act of hiding saved their lives. Some other Jews came to the United States, during and after World War II, yet still hid their Jewish identities for fear of what was happening across the ocean and the fear that it could happen in the new land of freedom. Moving out of an environment does not automatically lead to relief or a sense that one is not in danger. The idea that one continues to hide one's identity is symbolic of the continued pressures of trauma and traumatic experiences.

While some Jews outwardly show their identities with pride, others continue to hide it, impacting their sense of well-being. Being Jewish may be considered a concealable identity. Jews are removing their necklaces that have Stars of David or removing mezuzahs from their doors (Gottlieb & Steigerwald, 2024) to protect themselves.

Concealing one's identity may cause a person to have mental and physical health problems. Fear of being stigmatized or even discriminated against can cause an increased level of distress (Quinn & Earnshaw, 2013). Many young people suffer from a "suppression of personal identity" due to antisemitism. They fear that identifying themselves as Jewish will lead to being the victims of antisemitic comments directed at them in person or on social media. This fear can cause feelings of increased isolation. Young people who shared their identities state that they are being targeted with antisemitism (Facing History and Ourselves, 2022). The fear is a reality as incidents of antisemitism have increased.

Disclosing an identity can lead to additional social support. However, the disadvantage would be an increased risk of discrimination. Individuals who have "concealable stigmatized identities (CSIs)" report having increased depression and anxiety (Camacho et al., 2020).

Mental Health Problems

A recent study of the relationship of antisemitism to the mental health of Jewish people in the community found it associated with depression, survivor guilt-proneness, and self-hate, with 30% of respondents reporting they felt unsafe when identifying as Jewish (Kosdon et al., 2021). Among the group, Holocaust descendants had greater levels of trauma and guilt triggered by antisemitism. Additionally, concealing Jewish identity was associated with self-hate, proneness to guilt, and feelings of endangerment (Kosdon et al., 2021).

Antisemitic incidents incite anxiety and post-traumatic stress disorder for many Jewish people, creating a sense of insecurity and instability (NY State Office of Mental Health, n.d.). Other mental health outcomes include feeling alone, depressed, and anxious, resulting from micro-aggressions and also a need to hide one's identity (Greenfield, 2023).

Children and Antisemitism

With the surge in antisemitism, it has not ignored children who may be targeted in their schools and made to feel unsafe, afraid, vulnerable, excluded, and isolated. The Subcommittee Hearing of the House of Representatives held on May 1, 2024, "Confronting Pervasive Antisemitism in K-12 Schools," reflects the importance of the issue as antisemitism was viewed as infecting all institutions of learning, beginning in elementary schools. Incidents such as a two-hour riot in a public high school included threats made to a Jewish teacher, antisemitic harassment and intimidation that officials failed to address, antisemitic chants including "Kill the Jews" with no staff intervention were discussed along with the safety of Jewish children (Committee on Education and the Workforce, 2024). Examples of the fear that children may experience are "Is it ok to be Jewish?" Can I wear my kippah?" "Is it safe to go to school?" (Kandel, 2024).

Antisemitism can make children develop stress reactions that impact their overall well-being (ADL, 2024). Among these reactions are:

- Emotional Indicators: depression, anxiety, mood changes, detachment, physical indicators including nightmares, somatic complaints, fatigue.
- Physical Indicators: nightmares, somatic complaints, pains, sleep disturbance.
- Cognitive Indicators: negative feelings, persistent worries, loss of interest.
- Behavioral Indicators: regressive behaviors, social isolation, dropping out of activities.
- Academic Indicators: decline in grades, school avoidance, changes in peer groups.

In response to the rise in antisemitic incidents in schools, School Watch was developed as a platform where students, parents, and educators can report incidents (School Watch, n.d.). The organization collects data and offers assistance to administrators that raise awareness of antisemitism and discrimination in schools and the community.

College Students and Antisemitism

According to a survey done by Hillel and the ADL (2023), 73% of Jewish college students and 44% of non-Jewish witnessed or experienced antisemitism since the start of the school year (Hillel, 2023). In addition, prior to October 7, the survey found 64% of Jewish students stated their colleges were welcoming to them, with the proportion decreasing to 39% post-October 7. The survey also showed that 55% of the students had completed DEI training, but only 18% stated that it had any material on antisemitism.

A similar poll conducted by Hillel in 2024 found 61% of respondents stating that there had been antisemitic, threatening, or derogatory language toward Jewish students during campus protests with 63% feeling less safe and 40% feeling the need to hide their identity (Hillel International, 2024a, b). These students experienced bias and discrimination in their classrooms and were less safe on campus. Among the taunts to Jewish students included statements to go back to Poland, all you do is colonize, dirty Jews, they were spit on, and in some instances, professors were among the attackers (Christensen, 2024). Consequently, students felt threatened and intimidated and many were unable to complete their coursework.

Protests became particularly vehement at Columbia University (AMCHA Initiative, 2024).

> I've been screamed at because I wear a hostage tag and called a Zionist and a murderer. People aren't talking nearly enough about the anti-Zionism that is being pushed in the encampment and how that normalizes prejudice against Israelis and Jews. To force Jewish students to denounce Zionism? We don't do that to other students. We don't expect Chinese students to denounce their military at the start of every conversation. "Right now, Columbia is making us feel like we're not welcome. When they say, 'We don't want Zionists here,' that means we Jewish Zionists have to go back. It's a form of resistance.

Students were afraid for their well-being and disillusioned by the inaction of the university to quell antisemitism.

Comments from other campus protests included,

> "Before Oct. 7 I was cautious, but now I'm scared to walk around campus. I got yelled at by someone who saw my 'Bring Them Home' necklace." "I don't feel safe in my own dorm. It targeted me where I live. That's not just terrifying, that's outright harassment, that's antisemitism."

> Multiple guys came up to me from the bottom [of the fence], and they reached through the fence to grab the flag because I was on my side of the line. They punched me in the stomach, grabbed the flag and started a back and forth, and then one of them spit at me. And then I went to the cops, and apparently one of the guys that engaged in that had flashed his gun that he was carrying. (AMCHA Initiative, 2024).

One college student shared this experience when trying to get to his class at his university:

> Upon arriving at campus for my last day as an undergraduate, I saw signs boarding the glass windows to the main entrance. They said absolutely heinous things. One of them said "Israel? Is (not) real." Not even clever. Even still, I felt paralyzed. I immediately called my parents and told them I didn't feel safe going into class. My parents understood, but it was my last day of class and I had one more thing I needed to present to the class to finish up. They told me if I could, to try and walk by immediately and pay it no mind. I knew they were probably right. I walked closer to the foyer of the building when I realized the signs were the least of my problems. I saw movement. I saw marching. I

> entered the building and what I experienced almost felt cinematic. I'd seen it all over the news, but not right in front of me. Six huge camping tents lined the inside of the main entrance, with people marching, carrying picket signs, shouting antisemitic and anti-Zionist remarks. I wanted to stop walking inside, but I had to just keep moving. If I turned my head, I was worried they'd know I was their target. It was such a surreal experience. Could they tell I was Jewish? Would I have to fight? I knew I could probably defend myself, but would today be that day? I picked up speed and tried to get up to the second floor as fast as I possibly could. Their words stung in my ears like knives, even as the actual sound faded. I knew I couldn't stay. "How did they even get in here?" I asked myself. In order to enter into the building, students need to present their university IDs. And I realized in that moment what brought them inside our walls and what allowed them to bypass the "security" team: hatred for the Jewish people (Anonymous student #1, personal communication, June 20, 2024).

Colleges should expand mental health services to help those students who are experiencing anxiety and depression due to the rising antisemitism. Touro University, a large Jewish University in New York City, opened a free walk-in mental health clinic for their students. The purpose of this clinic is to help students at the University who have increased anxiety due to antisemitism. They expanded their mental health services to meet the increasing needs of their students (Rudy, 2023).

Social Work Students

Antisemitism not being discussed in the classes on diversity tells Jewish students that their experiences have no real importance and that they just do not matter (MacDonald-Dennis, 2006). This also gives non-Jews the message that Jews are not a discriminated group and do not require acknowledgment of being victims of discrimination.

Although social work emphasizes intersectionality, Jewish social work students are frequently discouraged and even silenced by their peers and professors when trying to discuss antisemitism (Cox & Marlowe, 2023). Jewish social work students are told that because they are white and have privilege, they cannot be oppressed. This goes against the concept of intersectionality and blatantly ignores antisemitism. In 2020, 10% of Jews in the United States did not identify as white. They identified as Asian, Black, Hispanic, Native American, or multiracial (Gottlieb & Steigerwald, 2024; Brandeis Cohen Center for Modern Jewish Studies, 2020). Consequently, calling all Jews White and privileged is in itself a misnomer.

Recently, one social work student said the following to a Jewish social work student in a social work class:

> Oh, I don't know if I ever told you, but I hate the Jews. I'm not trying to say the Holocaust was ok or anything, but I don't know… I really don't like them. I'm not like an antisemite or anything. (Anonymous Student #2, personal communication, April 29, 2024)

It seems unfathomable that the social work profession can blatantly discriminate against others. While social workers have a responsibility to fight social injustices, there cannot be a conscious decision to leave a specific group out of the discussion and have an acceptance of hatred in the classroom. The impact of antisemitism and the discrimination that it engenders continues, leading to further fear and trauma.

Helping Those Impacted by Antisemitism

Social workers can use a multidimensional approach to help those clients who are impacted by antisemitism and who are seeking help.

1. Utilizing social work skills

   To help clients dealing with the impact of antisemitism, social workers need to use their skills of active listening, showing empathy, and being where the client is. Social workers need to acknowledge that their client has experienced discrimination. With any client who has experienced any form of oppression, it is not the social worker's role to judge this experience or to give an opinion about it, but to listen to the client and to show cultural humility. The oppression should also not be minimized.

2. Not pathologizing the reaction

   A client's reaction of anxiety, depression, and/or trauma may be a very appropriate response to the antisemitism that is occurring. These symptoms should not be pathologized. These clients are reacting to extremely stressful situations and are reacting to them. It is our job as social workers to help these clients, but not to say that they have something wrong with them, when they are doing their best to deal with being discriminated against. The issues are with the systems around them. The threat to them is real, so responding to it is correct. Coming for help to deal with this is a true strength (Dale & Saunders, 2018).

3. Addressing real safety concerns

   In working with these clients, acknowledging and addressing real safety concerns can be a priority. Jews are being threatened now and many do not feel safe. Many Jewish clients will not be able to express themselves and address their feelings if they feel unprotected and at risk for danger. Ensuring their sense of safety in the agency is crucial for effective work.

4. Limiting social media

   Social media today is filled with antisemitic posts. Exposure to these can cause increased fear, depression, anxiety, and being in a state of hypervigilance. Limiting this exposure can decrease anxiety and improve one's sense of well-being. Part of working with a client impacted by antisemitism can be focused on the client limiting the use of social media. Having the client take some control of their social media use can also be empowering for the client.

5. Tools for coping

For any client seeking therapy services, evidence-based practices should be used. While acknowledging the antisemitism that the client has and is experiencing, social workers can use interventions that are shown to be effective for the client's symptoms. The social worker's role is not to tell our clients that antisemitism should not bother them. It is to help them cope with the circumstances around them.

One intervention that can be used is cognitive behavioral therapy (CBT). When using CBT with a client who is seeking help to cope with antisemitism, telling a client that their thoughts regarding marginalization are unhelpful or untrue would be ineffective and detrimental to the client. When working with the client on cognitive restructuring, the social worker must be culturally responsive to the client's experiences. Social workers need to acknowledge what is happening to the client, validate them, and then help the client to decrease their negative feelings associated with the thought so that they can cope with what is happening. Building resilience and focusing on strengths can be very effective (Suttenberg, 2016).

Another aspect of using CBT with a client who has been impacted by antisemitism is to focus on thoughts that are empowering for the client. Negative cognitions can be worked on to focus on strengths instead, such as the power that the client has to cope and that the client is not responsible for the oppression that they are experiencing. Social workers can also work with the client to see what coping mechanisms have worked for them in the past (Dale & Saunders, 2018).

Using distress tolerance tools of dialectical behavior therapy (DBT) can also be effective in coping with the impact of antisemitism. The emotional reaction to antisemitism can be very difficult to deal with. Providing clients with tools to decrease their feelings of being overwhelmed and to cope with their other negative reactions could be needed. These tools could be distress tolerance tools. These are part of crisis survival skills and help clients to cope with a crisis (Linehan, 2014), such as being oppressed and marginalized. Distress tolerance tools are used for the short-term in helping clients to cope with emotional pain and avoid poor coping that could lead to self-destructive behavior.

Mindfulness tools can also be very helpful with clients who have been impacted. These tools can help clients to live in the present, without focusing on the past and the future. Worry about the future can increase anxiety. Being fully present in the here and now can decrease negative feelings and thoughts. This can also help with emotional regulation and help one's mind and body to relax.

Mindfulness also encourages self-compassion and being non-judgmental toward oneself. This focus can also help to relax a person who is struggling with anxiety. Using breathing exercises, body scan meditations, mindful walking, and mindful eating are all mindfulness practices that can be important interventions in relieving stress and strengthening well-being.

It is important to note that none of these approaches discussed minimize the social injustice of antisemitism or its degree of hatred toward the Jewish people. The approaches are for social workers to use to help their clients to cope with what is happening around them.

Conclusion

Antisemitism is a particularly noxious form of oppression that impacts the mental health and well-being of Jewish people. It affects all ages, young children to adults, and can produce anxiety, feelings of insecurity, trauma, depression, and self-hate in its victims. However, in comparison to other types of oppression, there is relatively little research on the effects of antisemitism on mental health and psychological well-being. Jewish self-hatred and concealing one's identity are common means of coping that in themselves can result in further stress.

Interventions for college students as well as social work students who often encounter antisemitism in their classes are essential. Social work skills at all levels are important in dealing with the impact of antisemitism ranging from actual safety concerns to confronting social media sites that spread antisemitism. Specific therapeutic techniques such as CBT, DBT, and mindfulness can be important interventions in helping people to cope.

Main Points

- Oppression can negatively impact mental health. There is limited research on how antisemitism impacts the mental health of Jewish people.
- Because Jews are often seen as white, the perception of their history of being marginalized and discriminated against is often overlooked.
- Recent research shows that due to increasing antisemitism almost half of Jewish people in the United States are changing their behaviors.
- Intersectionality focuses on different parts of one's identity. Jewish people can be privileged in some ways, but still oppressed based on their religion.
- To cope with the ongoing antisemitism, Jewish people may develop self-hatred which can lead to mental health problems.
- Antisemitism can impact school-age children, causing issues in emotional regulation, physical symptoms, cognitive issues, behavioral issues, and issues in school performance.
- Antisemitism is often excluded from discussions in social work education, which can invalidate Jewish students' experiences.
- Social workers should not pathologize Jewish clients' reactions to antisemitism and should validate their experiences and feelings.
- Social workers can help clients affected by antisemitism by using a multidimensional approach. This approach includes using social work skills, encouraging limited social media use, addressing concerns around safety, and using evidence-based treatments for anxiety and depression.
- Tools from cognitive behavioral therapy, dialectical behavioral therapy, and mindfulness can help those impacted by antisemitism.

Discussion Questions and Short Assignments

The following suggested discussion questions can be done in class in small groups or by having students write their own short papers:

- Discuss why there is very little research on how antisemitism impacts Jewish people's mental health.
- How does the American Psychological Association's strategic plan to eliminate racism, excluding antisemitism, impact Jewish individuals?
- Jews are often characterized as having white privilege. How does this categorization impact a discussion of antisemitism and discrimination of Jews?
- How can people become more aware of how covert oppression is occurring?
- Discuss applying the concept of intersectionality to the experiences of Jewish people. Include factors such as religion, culture, and race in this discussion.
- Discuss how Jewish individual's mental health can be impacted as a result of antisemitism. How can social workers help these clients?
- Discuss how antisemitism in school settings impacts Jewish school-age children. What can schools do to create a safe environment for Jewish children?
- Discuss how you would implement Cognitive Behavioral Therapy with Jewish clients dealing with antisemitism.
- Discuss how you would implement Dialectical Behavior Therapy tools with Jewish clients dealing with antisemitism.
- Discuss how you would implement mindfulness with Jewish clients dealing with antisemitism.

In-Class Exercises

Goal: To work with clients impacted by antisemitism.

Exercise 1: Working with Cheryl
Phase I: Distribute the case of Cheryl to the class

Phase II: Role-play with Cheryl
Explain to the class that they will be doing a role-play. Break up the class into groups of 3. In each group of 3, one student will play Cheryl, one will play Cheryl's field placement supervisor, and one will be an observer.

Scenario: You are Cheryl's supervisor at her field placement. You find Cheryl to be an excellent student. She is very hard-working and very intelligent. She also is very committed to helping her clients. You really feel like you have been a mentor to her through her MSW program. She comes to you to tell you what she has been experiencing in her program. She is thinking about leaving the program to transfer to another one or just leaving the social work profession. She is asking you for your advice on what to do.

Phase III: Debrief
Ask the groups to share how the role-play went. What were the challenges and what went well?

Exercise 2: Working with Brian
Phase I: Distribute the case of Brian to the class

Phase II: Role-play directions
Explain to the class that Brian has come to you seeking therapy because of his increasing anxiety and depression related to antisemitism. Break the class up into groups of three. In each group, one student should play the social worker, one student should play Brian, and one student should be an observer.

Depending on which intervention will be utilized in the role-play(s), the instructor should review either CBT, DBT, and/or a Mindfulness tool with the class to be applied in the role-play.

Phase III. Using tools from a specific intervention
In this session, the social worker should use CBT cognitive restructuring to work with the client.

or

In this session, use DBT distress tolerance tools to work with the client.

or
In this session, use mindfulness tools to work with the client.

Phase IV: Debrief
Debrief with the students about the role-play. What went well in the role-play? What could have been better? What were the challenges?

Cases

Case 1: A Jewish Social Work Student

Cheryl is currently an MSW student in a highly respected program. Her Jewish identity has caused her to feel very isolated in her classes. She is committed in her fight against all kinds of discrimination and social injustices. However, when she tries to bring up antisemitism in her classes, she is met with anger and opposition from her classmates. She feels completely invalidated by her peers. Instead of feeling as though she is a member of the class, she feels completely alone and excluded in her class's discussions about oppression.

Cheryl was brought up in a Jewish home, where social justice was greatly encouraged. Both of her parents were very active in social justice activities and she felt inspired by this. This is why she ultimately decided to get an MSW. Cheryl was hoping that in the MSW program, she would be able to have meaningful conversations with her classmates and professors about injustices and how she could go about combating them. She was especially looking forward to her classes on oppression and advocacy.

As Cheryl went further into the program, she began to realize that antisemitism wasn't discussed and was not going to be discussed in any of her classes. Cheryl's professors and classmates also refused to acknowledge the fact that antisemitism is increasing in this country and is plaguing Jewish people all over the world. When Cheryl tried to bring up these issues, she was told that she was shifting the conversation away from people who were actually experiencing oppression.

When discussing different forms of discrimination in one of her classes, Cheryl tried to share her thoughts on current incidents of antisemitism. Her professor would not allow her to continue speaking about this topic. He said that antisemitism was not relevant to this course and that the course was designed to focus on marginalized races. Cheryl once again felt silenced. She felt that the oppression she experienced was completely neglected again.

Cheryl tried to address antisemitism in several of her assignments in her program. When Cheryl asked her professors for feedback on her research proposal about antisemitism in social work, her professors very much discouraged her from pursuing this topic. They didn't give her much feedback at all and told her that they were worried other MSW students might be offended. They also expressed their discomfort related to the topic. Cheryl felt a lack of support from the faculty and felt completely alone in her fight against antisemitism.

One of her professors assigned a group assignment, where students were asked to analyze how discrimination affects different communities. Cheryl said that they should evaluate the intersectionality of religion and ethnicity that Jewish people are grappling with today. Cheryl's group felt as though antisemitism was not relevant to the assignment and that they needed to focus on other groups. Cheryl tried to inform her group members of what was going on in the world today related to antisemitism and the rise in hate crimes against Jewish people. Her group members were not interested and said that they should focus on other topics.

The silencing of Jewish voices in social work education has a great deal of implications for Cheryl's sense of belonging in the social work profession. By erasing and denying an intrinsic part of Cheryl's identity, her peers are fostering an environment of ignorance toward the oppression faced by Jewish people every day. Cheryl is grappling with the fact that she does not want to remain silent about these issues, but that she also must somehow conform to the expectations of those around her, those who silence her. She is beginning to feel that she might need to drop out of the MSW program. She is beginning to look into other degrees in the helping profession.

Case 2: A Jewish College Student

Brian, a sophomore at a prominent university, is experiencing rising antisemitism on campus. He is a proud Jewish student who is actively involved in both his classes and activities on campus. When he began at the university, he felt a true sense of belonging with the community there. However, due to recent incidents of antisemitism, he is feeling very alone and vulnerable. His sense of belonging and feelings of security at the school are now gone.

Brian grew up in a Jewish community where community members were close and there was a focus on Jewish traditions and culture. He never considered himself to be religious, but did identify as Jewish. When he arrived at college, he got involved in his academics, he made new friends, and got involved in Jewish activities at Hillel. He initially loved his college experience, including his classes and friendships.

However, since October 7th, Brian has seen a real increase of antisemitism on campus. There was a swastika spray-painted on the wall in one dorm. There were also derogatory comments made at students during a gathering. Brian started feeling unwelcome on campus. Brian tried to speak to his peers and administration at the university about this but was met with resistance.

The antisemitic incidents continued to increase, with Brian feeling fearful and insecure. A swastika was painted on the outside of the Hillel House. During a discussion on the Middle East, Brian was silenced by antisemitic comments.

All of these incidents have had a negative impact on Brian's mental health. He is considering transferring to another institution that could be more inclusive. Brian is a resilient individual, but these prejudices have taken a toll on his well-being. He is having increased anxiety and depression and has even considered just dropping out and going home.

References

AMCHA Initiative. (2024). *About AMCHA Initiative.* Retrieved from https://amchainitiative.org/about/

American Jewish Committee (AJC). (2024). *The state of Antisemitism in America 2023.* Retrieved from https://www.ajc.org/news/new-ajc-report-46-of-american-jews-altered-behavior-out-of-fear-of-antisemitism

Anti-Defamation League (ADL). (2024). *Conversations that matter: Understanding and discussing Antisemitism with young people.* Retrieved from https://www.adl.org/sites/default/files/documents/2024-06/conversations-that-matter-understanding-and-discussing-antisemitism-with-young-people.pdf

Brandeis Cohen Center for Modern Jewish Studies. (2020). *American Jewish population project.* Retrieved from https://ajpp.brandeis.edu/faqs

Brenner, I. (2007). Contemporary anti-Semitism: Variations on an ancient theme. In H. Parens, A. Mahfouz, S. W. Twemlow, & D. E. Scharff (Eds.), *The future of prejudice: Psychoanalysis and the prevention of prejudice* (pp. 141–161). Rowman & Littlefield.

Camacho, G., Reinka, M. A., & Quinn, D. M. (2020). Concealment of stigmatized identities. *Current Opinion in Psychology, 31*, 28–32.

Christensen, J. (2024). Jewish students share harrowing experiences of campus antisemitism as they beg congress to hold universities accountable. *New York Post.* Retrieved from https://nypost.com/2024/02/29/us-news/jewish-students-implore-congress-to-stop-campus-antisemitism/

Committee on Education & the Workforce. (2024). *Hearing Recap: K-12 Antisemitism Edition.* Retrieved from https://edworkforce.house.gov/news/documentsingle.aspx?DocumentID=410551

Cox, C., & Marlowe, D. (2023). Antisemitism in social work findings from an exploratory national survey. *Journal of Religion & Spirituality in Social Work: Social Thought, 43*(1), 3–17. https://doi.org/10.1080/15426432.2023.2289435

Crenshaw, K. (1989). Demarginalizing the intersection of race and sex: A black feminist critique of antidiscrimination doctrine, feminist theory and antiracist politics. *University of Chicago Legal Forum, 1989*(1), 139–167.

Dale, S. K., & Saunders, S. (2018, September). *Using cognitive behavioral therapy approaches in assisting individuals coping with marginalization, oppression, and discrimination.* Retrieved from http://www.societyforpsychotherapy.org/using-cognitive-behavioral-therapy-to-assist-individuals-facing-oppression

Facing History and Ourselves. (2022). https://www.facinghistory.org/resource-library/antisemitism-its-impacts

Frankel, J. (2004). Identification with the aggressor and the 'normal traumas': Clinical implications. *International Forum of Psychoanalysis, 13*, 78–83.

Gottlieb, J. D., & Steigerwald, A. (2024). Editorial: Social work's role in ending antisemitism: If not us, who? *International Journal of Social Work Values and Ethics, 21*(1), 14–27. https://doi.org/10.55521/10-021-103

Greenfield, B. (2023). *How antisemitism affects mental health.* Retrieved from https://www.yahoo.com/lifestyle/how-antisemitism-affects-mental-health

Hillel International. (2023). *Nearly three-quarters of Jewish student experienced or witnessed Antisemitism om Campus, new survey finds.* Retrieved from https://www.hillel.org/nearly-three-quarters-of-jewish-students-experienced-or-witnessed-antisemitism-on-campus-new-survey-finds/

Hillel International. (2024a). *Majority of Jewish college students say the feel less safe Dur to Encampments: 61% report Antisemitism during campus protests.* Retrieved from https://www.hillel.org/majority-of-jewish-college-students-say-they-feel-less-safe-due-to-encampments-61-report-antisemitism-during-campus-protests/

Hillel International. (2024b). *Across college Hillels, mental health and wellness professionals make a difference.* Retrieved from https://www.hillel.org/across-college-hillels-mental-health-and-wellness-professionals-are-making-a-difference/

Hollinger, D. (2006). *Postethnic America.* Basic Books.

Kandel, I. (2024). *Six tools to respond to our children's fest.* Retrieved from https://aish.com/talking-to-your-kids-about-rising-anti-semitism/

Kosdon, S. M., Keller, A., Berry, J. W., Stiver, D. J., Whiteford, K., & O'Connor, L. E. (2021). The experience of being Jewish: Living with antisemitism. *Journal of Research in Social Psychology, 7*(1), 1–5.

Lewin, K. (1948). *Resolving social conflicts and field theory in social science* (p. 164). Harper.

Linehan, M. (2014). *DBT skills training manual.* Guilford Press.

Lipstadt, D. E. (2019). *Antisemitism: Here and now.* Schocken Books.

MacDonald-Dennis, C. (2006). Understanding anti-semitism and its impact: A new framework for conceptualizing Jewish identity. *Equity & Excellence in Education, 39*(3), 267–278. https://doi.org/10.1080/10665680600792794

Mallaly, B., & West, J. (2018). *Challenging oppression and confronting privilege: A critical approach to antioppressive and anti-privilege theory and practice* (3rd Ed.). Oxford.

New York State Office of Mental Health. (n.d.). *Spotlight on Jewish American's mental health.* Retrieved from https://omh.ny.gov/omhweb/cultural_competence/spotlight-on-jewish-americans.pdf

Ostow, M. (1997). *Judaism and psychoanalysis.* Karnac.

Quinn, D. M., & Earnshaw, V. A. (2013). Concealable stigmatized identities and psychological well-being. *Social and Personality Psychology Compass, 7*(1), 40–51. https://doi.org/10.1111/spc3.12005

Rubin, D. I. (2017). Whiter shade of pale: Making the case for Jewish presence in the multicultural classroom. *International Journal of Multicultural Education, 19*(2), 131–145.

Rudy, M. (2023). Jewish students struggling with antisemitism at college now have use of walk-in mental health clinic. *Fox News.* https://www.foxnews.com/health/jewish-students-struggling-antisemitism-college-walk-mental-health-clinic

Schlosser, L. Z. (2006). Affirmative psychotherapy for American Jews. *Psychotherapy: Theory. Research Practice, Training, 43*, 424–435.
School Watch. (n.d.). *Take action and get involved.* School Watch. https://www.schoolwatch.me/take-action
Suttenberg, L. P. (2016). Never forget: Cognitive restructuring limitations in holocaust related layered trauma. *Clinical Social Work Journal, 44*, 231–240.
Volkan, V. D. (2014). *Psychoanalysis, international relations, and diplomacy: A sourcebook on large-group psychology*. Routledge.
Walker, L. E. A., Cole, E., Friedman, S. L., Rom-Rymer, B., Steinberg, A., & Warshaw, S. (2024). The American psychological association and antisemitism: Toward equity, diversity, and inclusion. *American Psychologist*. https://doi-org.avoserv2.library.fordham.edu/10.1037/amp0001369
Williams, M., Osman, M., & Hyon, C. (2023). Understanding the psychological impact of oppression using the trauma symptoms of discrimination scale. *Chronic Stress (Thousand Oaks, Calif.), 7*, 24705470221149511. https://doi.org/10.1177/24705470221149511
Yad Vashem. (n.d.). *Remember your name: Surviving the Holocaust under a false name*. https://www.yadvashem.org/yv/en/exhibitions/false-identity/index.asp

Chapter 7
Antisemitism and Intergenerational Trauma

Discrimination and Its Relationship to Antisemitism

Most of the research on discrimination focuses on victimization, perceptions of the discrimination experienced, the relationship between discrimination and physical health or illness, such as diabetes or obesity, and how discrimination influences mental health problems and illnesses, such as depressive and anxiety disorders or poor coping (Abbott & Mollen, 2018; Doane & Elliott, 2015; Jordanova et al., 2015; Wu & Schimmele, 2021). As discrimination negatively shapes one's mental and physical health, it can result in anxiety, stress, and fear. Discriminatory actions or continued experiences of discrimination across the lifespan can result in mental illnesses, such as post-traumatic stress disorder, that can influence a person's overall sense of themselves and their well-being.

Discrimination commonly occurs due to an attribute, social identity, or religion, although little research examines religious discrimination (Wu & Schimmele, 2021). Not surprisingly, religious discrimination is tied to self-rated mental health problems, but further investigation is needed to expand an in-depth understanding of this negative social experience in societies around the world (Wu & Schimmele, 2021).

Antisemitism, a form of religious discrimination, is, "Prejudice or discrimination against Jews. Antisemitism can be based on hatred against Jews because of their religious beliefs or their group membership (ethnicity), but also on the erroneous belief that Jews are a race" (Echoes & Reflections, 2005–2024). Unfortunately, antisemitism is a prominent discriminatory experience for the approximately 15.7 million Jewish people around the world (The Jewish Agency for Israel, 2024). In comparison to all other religious groups in the United States, Jewish people continually experience more discrimination (Scheitle & Ecklund, 2020; Vang et al., 2019; Wu & Schimmele, 2021).

C. B. Cox, D. B. Marlowe, *Social Work and Antisemitism*,
https://doi.org/10.1007/978-3-031-72771-9_7

The Holocaust and Trauma

Between 1933 and 1945, the Nazi regime engaged in the systematic, state-sponsored murder of over six million Jewish people. As a result of discrimination, persecution, and almost total annihilation, the Jewish people have experienced a form of collective trauma throughout history, with the Holocaust being the most recent time of systemic hatred and violence. This trauma has also had an impact on future generations. A traumatic event can even change the life trajectory of the individuals most impacted by it. As with any traumatic event, there is "shrapnel" that comes out of the explosion, impacting those around it. With collective trauma, the "shrapnel" impacts entire communities, even those who are not a part of the targeted group can be directly impacted.

According to the Diagnostic and Statistical Manual of Mental Disorders (DSM-5-TR) (American Psychological Association [APA], 2022), "posttraumatic stress disorder (PTSD) is the development of characteristic symptoms following exposure to one or more traumatic events" (p. 305). Symptoms can include reliving experiences that are fear-based, symptoms affecting emotions and behaviors, having the inability to feel pleasure or to be happy, negative cognitions, externalizing symptoms, and dissociative symptoms. These symptoms can vary, from having one symptom to having a combination of symptoms (APA, 2022). Trauma reminders are reminders of the traumatic events and can bring up physical reactions and/or emotional reactions (Mayo Clinic, n.d.). Antisemitism today can be a trauma reminder to survivors, their children and grandchildren, and to anyone who was impacted by the Holocaust.

In this chapter, excerpts from interviews with three adult children of Holocaust survivors will be included. These interviews are referred to as interviews with Adult Child A, Adult Child B, and Adult Child C. The information given by the Adult Children provides examples of the impact of their parents' experiences on each of them and explains how they are responding to antisemitism today.

Intergenerational Trauma

The Holocaust is an acute illustration of intergenerational trauma. It shows how unconscionable horrors can be transferred from one generation to the next. It is an example of how trauma can impact children and even grandchildren of those impacted through the scars that continue to mold each generation. Research on the transmission of intergenerational trauma from Holocaust survivors to their children and grandchildren has uncovered the possible psychological impacts that can occur. These impacts may include increased rates of anxiety, depression, and PTSD (Sagi-Schwartz et al., 2003; Kellermann, 2001). Firestone (2019) describes the impact of the Holocaust and intergenerational trauma in this way:

> The residue of our ancestors' unresolved injury does not simply disappear. In fact, it often weighs most heavily on the introspective, sensitive members of the next generation (p. 5).

Intergenerational trauma is a specific kind of trauma, which occurs when traumatic events are "passed across generations without exposure to the original event" (Isobel et al., 2021, p. 631). Some might assume that the intergenerational transmission of trauma occurs because traumatized people raise traumatized children. This is a simplistic understanding of the phenomenon and does not consider the multiple ways that traumatic information gets "communicated" including behaviorally, socially, emotionally, psychologically, and genetically.

The transmission of trauma within Holocaust survivor families can occur through various mechanisms, including familial narratives, parental behaviors, attachment dynamics, and genetics. Rakoff (1966) was one of the first researchers to look at intergenerational trauma in Holocaust survivors and their children, finding increased levels of psychological distress. Since this research, numerous studies followed and identified higher levels of anxiety, depression, and PTSD (DeAngelis, 2023).

Epstein (2019), in her interviews with children of Holocaust survivors, shares their experiences of trauma and resilience and shows the intergenerational trauma that can be passed down. Her interviews also reveal how adult children look at their own identities and the impact of history on them. Some survivors might pass down their trauma through explicit or implicit communication of their experiences, as well as through their caregiving styles and relational patterns with their children and grandchildren (Kellermann, 2001; Bayer-Topilsky, 2018).

Storytelling and Communication

Families often pass stories on from one generation to another. My (Marlowe) own maternal grandparents both arrived in the United States before the beginning of WWII. However, the Holocaust still had a profoundly significant impact on my family, probably in many more ways that I am even aware of. My mother once told me that when she was a little girl, she had the same nightmare every night. She asked me if I was familiar with the meat grinder that my grandmother had that sat on her kitchen counter, which I did remember seeing. My mother shared, that in her dream, Hitler was standing next to a giant version of that meat grinder. There was a long line of Jews. They would go, one by one, into the meat grinder. I have never been able to forget my mother telling me about this dream. The talk of the war and the Holocaust was passed to my mother, which was evidenced in her daily nightmare. The story of her dream was then passed on to me. This was experienced by a family who did not lose any immediate family members in the Holocaust. And yet, there was a transaction of fear that was passed down from one generation to the next (Marlowe).

As survivors share their stories with their children and grandchildren, these experiences become encoded into their own self-views and worldviews. Generations internalize these stories and learnings. Other survivors may not share their stories, resulting in a kind of silence around the traumatic experiences. This silence can also lead to a transmission of the trauma without children and grandchildren even knowing the details of what actually occurred. Stories and narratives can inform future generations of a family's traditions, histories, and beliefs, but also of the traumas of their ancestors (Dever, 2023). The stories and narratives that are passed on to future generations are similar to how children, grandchildren, and great-grandchildren inherit intergenerational trauma.

Johns et al. (2022) explored the impact of family communication on the intergenerational transmission of Holocaust trauma among second- and third-generation survivors. The study, which involved 98 adults with relatives who experienced the Holocaust, investigated the associations among Jewish identity, historical loss awareness, and family communication about the Holocaust. The findings suggest that stronger Jewish identity and more frequent family communication predicted a greater awareness of the loss, supporting the idea that family narratives about trauma influenced the next generation. The study defined communication as healthy or unhealthy, with unhealthy communication linked to poorer mental well-being. While healthy communication was not directly associated with mental well-being, the results emphasize the significant negative impact of unhealthy communication, suggesting that communication type matters in the transmission of trauma.

The following interviews with the adult children of Holocaust survivors highlight the different ways that their parents shared their experiences of the Holocaust with them and the impact it has had on them.

Interviews with Adult Children of Holocaust Survivors

Adult Child A reported the following story about how her father hid during the Holocaust. Her father was able to conceal his Jewish identify and obtain papers under a Christian name. He was drafted into the Polish army and was able to hide in plain sight. During the next few years, he was captured by the Germans, was held in a POW camp, and was starved, with the dogs being fed before the prisoners. Eventually, he escaped into the woods and met partisans whom he helped to blow up some train tracks where Germans were shipping ammunition. He was then captured. He survived all of this and went to find his family, but all his family members who did not hide were murdered.

His mother and sister were murdered together when a Polish man told soldiers about them in exchange for a bottle of vodka. His older brother, who came back to check on them, was also murdered. His father was murdered in a Kristallnacht type of event. His one surviving brother never talked about how he survived. His brother's wife survived by living in a non-Jewish person's closet for a few years. Finally, her father made his way to America with nothing, sponsored by some cousins.

Adult Child A reported that her mother's story is "vaguer," mainly because she was much younger than her father. She spoke much more about it because her family survived. She and her parents hid in a bunker in the woods. They slept during the day and could leave at night to find food.

Adult Child A reported that she never thought that her parents were different from other parents. The first time she realized they were different was when they were in the Catskills. She was about 10 years old and remembers sitting at the kids' dining room table when someone asked about her parents having an accent. She thought, "Accent? They don't have an accent." Her parents actually had very thick Polish accents that she never noticed.

Although her parents did not talk about the Holocaust while she was growing up, they always went to the annual Holocaust remembrance ceremonies. Adult Child A and her sister were sent to yeshiva even though they were not religious. Her parents wanted them to get a Jewish education. Each year, the yeshiva acknowledged Yom Hashoah with films of the Holocaust that she found "horrible." There were also large gatherings in New York City for Yom Hashoah as well. Her family emphasized that the Holocaust was very important to remember. Each year, at these events, her father would cry. This was the only time she would see him cry. She remained reluctant to ask him what had happened because she did not want to upset him by bringing back the memories for him.

When Adult Child A was 22, after she had completed college, her father started talking about how he survived. After he told her his story, she ran to her bedroom and wrote it down so she would have it. He told her in a very factual manner, leaving out emotional details. She felt like he planned to wait until she was mature enough to handle it.

Adult Child A shared that when her niece was in college, she interviewed her aunt and uncle about their experiences. Adult Child A's sister sent her the video to watch. When her father started crying while talking about the last time he saw his own father, she had to turn off the video. Adult Child A's sister then hired a writer to write down their parent's story. Adult Child A stated, "I haven't read it because it's hard for me."

When Adult Child A was asked about the impact of growing up as the child of Holocaust survivors, she had the following responses:

When growing up, Adult Child A's family didn't have other family for support, but they had a group of Polish friends, who were also survivors, who were their family. They would go to each other's houses and the families really got to know each other and become like family.

> When we got together, they were so vibrant and full of life. They would dance and drink a little vodka. They just really appreciated life so much….My parents thought that life is so precious. They didn't take it for granted.

> My parents really gave us a happy childhood….not a sad tone in my house.

> We lived a block away from the synagogue. They were having second generation holocaust meetings and my mother said maybe you want to check it out. I was in my late teens. People were talking about the difficulties they had. I really couldn't relate.

When asked about the impact today on Adult Child A of growing up as the child of Holocaust survivors:

> …you have to have a suitcase ready (in case you have to run). Sometimes, I think that if they could be so resilient, so can I.

Due to my parents' lack of food,

> I do a lot of freezing and a lot of eating. My sister throws out things, but her husband doesn't have Holocaust parents.

When asked about how October 7th and current antisemitism are impacting her, Adult Child A stated:

> Maybe more frightened of another Holocaust than other people are.

She feels she might be a bit more alarmed by what's happening by her experience.

> After October 7th, I thought who is going to hide me. I was thinking about my Christian friends.

Adult Child A reported posting on Facebook, asking who would hide them, meaning that when the Jews are taken away, who would protect her and her family.

Adult Child B is the child of a father who is a Holocaust survivor, who was born in Vienna. Her paternal grandfather was murdered in a concentration camp. Her father was hidden in the South of France and was then on a kinder transport. He arrived in the United States and grew up in a Jewish orphanage in Milwaukee. His mother was able to get to England, where she was a domestic worker. Eventually, after several years, she was able to get to the United States and reunite with Adult Child B's father.

Adult Child B doesn't really know when she realized her father was a Holocaust survivor. She stated that her father was very "emotionally shut down, like he really is a trauma survivor…" It was much later in Adult Child B's father's life, when he began to reconnect with people from his past. He reconnected with the kids that he had been hidden away with. Her father had been one of the younger ones in hiding. The group came together and took a trip to the south of France to see where they had been hidden. "So my dad started to unfreeze a bit of his history."

When asked about the impact today on Adult Child B of growing up as the child of Holocaust survivors, she had the following responses:

Adult Child B stated that her father's behavior as a survivor impacted every aspect of her childhood. He would go on business trips, but not share where he was.

> I remember my mom telling me that she told his mother, my grandmother, he's doing this, he would basically disappear, which is interesting cause he disappeared, you know, as a kid.

> I guess that my dad would do this, like she [my mother] should just like to know where he is…she didn't know how to get in touch with her husband, and you know, his mother used to say to my mom, that's Hitler still at work.

Adult Child B feels that she grew up with a father that cared for her, but that he was emotionally unavailable and vacant. When speaking about her siblings, "I think everybody's life has been stunted to a great extent because of my dad's story, and how it then interplayed with my mom."When asked about the impact today of growing up as the child of Holocaust survivors:

> I've worked really hard not to let the damage affect me. I've had to work very hard to create the life that I've created for myself.

Adult Child B also states that she really values her friendships very much. She has a family that she feels would do anything for her, but not an "emotional family." She added that she does the opposite of how she was brought up.When asked about how October 7th and current antisemitism is impacting her, Adult Child B stated:

> I had this very strong sense of like, I'm not going anywhere… not a fear, not really fear, but more like a defiance. You can all go xxx yourself, we're not, I'm not going anywhere…like sort of this strengthening my sense. What really happened for me was a strengthening of my Jewish identity, I really got in touch with who I am.
>
> I felt like the child of a Holocaust survivor, and that was living in my body, like I could feel it physically in my hips and in my body, and I had to release it…I'm carrying this intergenerational trauma in my body…My ancestors are in my body.

Adult Child B began going to synagogue and had a need to be with other Jewish people, feeling a strong sense of comfort from doing this. She explained more about her reaction,

> But I think what was going on in my body was this fear the Holocaust that could happen again, but felt like I was living it in my body. And this could happen again. This could happen again.
>
> I just need to be around Jews… I would go to services and I would hear the prayers. I would sing the prayers or mumble the prayers and I would just cry, and it just felt, help me feel so connected to who I am.

Adult Child C's father was raised in Greece and her mother was raised in Bulgaria. All of her father's family, with the exception of one brother, were murdered in the Treblinka concentration camp. This included her father's parents, sisters, as well as aunts, uncles, and cousins. Her father survived because he was in a labor camp at the time and was not with his family. Her mother's family had been relocated from one area in Bulgaria to another area to make the process of transporting Jews to the concentration camps easier, but the War ended before the transport took place. The death rate of Jews in Northern Greece was over 95% so Adult Child C personally knows everyone from that area who survived.

The survivors in her mother's family moved to Israel, so Adult Child C's family had no family support in New York where they resettled. There was one family from her father's village who had survived by hiding in the mountains and they and a few others were like extended family to Adult Child C's family.

Her mother talked little about the Holocaust until about ten years before her death. She had saved all of these stories and she became enthusiastic about sharing her experiences and Adult C's father's experiences. Her father was very reluctant to discuss the War.

> My father would never talk about the war. But he would watch every single movie or news story intently, always looking at the pictures. I assume he was hoping that he would see someone that he knew, but he would never talk about his experiences.
>
> I don't remember when I learned of it, but I just knew some of my parent's friends had numbers tattooed on their arms. And I remember as a kid, overhearing my parents talk that the people with the number tattoos were people who had been in concentration camps.

When asked about the impact of growing up as the child of Holocaust survivors, Adult Child C responded:

> At any moment our lives can be uprooted is something that stayed with my family.
>
> Always have liquid assets. They never sat me down and said this to me, but till this day, I make sure I have cash on hand.

From the youngest age, Adult Child C recalls her family always being ready to leave, if necessary. For her this meant always having valid passports, cash, and other transportable valuables. Although the family owned their home and business, she remembers learning that she needed to be prepared for these to change at any time.

When asked about how October 7th and current antisemitism is impacting her, Adult Child C stated:

> And like this could happen again. This could happen again. Because of my family history, I know where it can go.
>
> Things are too well aligned with the playbook of what was happening in Germany, you know, when Hitler was preparing his strategy.
>
> ...My parents kind of raised us to always be questioning, cautious and critical right? And it took me years to shake that off, that everything was antisemitic. As an adult, I worked so hard to break out of that framework to see the world differently. What's happening today is just so painful because I can feel my parents saying, see, we told you to be careful.
>
> What I see now is that people do not really understand what antisemitism is and how it is being perpetuated.
>
> And how it evolved in Germany, right, and how it started in the universities, right? And it started with students and faculty. And eventually, first, there were no laws.
>
> They were just scapegoating professors, and that was all about controlling the intelligentsia so that you could then control the way people thought about things or saw things, and then the cartoons that started, and how it was all very subtle....
>
> No one's antisemitic here... But people started to slowly buy into these things. And I just see so many parallels in what's happening today.

Discussion

For each of the Adult Children of the survivors who were interviewed, there is a common theme of not being directly told, as children, the stories of what their parent(s) experienced during the Holocaust. Adult Child A attended Holocaust

Remembrance ceremonies each year, witnessing her father cry, knowing he was a survivor, but not knowing any details until she was 22 years old. Adult Child B experienced the unavailability of her father, knowing that something was wrong, but did not know any details of his experiences, until her father really started to address his own history 25 years ago. Adult Child C had an understanding from what she saw and heard in her house, but it was not until 10 years before her mother died that she really heard the stories.

Each of the Adult Children shared how their lives were impacted by growing up the child of a Holocaust survivor(s). Freezing extra food or keeping cash on hand may seem like small things, but these represent taking life-saving precautions based on past experiences. Adult Children A and C spoke about having a suitcase ready in case they must leave their homes quickly, reminiscent of the Jews during the Holocaust.

All three of the Adult Children shared how the terrorist attack on October 7th in Israel affected them, with each of them expressing fear that the Holocaust could happen again. They all implicitly expressed an understanding of what had happened in the past and how current events are reminders that these atrocities could again occur. Adult Child B had a somatic response, feeling the trauma in her body. Adult Child A's fear of needing to be hidden was so strong that she posted on social media requesting a safe hiding place. Adult Child C was able to see the historical cycling of what is currently happening. Each Adult Child was in touch with their fears on a palpable level.

Rituals

Mourning rituals aid in the transmission of stories that could be traumatic. These rituals are specific times where Holocaust survivors are going through rituals of mourning for their loved ones who were murdered during the Holocaust. Even if survivors are not talking about their experiences on a regular basis, when these rituals occur, their offspring are exposed to the grief and sadness. This is seen when Adult Child A describes attending the Holocaust remembrance ceremonies each year. This was a ritual for her family, and yet, there was not communication around it.

Rituals can also be places where survivors and their children and grandchildren can share emotions and stories. Second-generation individuals often find ways to create their own rituals, defining their own identities in that way, but also staying connected to their parents'/grandparents' past (Jacobs, 2011).

Parental Behavior and Attachment

Parental behavior and attachment are two variables impacting intergenerational trauma. Attachment theory can be used as a framework when examining the transmission of trauma from parent to child, with the idea that trauma can interrupt the attachment system, which would then impact the next generation (Alford, 2015).

Our ability to form attachments is essential for developing feelings of safety and the ability to connect to others. Disorganized attachment is understood as "not knowing who is safe or whom they belong to, they may be intensely affectionate with strangers or may trust nobody" (Van der Kolk, 2015, p.119). It is now evident that there is an intergenerational piece to this and that many survivors and their descendants suffer from disorganized attachment. If we can stop, and even prevent, the disorganized attachment, it will create healthier children and adults.

The information shared by Adult Child B provides an example of a parent whose parenting behavior was impacted by his experience during the Holocaust. Adult Child B describes her father as being emotionally unavailable and even disappearing. Adult Child B has made a conscious effort to parent in a completely "opposite" way, being emotionally available to her own child.

Epigenetics

The study of genes and their relationships to previous and current generations reveals that the traumatic experiences of one generation are genetically encoded and then passed onto subsequent generations (Bierer et al., 2020; Yehuda & Lehrner, 2018; Yehuda et al., 2016). Consequently, intergenerational trauma can be transferred to one's offspring through genetics. Epigenetics is basically the study of the effects of the environment and behavior on genes. This does not mean that there are changes in one's genes. This, instead, means that there is a change in the way that one's genes function. Epigenetics could say then that trauma is passed down because of the way that the trauma has impacted the genes' functioning.

Yehuda's (2022) research has found that even preconception can impact the next generation, with changes in sperm and eggs. Her research found that trauma had an impact on cortisol levels, lowering them for children of those impacted by 9/11 and by offspring of Holocaust survivors. While acute trauma may cause elevated cortisol levels, prolonged exposure to trauma may cause lower than normal cortisol levels. It is important to note that these changes may also help as an adaptation in being better able to cope with adversity and could build resilience.

Resilience and Healing

To survive the Holocaust and build a new life required resilience, strength, and healing. Resilience is "the process and outcome of successfully adapting to difficult or challenging life experiences, especially through mental, emotional, and behavioral flexibility and adjustment to external and internal demands" (American Psychological Association, 2014, p.1). Morgan et al. (2022) used a strengths-based perspective to examine the resilience of Holocaust survivors. While many survivors may have passed down their traumatic experiences, resilience and an ability to cope with adverse events may have also been passed down. Adult Child A talked about being resilient because her parents were. She talked about being brought up in a family where life was not taken for granted. Adult Child B showed an understanding of what she needed to do to be resilient, for example, going to temple and being with other Jewish people.

With resilience also comes the ability to heal from the traumas of their parents and grandparents. Adult Child C shared this story of healing,

> A couple of years ago I was traveling for work to Poland and went to Treblinka to pay respect to the family I lost there. We lit candles. My husband recited our Jewish prayers at gravesites, and I said the Mourner's Kaddish. This was my way of respecting all those who had perished. It helped me bring closure and heal. Afterward, it felt like a burden was lifted.

The ability to adapt and heal should not be overlooked, even when intergenerational trauma may be present.

The Effects of Intergenerational Trauma

Danieli et al. (2017) examined mental health issues of Holocaust survivors and found generalized anxiety disorder was the most common disorder, followed by depression and then PTSD. The survivors themselves had PTSD from their experiences. Their children were exposed to their parent's stories and their parent's general sense of fear about the world, contributing to their own anxiety.

Dashorst et al. (2019) reviewed 23 studies conducted between 2000 and 2018 on intergenerational trauma from Holocaust survivors to their children. The study looked at the mental health of the survivors, attachment and parenting, family structure including the impact of the Holocaust, other types of stress, and physiology. They found that mental health outcomes could not be determined by just one of these factors, but the impact would be from multiple factors and their interactions.

An important result of their review was that parental mental health issues are related to offspring's mental health issues. Perception of parenting and the quality of the attachment between the children and the parents were also related to offspring mental health. Having both parents as Holocaust survivors put offspring at higher risk for mental health issues than having one survivor as a parent. Mothers, who were survivors also had a more significant impact on their children's sense of well-being than their fathers did. The offspring also showed an increased vulnerability to stressful events, further supporting the findings of Yehuda and Bierer (2008), that cortisol levels were impacted. This article emphasizes the importance of the consideration of these factors when working with children of Holocaust survivors.

Research also examines the impact of the Holocaust on the grandchildren of survivors (Cohn & Morrison, 2018). While some children of survivors do not always pursue the stories of their parents, the grandchildren seem to seek it more. The grandchildren seemed connected to the trauma that their grandparents experienced. They also showed an understanding of their parent's silence regarding their family history and the Holocaust. Kahane-Nissenbaum (2011) studied the impact of grandparent trauma on third-generation Holocaust survivors. However, as opposed to looking at the intergenerational transmission of trauma from grandparent to grandchild, the research examined pride, strength, and gratitude. Stories of strength, instead of only pain and struggles, were also shared, helping to mitigate the impact of War.

Trauma Reminders

Acts of antisemitism can be trauma reminders of the history of discrimination or act as a reminder of the stories that have been told. Today, approximately 245,000 Jewish Holocaust survivors are living in 90 different countries. Almost half of these survivors live in Israel, while 18% live in North America and 18% live in Western Europe. The median age of these survivors is 86 years old (Claims Conference, 2024).

Since the October 7th terrorist attacks on Israel, Holocaust survivors have expressed fear and disbelief (Rubenstein et al., 2024). They are frightened that the increase in antisemitism is a sign of another Holocaust that is coming. There is concern that due to fear, Holocaust survivors may not go out of their homes to take care of basic needs, may withdraw, and may also feel isolated. Survivors may suffer from increased levels of anxiety and depression. Others may have nightmares or be unable to sleep. They also have great worries about their children, grandchildren, and great-grandchildren because of the atrocities they may be confronted with due to antisemitism (Giberovitch, 2021). They may also feel pain from memories of the losses of those close to them and memories of suffering (Rubenstein et al., 2024). In a talk about the increase of antisemitism for Miami Law students, Michael Banhidi, a Holocaust Survivor, stated that "World developments make Banhidi feel that 2024 will be like his past. He described learning about world events as rewatching a horror movie." (Rodriguez, 2024, p. 1).

Hanan Simhon, Vice President of the Holocaust Survivor Programs at Selfhelp Community Services, shared the reactions to October 7th and rising antisemitism of some of the survivors that he is working directly with,

> …this rise in anti-Semitism is very reminiscent of what they went through during the war and they're very concerned, very scared and very feeling helpless because of their age. They are saying…what can I do now?… I can't do anything. I'm 90 years old. What can I do?

> …and unfortunately, everything that you would fear that a survivor might go through or might feel is actually true, you know they're scared, they're angry…saying things like… why is this always happening to us? why won't people leave us alone? when will we ever have peace? (H. Simhon, personal communication, May 3, 2024).

Simply put, Jewish communities are feeling increased levels of fear and anxiety. For example, in colleges and universities across the United States, 37% of Jewish students reported having to hide their Jewish identity (Hillel, 2023). Jewish students are hiding their identities for fear of outward hate and violence on their college campuses (Anti-Defamation League, 2023). As antisemitism on college campuses grows, this hiding and concealment has increased. Jewish college students are feeling isolated, and are expressing fear and confusion (Meckler & Boorstein, 2024).

After the massacre on October 7th, The American Jewish Committee surveyed Jews and found that in the last year, approximately 1 in 4 Jews had experienced antisemitism. Almost 50% reported that they made intentional changes to their behavior so that others would not know they were Jewish to avoid antisemitism. This included changing where they went, what they wore, and what they posted online (Stanley, 2024).

Conclusion

This chapter has focused on the impact of antisemitism, specifically focusing on the Holocaust and intergenerational trauma. The effects of the Holocaust are an example of how trauma can be transmitted from survivors to their children and their grandchildren. The interviews with Adult Children A, B, and C show the impact that their parents' experiences had on them. Their reactions to current antisemitism also underscore how contemporary antisemitism brings up the trauma and fears from events that occurred more than 60 years ago.

The transmission of intergenerational trauma can be complicated and can happen through various ways, such as through family storytelling, rituals, parenting, and epigenetics. Adult Children A, B, and C shared their own experiences as well as their resilience and healing. The resurgence of antisemitism also acts as a trauma reminder for survivors and their family members. Increasing fears of events similar to another Holocaust are being felt.

Addressing antisemitism and providing effective interventions are crucial to prevent the transmission of trauma from occurring in future generations. We cannot allow the atrocities of the past to control future generations.

Main Points

- Both mental health and physical health can be negatively affected by discrimination. Anxiety, depression, and PTSD are examples of these negative mental health effects. Physical health effects can be issues such as diabetes and obesity.
- There is a lack of research focused on the impact of religious discrimination, and more specifically a focus on the impact of antisemitism.
- Acts of antisemitism are more common in the United States than any other kind of religious discrimination.
- The Holocaust is an example of a collective trauma that has had an intergenerational impact.
- Intergenerational trauma has been passed down to many children and grandchildren of Holocaust survivors. Symptoms of PTSD, anxiety, and depression have been found in these descendants.
- Parenting behaviors, such as being emotionally unavailable, are ways that trauma can be transmitted from a survivor to their children.
- Trauma can negatively impact attachment, which can cause difficulty in relationships between survivors and their children.
- Storytelling can impact the transmission of trauma and family members' worldviews.
- Changes in gene function, known as epigenetics, can be a response to trauma and can be passed down to the next generation.
- Rituals can act as both a place where trauma transmission can occur and where healing can happen.
- Many Holocaust survivors and their descendants show resilience and the ability to heal.
- Increasing antisemitism can act as a trauma reminder to Holocaust survivors and their family members.
- Discrimination and trauma shape the identities and behaviors of survivors and their descendants, influencing how they navigate the world and perceive their safety.
- The children and grandchildren of Holocaust survivors may be at higher risk for mental health issues due to the intergenerational trauma they may experience.
- Family communication can decrease the impact of intergenerational trauma and increase well-being.

Discussion Questions and Short Assignments

The following suggested discussion questions can be done in class in small groups or by having students write their own short papers:

- How can discrimination impact one's mental and physical health?
- What is different about those who experience antisemitism versus other types of discrimination?

- How has the trauma experienced by Holocaust survivors been passed down to their descendants?
- How do parenting behaviors affect the transmission of trauma to Holocaust survivors' descendants?
- How do storytelling and family narratives affect the transmission of trauma to Holocaust survivors' descendants?
- How do rituals affect the transmission of trauma? How do rituals contribute to healing?
- What is epigenetics and how does it explain intergenerational trauma transmission?
- How do the stories and experiences shared by the Adult Children of Holocaust survivors demonstrate what it is like to be a child of a survivor?
- What coping strategies and resilience were shown by the Adult Children of Holocaust survivors who were interviewed?
- How do antisemitic incidents today act as trauma reminders for Holocaust survivors and their family members?
- How can intergenerational trauma impact the mental health of the children and grandchildren of Holocaust survivors?
- How can attachment theory be applied to intergenerational trauma?
- How do the personal experiences shared by the children of Holocaust survivors provide a better understanding of trauma?
- How can mental health practitioners support individuals and communities that are impacted by intergenerational trauma?
- What can be done to decrease antisemitism today?

In-Class Exercise

Goal: To understand antisemitism and intergenerational trauma.

Phase I: Reviewing the literature (30–45 min).

Break the students up into pairs or groups of 3–4. Ask them to do the following:

(a) Research the Holocaust, contemporary antisemitism, and intergenerational trauma. Focus on the effects of the intergenerational trauma today. Include case studies in your research.
(b) Create a 15-minute PowerPoint to present to the class to teach them what your group learned about the Holocaust and intergenerational trauma.

Phase II: Presentations (30 min).

Each group should present to the class, showing their PowerPoint and explaining their findings.

Phase III: Debrief (15–20 min).

Debrief with the class. Possible discussion questions during the debrief:

(a) What was it like to research this topic?
(b) What did you learn that you had not known before?
(c) If you included case studies, how did learning about these individuals impact you?

References

Abbott, D., & Mollen, D. (2018). Atheism as a concealable stigmatized identity: Outness, anticipated stigma, and well-being. *The Counseling Psychologist, 46*(6), 685–707.

Alford, C. F. (2015). Subjectivity and the intergenerational transmission of historical trauma: Holocaust survivors and their children. *Subjectivity, 8*(3), 261–282.

American Psychiatric Association. (2022). *Diagnostic and statistical manual of mental disorders: DSM-5-TR* (5th ed., text rev.). American Psychiatric Association Publishing.

American Psychological Association. (2014). *The road to resilience*. American Psychological Association. Retrieved from http://www.apa.org/helpcenter/road-resilience.aspx

Anti-Defamation League. (2023). *Campus antisemitism: A study of campus climate before and after the Hamas terror attacks*. https://www.adl.org/resources/report/campus-antisemitism-study-campus-climate-and-after-hamas-terrorist-attacks

Bayer-Topilsky, T. (2018). The effects of intergenerational transmission of holocaust trauma on the severity of PTSD and depressive symptoms among second and third generation holocaust survivors. *Journal of Loss and Trauma, 23*(1), 76–89.

Bierer, L. M., Bader, H. N., Daskalakis, N. P., Lehrner, A., Provençal, N., Wiechmann, T., Klengel, T., Makotkine, I., Binder, E. B., & Yehuda, R. (2020). Intergenerational effects of maternal holocaust exposure on *FKBP5* methylation. *American Journal of Psychiatry, 177*(8), 744–753. https://doi.org/10.1176/appi.ajp.2019.19060618

Claims Conference. (2024). *Holocaust survivors worldwide: A demographic overview*. Retrieved from https://www.claimscon.org/demographics/

Cohn, I. G., & Morrison, N. M. V. (2018). Echoes of transgenerational trauma in the lived experiences of Jewish Australian grandchildren of holocaust survivors. *Australian Journal of Psychology, 70*, 199–207. https://doi.org/10.1111/ajpy.12194

Danieli, Y., Norris, F. H., & Engdahl, B. (2017). A question of who, not if: Psychological disorders in holocaust survivors' children. *Psychological Trauma: Theory, Research, Practice, and Policy, 9*, 98–106.

Dashorst, P., Mooren, T. M., Kleber, R. J., de Jong, P. J., & Huntjens, R. J. C. (2019). Intergenerational consequences of the holocaust on offspring mental health: A systematic review of associated factors and mechanisms. *European Journal of Psychotraumatology, 10*(1), 1654065. https://doi.org/10.1080/20008198.2019.1654065

DeAngelis, T. (2023). War's enduring legacy: How does trauma haunt future generations? *American Psychological Association*. https://www.apa.org/topics/trauma/trauma-survivors-generations

Dever, A. (2023). *Holocaust Remembrance Day: How trauma persists*. CU Boulder today. https://www.colorado.edu/today/2023/01/26/holocaust-remembrance-day-how-trauma-persists#:~:text=Intergenerational%20trauma%20describes%20the%20phenomenon,been%20traumatized%20by%20this%20past

Doane, M., & Elliott, M. (2015). Perceptions of discrimination among atheists: Consequences for atheist identification, psychological and physical Well-being. *Psychology of Religion and Spirituality, 7*(2), 130–141.

Echoes & Reflections. (2005–2024). *A Holocaust education partnership of ADL, USC Shoah Foundation, and Yad Vashem*. https://echoesandreflections.org/studentactivities/?gad_source=1&gclid=CjwKCAjwr7ayBhAPEiwA6EIGxCF7nnluM5YQslZiqovFHxUOkasJPBJDcjpct52Ej8tu

Firestone, T. (2019). *Wounds into wisdom: Healing intergenerational Jewish trauma*. Adam Kadmon Books/Monkfish Book Publishing Company.

Giberovitch, M. (2021). *Supporting survivors amid attack against Israel and a rise in antisemitism*. The Center for Holocaust Survivor Care Institute on Aging and Trauma, Jewish Federations of North America. https://holocaustsurvivorcare.jewishfederations.org/supporting-survivors-amid-attacks-against-israel%2D%2Da-rise-in-anti-semitism

Hillel International. (2023). *More than one-third of Jewish college students are forced to hide their Jewish identity, new Hillel poll show*. https://www.hillel.org/more-than-one-third-of-jewish-college-students-are-hiding-their-jewish-identity-on-campus-new-hillel-international-poll-finds/#:~:text=More%20than%20one%20in%20three,violence%20on%20campus%20against%20Jews

Isobel, S., McCloughen, A., Goodyear, M., & Foster, K. (2021). Intergenerational trauma and its relationship to mental health care. *Community Mental Health Journal, 57*, 631–643.

Jacobs, J. (2011). The cross-generational transmission of trauma: Ritual and emotion among survivors of the holocaust. *Journal of Contemporary Ethnography, 40*(3), 342–361.

Johns, A. N., Brown, L. S., & DeMarni Cormer, L. (2022). Examining intergenerational transmission of holocaust trauma as it relates to Jewish identity, communication type, and mental Well-being. *Journal of Traumatic Stress, 35*(5), 1497–1507. https://doi.org/10.1002/jts.22856

Jordanova, V., Crawford, M., McManus, S., Bebbington, P., & Traolach, B. (2015). Religious discrimination and common mental disorders in England: A nationally representative population-based study. *Social Psychiatry and Psychiatric Epidemiology, 50*, 1723–1729.

Kahane-Nissenbaum, M. C. (2011). *Exploring intergenerational transmission of trauma in third generation holocaust survivors* (Doctoral dissertation, University of Pennsylvania).

Kellermann, N. P. F. (2001). Transmission of holocaust trauma—An integrative view. *Psychiatry: Interpersonal and Biological Processes, 64*(3), 256–267.

Mayo Clinic. (n.d.). *Post-traumatic stress disorder (PTSD)*. https://www.mayoclinic.org/diseases-conditions/post-traumatic-stress-disorder/symptoms-causes/syc-20355967

Meckler, L., & Boorstein, M. (2024). *For Jewish students, protests stir fear, anger, hope and questions*. https://www.washingtonpost.com/education/2024/04/28/jewish-students-campus-protests-israel-gaza/

Morgan, M. L., Franco, V., Felix, E., & Ramirez, N. M. (2022). "And the ones that survived had hope": Resilience in holocaust survivors. *Journal for Social Action in Counseling and Psychology, 14*(2), 111–126.

Rakoff, V. (1966). A long term effect of the concentration camp experience. *Viewpoints, 1*, 17–22.

Rodriguez, S. (2024). *Cardozo Jewish legal society and holocaust survivor discuss the rise of antisemitism*. University of Miami School of Law. Retrieved from https://news.miami.edu/law/stories/2024/02/holocaust-survivor-discusses-the-rise-of-antisemitism7.html

Rubenstein, V., Rabin, C., & Wernick, S. R. (2024). *Aging with a history of trauma: How service providers can help*. Generations, American Society on Aging. https://generations.asaging.org/aging-history-trauma-how-service-providers-can-help

Sagi-Schwartz, A., Van IJzendoorn, M. H., Grossmann, K. E., Joels, T., Grossmann, K., Scharf, M., Koren-Karie, N., & Alkalay, S. (2003). Attachment and traumatic stress in female holocaust child survivors and their daughters. *American Journal of Psychiatry, 160*(6), 1086–1092. https://doi.org/10.1176/appi.ajp.160.6.1086

Scheitle, C. P., & Ecklund, E. H. (2020). Individuals' experiences with religious hostility, discrimination, and violence: Findings from a new national survey. *Socius, 6*. https://doi.org/10.1177/2378023120967815

Stanley, T. (2024). *Majority of American Jews feel less safe than they did a year ago, survey finds*. PBS News Hour. https://www.pbs.org/newshour/nation/majority-of-american-jews-feel-less-safe-than-they-did-a-year-ago-survey-finds

The Jewish Agency for Israel. (2024). *The Jewish agency for Israel*. Retrieved from *www.jewishagency.org* on 15 May 2024.
Van der Kolk, B. (2015). *The body keeps the score: Brain, mind, and body in the healing of trauma*. Penguin.
Vang, Z. M., Hou, F., & Elder, K. (2019). Perceived Religious Discrimination, Religiosity, and Life Satisfaction. *Journal of Happiness Studies*, Springer, *20*(6), 1913–1932.
Wu, Z., & Schimmele, C. M. (2021). Perceived religious discrimination and mental health. *Ethnicity & Health, 26*(7), 963–980. https://doi.org/10.1080/13557858.2019.1620176
Yehuda, R. (2022). How parents' trauma leaves biological traces on children. *Scientific American*. https://www.scientificamerican.com/article/how-parents-rsquo-trauma-leaves-biological-traces-in-children/
Yehuda, R., & Bierer, L. M. (2008). Transgenerational transmission of cortisol and PTSD risk. *Progress in Brain Research, 167*, 121–135. https://doi.org/10.1016/S0079-6123(07)67009-5
Yehuda, R., & Lehrner, A. (2018). Intergenerational transmission of trauma effects: Putative role of epigenetic mechanisms. *World Psychiatry, 17*(3), 243–257. https://doi.org/10.1002/wps.20568
Yehuda, R., Daskalakis, N. P., & Bierer, L. M. (2016). Holocaust exposure induced intergenerational effects on FKBP5 methylation. *Biological Psychiatry, 80*, 372–380.

Chapter 8
Antisemitism and Trauma-Focused Interventions

To address the impact of antisemitic-related trauma, depression, anxiety, and other responses, social work must first take a stand against antisemitism, similar to the stand it has taken against other forms of injustice. The profession cannot choose which social injustices to address.

Informed care implies equity and inclusivity which enables clients and practitioners to work together regardless of diverse backgrounds or cultures. A client should be able to seek social work services from a social worker who has a different ethnic or religious background from themselves without feeling any kind of biased treatment. Social workers must be well trained in their social work programs on social justice and understanding intersectionality. Without this knowledge, they cannot work effectively. According to the Council on Social Work Education (CSWE, 2022),

> social workers demonstrate cultural humility by applying critical reflection, self-awareness, and self-regulation to manage the influence of bias, power, privilege, and values in working with clients and constituencies, acknowledging them as experts of their own lived experiences (p. 10).

Social workers may specialize in working with specific populations, but this does not mean that they are then biased against other populations. Practitioners may sometimes report that a client is resistant, non-compliant, or in denial because they are not disclosing information or are resistant to a more in-depth discussion on a certain topic. However, if a client believes that they are not permitted to share their experiences of discrimination with a practitioner, social workers are failing their clients. It is essential for social workers to be unbiased and nonjudgmental, showing respect to each client.

In this chapter, different types of therapeutic approaches that address antisemitism will be discussed. This chapter will also specifically focus on trauma treatment.

C. B. Cox, D. B. Marlowe, *Social Work and Antisemitism*,
https://doi.org/10.1007/978-3-031-72771-9_8

Intergenerational Trauma

Isobel et al.'s (2021) study of psychiatrist's understanding of intergenerational trauma and effective interventions illustrates two very important points in understanding the treatment of intergenerational trauma. One theme is "thinking differently," meaning that if intergenerational trauma is present, the social worker must be deliberate in making the distinction between mental illness and trauma transmission. Symptoms must be considered in a much broader context, with consideration of familial history. The choice of interventions must then also change in response to this understanding of the client so that the client's experience is not invalidated and so that the risk of re-traumatization through treatment is decreased.

The second theme, "looking backward and looking forwards," focuses on both the client's past and future and its impact on their present. Clients are helped to gain an understanding of their past and gain insight into how it impacts their present lives. When appropriate, there is also an emphasis on the parenting of their children so that any intergenerational trauma would be stopped. This is a form of prevention in keeping the cycle from continuing.

Trauma-Informed Care Approach

Jewish individuals can experience antisemitism directly or indirectly. This means that their experiences may not be apparent to the individual and/or agency trying to help them. Discrimination can be more explicit, or it can be more subtle. When utilizing the approach of universal precautions, the assumption is made that there is a likelihood that the person has experienced trauma and, thus, they need to be treated in that way. Being trauma-informed means going beyond having cultural sensitivity and cultural competence. It demands that social workers pay attention to historical traumas. Practitioners must recognize and respond to the complex intersectionality and multiple layers of identities of individuals.

A trauma-informed care approach in an organization is pertinent to addressing antisemitism, as this approach is helpful for any marginalized population. This approach is an important reminder for agencies to be fully inclusive to all groups.

According to SAMHSA (2014),

> A program, organization, or system that is trauma-informed realizes the widespread impact of trauma and understands potential paths for recovery; recognizes the signs and symptoms of trauma in clients, families, staff, and others involved with the system; and responds by fully integrating knowledge about trauma into policies, procedures, and practices, and seeks to actively resist re-traumatization (p. 9).

A trauma-informed care approach (TIC) is a change in an organization where trauma is addressed at all levels. The approach is seen as using universal precautions, in that everyone is involved in acknowledging and addressing trauma (Bloom, 2013). By creating a healing environment for all staff and clients of an agency, universal precautions are taking place, decreasing the risk of re-traumatization.

In a TIC approach, the organization asks, "What happened to this person?" instead of "What is wrong with this person?" (Bloom, 2013; Harris & Fallot, 2001). Trauma-informed care is based on organizational models where every staff member within an organization and all organizational policies and procedures are designed so that every client and staff member feel safe and not at risk for re-traumatization.

The constructs of self-view and worldview for an individual reflect their personal perceptions of current experiences. These perceptions become a personal narrative that has been influenced by personal experiences and historical and systemic traumas. Self-views and worldviews are created in childhood but can be impacted as we experience various life events, which can be either positive or negative. These experiences may result in re-traumatization. Being re-traumatized can cause one's trauma narrative to become reactivated, resulting in one's sense of self and the world being negatively impacted (The Institute on Trauma and Trauma-Informed Care, 2022).

In applying a trauma-informed care approach in agencies, it is essential to ensure that the agency shows true inclusivity and that groups that are being discriminated against are also included. This would specifically include those impacted by antisemitism either through intergenerational transmission, by being current victims, or being part of an oppressed group. Because antisemitism has often been excluded from most Diversity, Equity, and Inclusion (DEI) and other organizational efforts to address social injustice, this inclusion in TIC is critical. An individual should be "validated and affirmed" by every staff person at the agency. This means that antisemitism needs to be recognized by every person who works in the organization and by the organization as an institution itself.

SAMHSA's (2014) approach to trauma-informed care consists of four assumptions and six principles that lay the foundation for this approach. These can be applied to working with all populations in all agencies. They can also be specifically applied to agencies to be fully inclusive of all Jewish clients and to address antisemitism. By doing this, social workers can facilitate the process of healing and decrease the risk of re-traumatization. Trauma-informed care includes addressing historical and intergenerational trauma, so this approach is an appropriate fit for those impacted by antisemitism in the past and those impacted by current incidents.

The four assumptions, also known as the four R's, are realization, recognize, respond, and resist re-traumatization.

> A program, organization, or system that is trauma-informed realizes the widespread impact of trauma and understands potential paths for recovery; recognizes the signs and symptoms of trauma in clients, families, staff, and others involved with the system; and responds by fully integrating knowledge about trauma into policies, procedures, and practices, and seeks to actively resist re-traumatization (SAMHSA, 2014, p. 9).

Agencies must recognize that trauma can be prevalent among their Jewish clients and Jewish staff members. They must also understand the symptoms of trauma that can occur and that are specific to this population. There is a historical aspect and a current response to the reminders that are so public today. This understanding must be integrated into the policies and procedures of the organization. Safety and collaboration in the organization can lead to decreasing the risk of re-traumatization for Jewish clients and staff.

1. *Safety*—"Safety in physical settings and interpersonal interactions" (SAMHSA, 2023, p. 10). This principle dictates that the environment is safe and supportive for all Jewish clients and staff. This would include all individuals impacted by antisemitism. This can include providing physical safety measures in spaces where antisemitic incidents may occur, as well as creating emotionally safe spaces where individuals feel comfortable expressing their experiences and emotions. This also means that Jewish individuals do not feel that they need to conceal their Jewish identity to protect themselves. They are free to express themselves as being Jewish without feeling any threat to their safety.
2. *Trustworthiness and Transparency*—"Operations are conducted, and decisions are made with transparency, consistency, respect, and fairness, in order to build and maintain trust" (SAMHSA, 2023, p. 10). Organizations need to build trust in their relationships with clients so that the clients feel comfortable sharing their experiences of antisemitism. This trust needs to extend to family members, staff, and other organizational stakeholders. To do this, the organization needs to have visible and clear operations and decision-making related to antisemitism, which will build and maintain trust.
3. *Peer Support*—"Peer support from those with lived experiences of trauma or, in the case of children with a history of trauma, their family members" (SAMHSA, 2023, p. 10). Peer support and mutual aid can play crucial roles in creating a sense of safety, fostering trust, and leveraging personal narratives and firsthand encounters to encourage recovery and well-being. This can be directly applied to individuals who have intergenerational or current experiences with antisemitism. Coming together to share narratives with others who truly understand you can bring about healing and support. Peer support can decrease feelings of isolation brought on by experiences of trauma. It is in applying this principle that individuals who have experienced oppression and discrimination should be brought together. Instead of dividing groups of people and encouraging competition between groups, "peers" can denote individuals who have undergone trauma and who can support each other.
4. *Collaboration and Mutuality*—"Partnering, leveling of power differences between and among staff and clients" (SAMHSA, 2023, p.10). Applying this principle means fostering a relationship between the organization, its staff, and the individuals who have experienced antisemitism so that there is a partnership in addressing antisemitism. Input should be requested from impacted individuals, and they should be included in decision-making. This collaboration can be

effective in fighting social injustice and promoting inclusivity for everyone at the agency.

5. *Empowerment, Voice, and Choice*—"Individuals' strengths and experiences are recognized and built upon" (SAMHSA, 2023, p. 10). Individuals need to be empowered and given autonomy. Individuals who have been impacted by antisemitism must be given the autonomy to make their own decisions on how they want to deal with their experiences. While some individuals may choose to disclose antisemitic incidents, others may choose not to. While some individuals may want to get support for their experiences, others may want to pursue legal action. Providing a range of services and options for support so that an individual may make choices is empowering. Within these options, individuals need to be provided with information about their rights in a well-defined and correct way.
6. *Cultural, Historical, and Gender Issue*—"Organization moves beyond the cultural stereotypes and biases" (SAMHSA, 2023, p. 10). In a trauma-informed organization, policies and procedures are responsive to historical trauma and acknowledge and respect the differences of individuals. This principle clearly infers that a true TIC organization would not allow antisemitism to exist within its walls.

Grandchildren of Holocaust survivors have been studied in the application of Trauma-informed care (Greenfeld et al., 2021). Their research shows the necessity of understanding the persistent impact of Holocaust-related trauma. It also recognizes the complexities that are inherent to families and encourages communication that is open and honest. The grandchildren may have distinct challenges, which could include anxiety about annihilation and genocide and about separation from their loved ones. A trauma-informed care approach can help these grandchildren by looking at their ancestry and helping them to heal.

Person-Centered, Trauma-Informed Treatment

The Administration for Community Living (ACL) created the term, "Person-Centered, Trauma-Informed (PCTI)" as an approach to providing services to those impacted by trauma, particularly survivors of the Holocaust. Congress directed the ACL to award grants to the Jewish Federation of North America's (JFNA) Center on Survivor Care and Institute for Aging, to develop this approach and to award grants to organizations to implement these programs. "PCTI was envisioned as a holistic approach to providing services. It would promote dignity, strength, and empowerment of trauma victims by incorporating knowledge about trauma in victims' lives into agency programs, policies, and procedures" (ACL, 2023, p. 1).

PCTI is a combination of the six principles of trauma-informed care (SAMHSA, 2014) and the principles of person-centered care (self-determination, choice, empowerment, and individual preference). The PCTI approach was first introduced in services for Holocaust survivors in 2016 through the work of the JFNA center. It uses a "universal precaution" approach, assuming that everyone that they are providing services to has trauma. While some Holocaust survivors may have PTSD symptoms throughout their lives, others do not show symptoms until they become older adults. As the survivors age, feelings of loss and vulnerability may bring up emotions related to their survival.

Holocaust survivors can also be re-traumatized by the agencies providing services to them. Having a Holocaust survivor undress or have to say goodbye to a spouse or child can be a trauma reminder of their experience in a concentration camp (Rubenstein et al., 2024). Even asking a Holocaust survivor for a family history can be retraumatizing (Eisenger & Bedney, 2018). The PCTI approach has been especially important since the October 7th terrorist attacks on Israel when many Holocaust survivors became re-traumatized, reliving memories of the Holocaust.

JFNA has awarded 84 grants to non-profit organizations to develop PCTI care for Holocaust survivors. Included in these programs are support for family caregivers, and a focus on socialization, health, and wellness. Trainings have been provided to professionals on how to provide PCTI care. Those trained include social workers, doctors, nurses, dentists, lawyers, and home health workers. Over 13,000 Holocaust survivors and over 2300 family caregivers have received services, and over 9400 professionals have been trained in PCTI care. The results of these programs have been overwhelmingly positive, delivering outcomes such as decreased depression and decreased anxiety shown by survivors.

Caregiving for these older family members can be very depleting, but family members have reported feeling more skillful in taking care of their family members and improving their own self-care. There has also been an increased knowledge of effectively implementing this program. Further adaptations for other older adults who are dealing with other types of issues can be made as well (Administration for Community Living, 2023).

An example of an agency that has implemented PCTI care is Selfhelp Community Services, a New York City-based agency, providing services to aging Holocaust survivors.

> Selfhelp's services for Holocaust survivors honor the sacred pledge made by [their] founders: to serve as the last surviving relative of victims of Nazi persecution. This promise remains [their] imperative. [Their] overarching goal is to provide Holocaust survivors with the services they need so that they may live with the comfort and dignity they so richly deserve (Selfhelp Community Services, 2022).

> Selfhelp began in 1936 and was run by volunteers who were trying to help Jews who were being persecuted in Europe by the Nazis. After the War, the agency focused on helping the survivors to adjust and rebuild their lives.

> Selfhelp continued to play this role welcoming these Holocaust survivors, helping them find jobs, helping them find housing, even getting clothing, anything to get them on their feet and get a good start in life and be connected to the community. Since then, after the war ended, it became more of a formal organization that hired staff and social workers to work with these survivors on a host of issues related to their trauma and related to their needs because survivors came in all ages and sizes at that time.

> Now it's mostly related to the direct care needs, so that they can remain in the community at the age that they are, given the frailty and the trauma that they've been through. Fast forward all these years – we've continued to remain as an organization that provides comprehensive services to Holocaust survivors (H. Simhon, personal communication, May 3, 2024).

Today, Selfhelp provides services to 5400 Holocaust survivors. According to Simhon (2024), since 1936, Selfhelp has been informally providing trauma-informed care because of the horrific traumas that the survivors went through, although TIC was not a formalized program. Over the last 8 years, Selfhelp has worked with Jewish Federations of North America and through a grant has implemented PCTI. Over the last two years, the agency has expanded this approach to all of its programs through the National Council for Well-Being.

An example of the PCTI approach at Selfhelp is the agency formally integrated the PCTI care into onboarding for all new staff. Included in onboarding new social workers is educating them about the trauma that these survivors experienced and the potential trauma reminders. These reminders can occur when working with the social workers or other individuals providing services to them (i.e., doctors, and home attendants).

The agency has also developed a trauma-informed mentoring program for its home care programs. Home health care workers are educated about the trauma that the survivors experienced, trauma reminders, and their possible reactions to these reminders. There is also education provided on cognitive issues or mental health issues that the survivor may also exhibit more as they age, related to the trauma. As the survivors age, for some, happy memories of childhood may not come up. Instead, the horrors of the Holocaust may be the memories that become more vivid. Without an understanding of this, the reactions or statements of the survivor may be difficult to understand.

Some survivors, who were reliving the trauma of the Holocaust, began to scream that the Nazis are coming or suddenly spoke in another language. They were then placed in nursing homes or institutional facilities because of a lack of understanding of their cognitive changes and behaviors when their trauma should have been addressed. Keeping survivors at home is important and necessitates that everyone understands the trauma that these survivors have been through, how to react to those behaviors, and how to work with the survivor whether they have cognitive issues or not.

One of Selfhelp's educational programs incorporates a PCTI approach. Witness Theater is one of their educational programs where survivors and high school students come together. The two groups get to know each other while students learn stories from the Holocaust. This work results in a play that is performed on Yom Hashoah. The program itself follows a drama therapy model and a trauma-informed approach. Students are taught to learn about the survivors as human beings first, instead of just being passive learners and listening to a story. Exercises are built into the program to allow students to learn about the survivors as individuals, hear their stories, and thus feel the impact of their experiences (H. Simon, personal communication, May 3, 2024).

Evidence-Based Treatments for Trauma

If individuals are able to address and process their trauma, then the possible transmission of trauma can be stopped. The American Psychological Association (APA) recommends specific evidence-based treatments to treat trauma. The APA strongly recommends Cognitive Behavioral Therapy, Cognitive Processing Therapy, Cognitive Therapy, and Prolonged Exposure. Conditionally recommended are Brief Eclectic Psychotherapy, Eye Movement Desensitization and Reprocessing, Narrative Exposure Therapy, and medications (APA, 2024). With the exponential increase of antisemitic incidents (Rubenstein et al., 2024), all practitioners must be prepared to help clients who have symptoms of PTSD as a result. In this chapter, a sampling of the treatments will be highlighted. Practitioners should be encouraged to use these and other effective treatments.

Eye Movement Desensitization Reprocessing Eye movement desensitization reprocessing (EMDR) can help clients to process their trauma and loss. With intergenerational trauma, there is a cycling of the trauma from one generation to another. EMDR stops the cycle and as a result, the trauma is not passed down to the next generation. Part of the passing down of trauma is related to one's unconscious behavior patterns. Resolving the trauma can also stop these behaviors. Grief, loss, and the repetition of events that are seen in one's mind can also be resolved. EMDR may build resilience and positive cognitions, additional factors that can decrease the risk of passing down the trauma (Melo, 2023).

EMDR has components that can be expanded upon to specifically address the transgenerational impact of antisemitism. This would include the history taking, preparation for reprocessing, and case conceptualization. The history taking part of this intervention needs to include a transgenerational history. This would consist of: "(a) pre-trauma experiences of the survivor's family including resources within the family and religious/cultural identifications before anti-Semitic genocide, (b) the specific genocide trauma experiences, and (c) post-trauma experiences including displacements, adaptations made in the host culture, and resiliency" (Alter-Reid & Heber, 2023, p. 227).

It is not uncommon for people to have some knowledge of their ancestral history, but not to have the details of what specifically happened. Clients can be asked to speak to family members and find out more details and stories about their family history. Obtaining positive and negative memories will contribute to a comprehensive narrative of the family and a more highly functioning individual.

Through this process, themes and targets can be established, creating a treatment plan. Targets for the intervention may not only include the client's traumatic memories. They would also include how the client would imagine the traumatic experiences of their family members. When participating in EMDR, the client can use their traumatic memories or those traumatic stories of their parents and/or grandparents which they have internalized (Alter-Reid & Heber, 2023).

Narrative Exposure Therapy Intergenerational trauma can be addressed through narrative exposure therapy (NET) by using it as part of the narrative of the memory. This involves adding the experience of learning about past generations' trauma as a personal narrative on the participant's lifeline. The goal is the acknowledgment that past historical events can have a profound impact on a person. Individuals can share the stories of their family's experiences in the Holocaust as part of their narrative.

NET not only acknowledges the intergenerational trauma, but it documents it for the client. It focuses on the individual's dignity and on their human rights. For many clients, receiving a written biography when treatment is completed is very motivating (American Psychological Association, 2024).

This intervention can be very empowering for a Jewish individual impacted by antisemitism, either through intergenerational trauma or due to current incidents of antisemitism. Knowing and understanding the stories that have impacted them, while focusing on human rights, is clearly representative of social work ethics and its mission to fight for social justice.

Intergenerational Trauma Treatment Model The intergenerational trauma treatment model (ITTM) (Scott & Copping, 2008) is a 21-session manualized intervention aimed at decreasing the impact of trauma in children. This model has a specific focus on intergenerational trauma with a focus on the parent(s) as the change agent(s) in the process. Although aimed at the child (between the ages of 3 and 18), the intervention improves the functioning of the child and the parent, thus impacting two generations at once. This model directly addresses the caregiver's traumatic experiences and their impact on the child. Helping the caregiver to process their own trauma impacts their ability to be a better parent in having empathy and emotional regulation in their parenting (California Evidence-Based Clearinghouse, n.d.).

There are three distinct phases to the treatment. The first phase is group sessions for parents focusing on psychoeducation. These are considered to be trauma information sessions. The second phase of treatment is individual sessions with the parent. This part of the intervention helps the parent to deconstruct their trauma, gain a better understanding of the trauma, and its impact on parenting. The final phase of the model is interventions with the parent and child, with the goal of strengthening the relationship. Symptoms and behaviors related to trauma are addressed during these sessions (Scott & Copping, 2008).

This model specifically looks at two generations (parent to child). If trauma has been passed down from a Holocaust survivor to their descendants, then an adult descendant and child, who have been impacted by intergenerational trauma, could benefit from this model. This model also differs from other interventions for children who have experienced trauma. Although some trauma treatments for children include the parent, this model focuses on the empowerment of the parent in helping their child. Another distinct feature of this model is the recognition of intergenerational trauma and how it impacts families.

Additions to Evidence-Based Practices

For the evidence-based treatments that SAMHSA lists as being effective for trauma, for some, certain modifications or additions can be made to specifically address intergenerational trauma. As an example, if using cognitive behavioral therapy with a client to address intergenerational trauma, it is essential to assess layers of core beliefs because of the layers of traumas. While some automatic thoughts may seem maladaptive with one trauma, they may be appropriate for another trauma. Cognitive restructuring may have to focus on one layer of trauma at a time until the multiple traumas are all addressed (Suttenberg, 2016).

Transgenerational Trauma Resilience Genogram

The Transgenerational Trauma Resilience Genogram (TTRG) is an expansion of a genogram that can assess clients through a lens of resiliency and intergenerational trauma. The TTRG has a strengths-based approach, considering the whole person and the environment. The TTRG was designed to assess the impact that can occur on the micro, mezzo, and macro levels as a result of transgenerational trauma. It has a view of trauma using a lens that incorporates culture and political concerns that can impact trauma and healing. The TTRG is also culturally responsive, considering different traditions, customs, beliefs, and perspectives (Goodman, 2013).

Responsive Services

Services should be created in response to changing needs as antisemitism increases. An example of a responsive service is the creation of a group at Selfhelp for Holocaust survivors after the October 7th terrorist attacks. The purpose of the group is to discuss current events in Israel. Discussions also include topics such as the rise of antisemitism, the United Nation's response to the crisis, and what is currently happening on college campuses. Discussions are based on the needs of the participants.

Conclusion

Clients who are impacted by trauma related to antisemitism have a right to receive services from a social work practitioner who understands trauma, intergenerational trauma, and the impact of antisemitism. As social workers, we must be prepared to not only fight for social justice but also to help those impacted by social injustice.

Antisemitism is a social injustice, a form of discrimination, and a violation of human rights. Integrated within effective treatment are social work's core values of inclusivity and unbiased treatment of all people and groups.

There is an ethical imperative for social work practitioners to continue their commitment to social justice while having clinical expertise in providing effective interventions. For Jewish people, this necessitates an understanding of antisemitism and its many manifestations. To effectively work with and treat Jewish clients, this knowledge is critical and must include an understanding of the significance of the October 7th terrorist attacks.

Main Points

- Antisemitism can lead to depression, anxiety, and trauma in Jewish individuals.
- Social workers need to use evidence-based treatments and trauma-informed care to work with those impacted by antisemitism.
- There are specific evidence-based treatments for trauma. Some of these treatments can be adapted to treat intergenerational trauma.
- Social workers need to work to prevent re-traumatization of their clients.
- Using the trauma-informed principles of realize, recognize, respond, and resist re-traumatization can create a safe environment in an agency.
- Using universal precautions is an essential part of a trauma-informed care approach.
- Person-centered, trauma-informed care is an approach that was established for agencies providing services to Holocaust survivors and now has been expanded to serve other populations.
- Person-centered, trauma-informed care promotes dignity, empowerment, and individual preferences.
- There are specific evidence-based treatments for trauma. Some of these treatments can be adapted to treat intergenerational trauma.
- Eye movement desensitization reprocessing (EMDR) can help to stop the transmission of trauma from one generation to the next.
- Phases of EMDR need to be expanded and adapted in order to address the intergenerational trauma.
- Narrative exposure therapy (NET) can be used to help Jewish clients who have experienced intergenerational trauma and/or who are impacted by current antisemitism, focusing on the stories of the trauma and on human rights.
- The intergenerational trauma treatment model (ITTM) involves children and their parents in the therapeutic process to reduce the impact of trauma across generations.
- Programs and services should be implemented to meet the needs of those impacted by increasing antisemitism.

Discussion Questions and Short Assignments

The following suggested discussion questions can be done in class in small groups or by having students write their own short papers:

- What are the key principles of trauma-informed care? How are these principles specifically applicable to individuals impacted by antisemitism?
- How can social workers distinguish between symptoms of depression and anxiety and intergenerational trauma?
- Explain how person-centered, trauma-informed care encourages dignity, strength, and empowerment.
- What are some evidence-based treatments that can be effectively used for working with clients who have intergenerational trauma?
- How can a transgenerational trauma resilience genogram be helpful in working with a client who has intergenerational trauma?
- Explain what "universal precautions" mean in a trauma-informed care approach.
- How can agency policies effectively address antisemitism? How can agency practices be inclusive of Jewish staff and clients?
- What is the role of peers in helping clients and staff in an agency that is using a trauma-informed care approach?
- What are some challenges that social workers might confront in their practices when working with individuals who are experiencing intergenerational trauma?
- What are some services that can be implemented now to help clients who are impacted by antisemitism?

In-Class Exercises

Exercise 1: Addressing a Client's Intergenerational Trauma (based on cases)

Goal: To provide students with an opportunity to learn about intergenerational trauma with a specific focus on the intergenerational trauma of the family members of Holocaust survivors. An additional goal is to have students learn about different strategies for helping these descendants.

Phase I: Introduction to intergenerational trauma (15 min)

(a) Introduce the concept of intergenerational trauma through lecture and PowerPoint, providing concrete definitions and examples.
(b) Include information on how trauma is passed down from one generation to the next.
(c) Explain intergenerational trauma and its impact on the children and grandchildren of Holocaust survivors.

Phase II: Share the case of Lisa (The case of Adam can also be used for his exercise) (15 min)

Review key points of the case with the class. This can include history (family's history) and current symptoms.

Phase III: Discussion in small groups (15–20 min)

Break up the class into groups of 3–4 students and ask one student in each group to be responsible for reporting the group's discussion back to the class.
Ask each group to do the following:

(a) Focus on one aspect of Lisa's case for the discussion.
 (Group 1—Lisa's symptoms, Group 2—Lisa's need to be perfect and its impact professionally, Group 3—Lisa's personal and professional relationships. If this is a large class, more than one group can focus on the same aspect).
(b) Discuss how the aspect they are focusing on is a possible result of intergenerational trauma.
(c) Discuss interventions that could be helpful to Lisa.

Phase IV: Groups report back to the entire class (15 min)

(a) Each group should report their responses to the class.
(b) Further discussion can occur, led by the instructor, discussing the themes that have come up.
(c) Discussion of vicarious trauma and self-care when working with clients who have intergenerational trauma.

Exercise 2: Role-Play with a Client Who Has Intergenerational Trauma.

Goal: To provide students with an opportunity to practice working with a client who has intergenerational trauma, with a specific focus on the intergenerational trauma resulting from the Holocaust.

Phase I: Role-play (20 min)

(a) Divide students into groups of 3 students for this exercise. One student should play the social worker, one should role-play the client, Lisa, and one should be an observer of the role-play.
(b) Ask the students to role-play a situation where Lisa has come to see a social worker to address her symptoms and intergenerational trauma.

**Empathy and active listening should be emphasized in this role-play.

Phase II: Debrief (15 min)

(a) Ask the students to report back on their role-play experience. Prompt the observers to report back on their observations of the role-play.
(b) Ask students what went well, what the challenges were in the role-play, and what could be done differently.

(c) Ask students how the intergenerational aspect of the trauma impacted the role-play.

Exercise 3: Implementing Trauma-Informed Care as a Response to Antisemitism.

Goal: To provide students with a deeper understanding of how to implement a trauma-informed approach to their agency.

Scenario: Becoming aware of the increase of antisemitism and the related anxiety and depression experienced by the Jewish clients and staff in your agency, you have decided that implementing trauma-informed care in your agency would be very effective in helping both clients and staff. You also feel that once implemented, this approach can be helpful to any oppressed population seeking services at your agency or working at your agency.

Create a step-by-step plan to implement this approach in your agency. This plan should include goals and objectives, your proposal to your supervisor, changes or additions to agency policy and procedures, and ideas for trainings.

Cases

The following two cases were created as examples of clients who have been impacted by antisemitism. These cases can be used for teaching about clinical interventions for Jewish individuals impacted by antisemitism. They can also be used to gain a better understanding of the experience that some Jewish clients are experiencing. The first case, Lisa, is an example of intergenerational trauma experienced by an adult child of a Holocaust survivor. The second case, Adam, is an example of the intergenerational trauma experienced by a grandchild of a Holocaust survivor.

The main goal of treatment for these clients would be for healing and building resilience. For the cases, the clients would best be served by an agency or practice that has a trauma-informed care approach. The clients should also be provided with an evidence-based practice that is effective for treating PTSD.

Case 1: The Intergenerational Trauma of a Holocaust Survivor's Adult Child

Lisa is looking for a therapist to help her deal with her feelings of anxiety and depression. She is a 55-year-old woman living in a suburb of Chicago. Lisa's parents were both survivors of Auschwitz during the Holocaust. Lisa reports that she often feels hypervigilant and has sleep disturbances. She also reports significant feelings of self-blame and guilt, although she was not directly involved in the Holocaust at all. She has difficulty trusting others, which negatively impacts her personal and professional relationships. Lisa is professionally successful, however, she constantly strives for success often to the point of total exhaustion, due to her profound fear of complete failure.

Lisa's parents, Charlotte and Leon, were both born in Poland. When they were teenagers, they were both sent to Auschwitz. They survived horrific acts of terror, were witnesses to loved ones murdered, and were starved. They were able to survive and came to the United States right after the war. They created a new life for themselves, but they continued to be plagued by their traumatic experiences.

Lisa feels like her parents' trauma was always hanging over her head. Her parents rarely spoke about what happened to them, however, it felt like their trauma was somehow integrated into every part of her life. Growing up, her home was defined by what she describes as a deafening silence. She felt an all-encompassing fear and an ever-present sense of loss in her home as well. Lisa took on her parents' issues and developed a sense of survival guilt. She intensely felt the legacy of her parents' experiences that she could not even comprehend.

Assessment

Lisa presents with symptoms of complex post-traumatic stress disorder (C-PTSD), as a result of intergenerational trauma. These symptoms consist of dissociation, emotional dysregulation, and challenges creating secure attachments. She has intrusive memories of events that she did not experience, and yet she feels as if she did. Lisa struggles with an overwhelming ownership of her parents' pain. She also feels a deep sense of loneliness and disconnection.

Lisa's describes herself in relationships as consistently emotionally distant and avoidant. It is difficult for her to trust others as she fears betrayal and abandonment. While she wants relationships, Lisa tends to self-sabotage her relationships based on a fear of pain and loss. Professionally, Lisa strives for perfection and worries about failure. This drives her to work too much and overmanage, creating additional stress and anxiety for herself.

Case 2: Intergenerational Trauma in the Grandchild of a Holocaust Survivor

Adam reached out to your agency looking for a therapist to help him to address his feelings of depression, anxiety, and uncertainty about his life. He is a 32-year-old Jewish man living in Manhattan. Since completing law school, he has worked as an attorney with a private law firm.

During Adam's initial intake, he shared that his maternal grandparents are Holocaust survivors. Although he never obviously experienced the trauma of living through the Holocaust, he truly feels impacted by his family's history. He discusses having nightmares, intrusive thoughts, and lingering feelings of nervousness. He also expresses feeling guilt over the suffering his grandparents experienced during the Holocaust. Adam continually looks for purpose in his life and feels frustrated with this constant struggle. He also at times does not feel connected to other people.

Adam's grandparents, Dori and Sam, were both survivors of Auschwitz. They came to the United States immediately after the war and were able to start a new life in New York City. Adam believes that his grandparents were incredibly resilient to be able to build the life that they had in the United States. However, he feels that they were still haunted by their experiences during the Holocaust. He rarely heard them speak about it, but over time, he became aware of their experiences. He also believes that their own PTSD symptoms were somehow passed down to his parents and to himself, although he feels confused about how this could happen.

Adam feels that he was born into a family with unspoken anguish. Although his parents did not share the details of his grandparent's experience in the Holocaust, trauma seemed to weave its way through every aspect of Adam's life. The dynamics in Adam's family had an underlying tone of sadness. Adam always felt like there were family secrets and great pain that was not spoken about.

Assessment

Adam shows symptoms that are characteristic of having complex post-traumatic stress disorder (C-PTSD), as a result of intergenerational trauma. These symptoms include avoidance behavior, dysregulated emotions, and hypervigilance. He states that he has trauma reminders of places that he has never been to and things that really don't mean anything to him. He admits to feelings of guilt over the fact that he did not have to suffer the way his grandparents did. Adam has trouble trusting others and committing to relationships. He has fears of rejection and so will reject others first, avoiding intimacy and connection.

References

Administration for Community Living (ACL). (2023). *Person centered, trauma-informed services*. https://acl.gov/programs/strengthening-aging-and-disability-networks/advancing-care-holocaust-survivors-older

Alter-Reid, K., & Heber, R. (2023). The transgenerational impact of antisemitism. In M. Nickerson (Ed.), *Cultural competence and health culturally based trauma with EMDR therapy* (2nd ed.) pp. 225–237. Springer Publishing Company.

American Psychological Association. (2024). *PTSD treatments*. https://www.apa.org/ptsd-guideline/treatments

Bloom, S. (2013). *Creating sanctuary: Toward the evolution of sane societies*. Routledge.

California Evidence Based Clearinghouse. (n.d.). *The intergenerational trauma treatment Model (ITTM)*. https://www.cebc4cw.org/program/the-intergenerational-trauma-treatment-model-ittm/

Council on Social Work Education (CSWE). (2022). *Educational policy and accreditation standards*. https://www.cswe.org/accreditation/policies-process/2022epas/

Eisenger, M. A., & Bedney, B. J. (2018). Teaching about trauma: Models for training service providers in person-centered, trauma-informed care. *Kavod a Journal for Caregivers and Families, 8*, 1–8.

Goodman, R. D. (2013). The transgenerational trauma and resilience genogram. *Counseling Psychology Quarterly, 26*(3–4), 386–405.

Greenfeld, D., Reupert, A., Harris, N., & Jacobs, N. (2021). Between fear and Hope: The lived experiences of grandchildren of holocaust survivors: A qualitative systematic literature review. *Journal of Loss and Trauma, 27*(2), 120–136. https://doi.org/10.1080/15325024.2021.1905320

Harris, M., & Fallot, R. D. (Eds.). (2001). *Using trauma theory to design service systems. New directions for mental health services*. Jossey-Bass.

Isobel, S., McCloughen, A., Goodyear, M., & Foster, K. (2021). Intergenerational trauma and its relationship to mental health care: A qualitative inquiry. *Community Mental Health Journal, 57*, 631–643.

Melo, V. U. (2023). EMDRIA EMDR National Association. *Healing across generations: Using EMDR therapy for intergenerational trauma.*

Rubenstein, V., Rabin, C., & Wernick, S. R. (2024, Feb 20). *Aging with a history of trauma: How service providers can help. Generations, American Society on Aging.*

Scott, K., & Copping, V. E. (2008). Promising direction for the treatment of complex childhood trauma: The intergenerational trauma treatment model. *Journal of Behavior Analysis of Offender and Victim – Treatment and Prevention, 1*(3), 273–283. https://doi.org/10.1037/h0100449

Selfhelp Community Services. (2022). Retrieved https://selfhelp.net/holocaust-survivor/

Substance Abuse and Mental Health Services Administration. (2014). *SAMHSA's concept of trauma and guidance for a trauma informed approach.* HHS Publication no. (SMA) 14–4884.

Substance Abuse and Mental Health Services Administration. (2023). *Practical guide for implementing a trauma-informed approach.* SAMHSA Publication No. PEP23-06-05-005. National Mental Health and Substance Use Policy Laboratory.

Suttenberg, L. P. (2016). Never forget: Cognitive restructuring limitations in holocaust related layered trauma. *Clinical Social Work Journal, 44*, 231–240.

The Institute on Trauma and Trauma-Informed Care. (2022). *Trauma-informed organizational change manual.* University of Buffalo School of Social Work.

Chapter 9
Antisemitism: A Guide for Teaching and Social Work Practice

Purpose

A key principle of the social work profession is to challenge social injustice while promoting sensitivity to and knowledge about oppression and cultural and ethnic diversity (NASW Code of Ethics, 2021). The profession's ethical responsibilities call upon social workers to be culturally aware and understanding of diversity and oppression as it occurs in many forms, including race, ethnicity, sex, sexual orientation, gender, status, ability, and religion. Cultural competency, the ability to understand the unique experiences of diverse groups with an awareness of one's own privilege and power, is essential to combating oppression (NASW Standards and Indicators for Cultural Competence, 2015).

The Council on Social Work Education (CSWE, 2022) specifies nine competencies expected of graduating students. Among these competencies, Competency 2: Engage diversity and difference in practice and Competency 3: Advance Human Rights and Social, Economic, and Environmental Justice offer a foundation for anti-oppressive practice. Both of these competencies attest to the importance of social work's role in combating all forms of oppression, including antisemitism.

Organization

This Teaching Guide is organized to enable educators to understand antisemitism, its manifestations, and its impact on Jewish people and societies. Such education is critical to assuring that social work students and practitioners can understand and be knowledgeable about the harm caused by antisemitism both to Jewish people and others. Such knowledge is crucial for counteracting it and ensuring that this specific

C. B. Cox, D. B. Marlowe, *Social Work and Antisemitism*,
https://doi.org/10.1007/978-3-031-72771-9_9

oppression is diminished. Each section of the guide includes exercises and resources that can be used in the teaching.

Definition of Antisemitism

Antisemitism is defined by the International Holocaust Remembrance Alliance (2016) as a certain perception which may be expressed as hatred toward Jews. Rhetorical and physical manifestations of antisemitism are directed toward Jewish or non-Jewish individuals and/or their property, toward Jewish community institutions and religious facilities.

It is a form of social injustice, discrimination, and a violation of human rights. Antisemitism, hatred that targets Jewish people and Jewish institutions, is a prejudice built on discrimination and oppression.

It is an ancient form of oppression that has dramatically increased in recent years both in the United States and globally. Data from the Anti-Defamation League (ADL, 2024) reports 3697 antisemitic incidents in 2022, an increase of 36% from the previous year and the highest number since 1979, the first year that data on incidents was collected. Within the first 2 months of 2023, attacks, including harassment, vandalism, and assaults, occurred in the United States. a 140% increase from 2022 (ADL, 2024). Globally, harassment of Jews has increased since 2020 in 94 countries with incidents ranging from verbal and physical assaults to vandalism of cemeteries as scapegoating of Jews as responsible for the COVID-19 pandemic (Diament, 2023).

Since the attacks in Israel by Hamas in October 2023, antisemitic attacks in the United States surged, with an average of nearly 34 incidents per day with explicit antisemitic anti-Zionist rhetoric at rallies across the country (ADL, 2024). Attacks on institutions, businesses, and vandalism also increased with particular harassment of Jewish students on college campuses. These incidents have resulted in fear among Jewish people about their security and ability to participate fully in society.

History

The persecution of Jewish people has a long history. In the Old Testament, the Hebrews were often persecuted because they refused to worship idols. With Christianity and the subsequent conversion of the Roman Emperors, Jews who refused to convert were seen as a threat to society, a threat that was strengthened by the Church's charge that the Jews were responsible for the death of Jesus.

In the early Middle Ages, Jews were excluded from intermarriage with Christians, holding political positions, and appearing as witnesses in courts. In most European cities they were restricted to living in specific areas. In the thirteenth century, they were required to wear a distinctive symbol so that they could easily be recognized (Abrahams, 2005). As it was forbidden for them to own land, they often became money lenders, an occupation that Christians could not assume but one that also led to further bias and stereotypes. Beliefs and myths developed to substantiate these prohibitions, such as "blood libel," which claimed that Jews ritually murdered Christian children and used their blood in making matza. Ostracized from society, Jews became an easy scapegoat and were frequently viewed as the causes of disease, including the Black Death, which killed thousands throughout Europe in the Middle Ages. In the 1400s Jews in Spain were forced to convert, leave the country, or be executed (Abrahams, 2005).

With the enlightenment of the eighteenth century, Jews were more accepted into Western European society while their activities continued to be restricted in Eastern Europe. Fears that Jews were trying to take over the governments in Germany and Russia led to further attacks and violent pogroms against Jewish communities. In France, the Dreyfus Affair, the false accusation against a Jewish French lieutenant of spying for the Germans, resulted in increased antisemitic attacks (Jewish Virtual Library, n.d.).

In the early 1900s, *The Protocols of the Elders of Zion*, a hoax that was used to discredit revolutionary forces hostile to the Tsar, published in Russia, described a Jewish plan for global domination (Whitfield, 2020). The fact that several of the leaders of the revolution were Jewish gave support to the accusations. In the 1920s, the Dearborn Publishing Company, owned by Henry Ford, published *The International Jew*, a four-volume set of anti-Semitic booklets based on the *Protocols*, which included "The American Jew: The World's Foremost Problem," contributed to increases in antisemitism in the United States (Whitfield, 2020).

Although there is no evidence for any international conspiracy, the works were influential in Hitler's belief that the Jews were dangerous and skilled at deception as they worked for world domination. Even with no support, the *Protocols* continue to be influential today. For example, the Rothschilds who played key roles in the development of finance capitalism in nineteenth century Europe, and the success and influence of George Soros, an investor, who spends billions on progressive causes, are used to personify the power of the Jew and may contribute to today's antisemitism (Whitfield, 2020).

During the Second World War, antisemitism in the United States had a major impact on immigration policy as it limited the number of Jewish immigrants that the country would accept from Germany (Welch, 2014). Even with knowledge of the genocide occurring in Europe, the American public overwhelmingly opposed accepting more Jewish refugees (Wyman, 2018) resulting in strict quotas that limited Jewish immigration.

The rising visibility of the White Nationalist movement in the United States continues to empower antisemites (Cox, 2023). Classifying Jews as a race threatens American society and building on stereotypes and empowers these extremists. In addition, the COVID-19 pandemic as it has isolated people at home has increased the groups' antisemitic expressions online, raising concerns about more antisemitic attacks (Kampeas, 2020). The virulence of these attacks was found in an FBI report documenting neo-Nazis and white nationalists' intent to infect Jews and policemen with the Coronavirus by spitting in their faces (Folley, 2020). The virus also accentuated antisemitic stereotypes and myths that contribute to violence by fueling beliefs, spread through social media, that Jews are responsible for the virus and using it to make money (Greenblatt, 2023).

Israel

Creation of Israel

Israel has been called a colonizing country which implies that Israel took control of an existing country, overpowering the residents, and claiming the land for itself (Lowry, 2023). Calling it a colonizing country ignores the fact that Jews have been in the land of Israel for over 3000 years during which time they were always self-governing. During the period of King David in the Old Testament, Jerusalem was the capital of the Jewish state.

The Kingdom was conquered by the Babylonians and large numbers of Jews were exiled to Babylon in the sixth century BCE. Following the fall of Babylon to the Persians, many Jews returned to build the Second Temple and the Jewish kingdom of Judea, which is recognized in the holiday of Chanukah.

The country was conquered in 70 AD by the Romans who changed the name from Judea to Palestina. Subsequently, the country was conquered by the Byzantines, Crusaders, and the Ottomans and finally became part of the British Empire in 1917. Under the British mandate, due to pogroms and increased antisemitism in both Europe and Russia, the Jewish population dramatically increased (Halevi, 1983).

Palestine

The Balfour Declaration (1917) issued by the British supported the establishment of Palestine as the national home for Jewish people, stating that nothing should be done that would prejudice the civil and religious rights of non-Jewish communities living in the country. The Declaration was approved by the League of Nations in 1922 with Britain recognizing the Jews as indigenous people and Palestine as the Jewish home (Kramer, 2017).

With the British Mandate, all residents, Muslims, Jews, and Christians, were considered Palestinians within the mandated territory. In 1947, The United Nations created a Partition Plan for Palestine which included the termination of the British Mandate and the partition of Palestine into two states, one Arab and one Jewish, with Jerusalem and Bethlehem areas administered by the United Nations. Most parts of the Plan were accepted by the Jewish Agency for Palestine while they were all rejected by the Arab leaders (Kramer, 2017).

In 1948, the British gave up the Palestinian Mandate and on May 14, 1948, Israel declared independence as the state of Israel. According to international law, the borders, Gaza, and Judea, and Samaria, matched those of the British mandate. Israel was accepted as a nation into the United Nations on May 11, 1949.

Shortly after the end of the British Mandate and the call for partition of Palestine, a civil war broke out between Jews and Arabs regarding the British plans for partition. In 1948, directly after the Israeli Declaration of Independence, the country was invaded by Egypt, Transjordan, Syria, and Iraq. After 10 months of fighting, Israel declared victory and over 100,000 Arabs evacuated to Arab countries. Jordan occupied parts of Jerusalem, Judea, and Samaria which they called the West Bank and Egypt controlled Gaza. These areas, which were never under Palestinian rule, were taken over by Israel in the 1967 War.

The 1968 War was followed by a war in 1973, known as the Yom Kippur War, which also ended in an Israeli victory. In 1978, President Jimmy Carter, President Anwar Sadat of Egypt, and Prime Minister Menachem Begin of Israel signed the Camp David Accords, resulting in the 1979 peace treaty between Israel and Egypt. Subsequently, in 1993, the Oslo Accords were signed between the Israelis and the Palestinian Authority. The Accords agreed that the Palestinian Authority would be established and would be responsible for governing the West Bank and Gaza for five years (US Department of State, Office of the Historian, 2018).

The Accords were significant as they cemented a framework for peace between Arabs and Israelis. However, they failed to maintain peace as the expectations of both sides, security for Israel and the expansion of Israeli settlements, led to claims and counter-claims resulting in anger, mistrust, and even violence between the two sides.

Whether or not Israel is an occupying country remains a debatable issue. Gaza remains under the administration and control of the Palestinian Authority along with the West Bank. However, Israel has maintained a military presence due to terrorist threats and concerns about security while the Palestinians have been free to govern themselves and their economy.

Hamas, the militant group in the territory formed in 1987, is committed to armed resistance against Israel and replacing it with an Islamic Palestinian state and was designated (1997) by the U.S. State Department as a foreign terrorist organization (Counter Terrorism Guide, 2022). The October 7, 2023, attacks on Israel are evidence of their efforts.

Apartheid

An apartheid state is one in which minority populations are segregated and oppressed by law. Over 20 percent of Israelis are non-Jewish Arabs, who receive the same benefits and services as all other citizens. They are represented in the Knesset (Parliament) and have the same rights as others. Israeli health services are available to them, including the medical care of persons in Gaza.

However, many, including Israeli's, consider Israel's policies as being apartheid particularly with regards to the occupation of the West Bank and the expansion of settlements. The claim has been supported by Amnesty International and Human Rights Watch (2023). At the same time, the charges are refuted by those who claim that the measures were taken to increase the security of Israel, are not racist, and that a double standard applies to Israel which promotes antisemitism (Carey, 2022).

Genocide

The term genocide was coined after the Holocaust and refers to the deliberately planned murder of people from a particular nation or group with the aim of destruction. Applying the term to the war with Hamas is inaccurate as Israel has tried to prevent harming citizens through notifications of attacks and permitting citizens to move from targeted areas. Israel is not focused on obliterating the people of Gaza; it is focused on combatting Hamas. In contrast, the October 7 attacks by Hamas, which killed over 1200 civilians and included the taking of more than 240 hostages, and the rape and sexual assault of women, are representative of a genocidal intent (Curtis, 2024). It is this attack that led to the War in Gaza rather than a genocidal motive on the part of Israel.

Israel's responses to the attacks continue to be a controversial issue. However, when pro-Palestinian protesters carry signs "Gas the Jews" and "From the River to the Sea," they are calling for the deaths of millions of people, wherever they are, and the eradication of an country, statements that may be perceived as having a genocidal intent.

Teaching Plan

We are providing several resources for education. We recommend that you review these and find which would be most effective for your teaching objectives and for the students that you are teaching. Please note that some of these resources state that they are for younger students. We have included resources that can be modified for the age and developmental level of the population that you are teaching (i.e., college and graduate students).

Defining Antisemitism

To begin education about antisemitism, students need to have a clear understanding of what antisemitism is. This includes having students recognize their own biases and stereotypes as well as how they reflect them in their interactions.

Factors Contributing to Antisemitism

Antisemitism is based on biases and stereotypes that depict Jews as an inferior and/or a malicious race or a group that seeks to dominate societies. However, there is no such entity as a Jewish race, Jewishness is a religion or culture and not a distinct racial group. In fact, the concept of Jewishness itself is debatable due to the diversity of the Jewish population. In addition, the concept of race itself has been disputed as race is viewed as a social construct used to distinguish people and social hierarchy and not a biological classification (Simama, 2023). Thus, Jews may be considered an ethnic group or cultural group as they share a certain membership in as they maintain specific cultural traditions and ties (APA, 2023).

When societies are threatened or those in power perceive themselves to be threatened, history shows that antisemitism tends to reveal itself. It reflects broad social and political issues and regressive, dangerous tendencies in the fabric of society (United Nations Educational, Scientific and Cultural Organization [UNESCO], 2017). Antisemitic tropes and beliefs continue to be powerful conduits of antisemitism as Jews remain a traditional target on which to place all of the ills and problems in society. For example, "The Great Replacement Theory" sees people of color, immigrants, and Jews as specific groups that threaten to pollute the white race (Clark, 2020). Stereotypic tropes based on claims that Jews caused the COVID-19 pandemic and that Jewish bankers are using lasers to start forest fires to finance railroads reflect these historical stereotypes (Zipperstein, 2020).

Resources

(a) American Jewish Committee (AJC) Translate Hate Glossary: https://www.ajc.org/translatehateglossary
(b) Rabbi Jonathan Sacks—Rabbi Sacks on the Mutation of Antisemitism: https://www.youtube.com/watch?v=3UAcYn4uUbs
(c) United States Holocaust Memorial Museum - Antisemitism Explained: https://www.ushmm.org/antisemitism/what-is-antisemitism/explained
(d) American Jewish Committee (2024b)—The Working Definition of Antisemitism: https://www.ajc.org/the-working-definition-of-antisemitism

The Holocaust

The Holocaust, the Nazi's war against and almost total destruction of the Jewish population of Europe, has been labeled the greatest genocide in history. The term Holocaust, derived from the Greek "a burnt offering" was first used in the 1960s to describe the murder of almost 6,000,000 Jews by the Nazis and their collaborators during World War II (Bergen, 2009).

Germany began its persecution of the Jews in 1933 with the rise to power of the Nazi party. The Nazis divided people into two racial groups, Aryans, who they considered superior to all, and those who were inferior, Jews, Slavs, Romas, and Blacks. The inferior groups, particularly the Jews, were seen as poignant threats to the Aryan race which needed to be controlled and eliminated. The restrictions on the Jews went through steps that continued to limit and ostracize them from German society.

Between 1933 and 1939, a series of laws and restrictions were introduced in Germany that directly Jewish people who composed less than 1% of its population (Montreal Holocaust Museum, n.d.). The restrictions on the Jewish population began with a German boycott of all Jewish business in April 1933 followed quickly by the removal of Jews from all civil service professions and the banning of Jewish teachers from public schools. Within the same month, Jews were forbidden from taking the bar for the legal profession, and universities and schools.

The Final Solution to the Jewish Problem was instituted in 1941 and lasted through 1945. The ultimate goal was the murder through mass extermination of all of the Jews of Europe in contrast to Aryans, who saw work as a moral duty and virtue, Jews were a nomadic people who abhorred work, lived as parasites, and were incapable of culture (Browning, 2004).

In July 1942, extermination camps were created in Poland and Germany to which Polish Jews were deported and murdered. Extermination centers, Sobibor, Belzac, Chelmo, Treblinka, and Auschwitz were created in the Spring of 1942 (Yad Vashem, n.d.). Jews were transported across Europe to these killing centers, usually by train and in freight cars, under the guise of being resettled. The cars were overcrowded, often forcing people to stand for days without food. The cars lacked bathrooms or heat, many died before reaching the camps. Upon reaching the camps, those who looked able were often selected for labor, while the majority, were immediately gassed. Jews were also forced to assist with the killings by removing bodies from the gas chambers, sorting through belongings, and burning the bodies in specially designed ovens.

The Holocaust ended in 1945 with the surrender of Germany. As well as the near-extermination of the Jews of Europe, millions of others were murdered. This includes over three million Soviet prisoners of war, more than 250,000 Romani (gypsies), approximately 300,000 people with disabilities, thousands of homosexual men, Black people, and Jehovah's Witnesses (Jewish Virtual Library, n.d.). All groups were viewed as threats to Germany and the purity of the Aryan race.

Holocaust Education

The United States Holocaust Memorial Museum (n.d.) provides guidelines for teaching about the Holocaust. These guidelines can apply to any educational resources that are used for teaching about this topic. As one would teach any topic effectively, a deep understanding of how complex this topic is combined with compassion needs to be included. Their guidelines are the following:

- Define the term "Holocaust."
- The Holocaust was not inevitable.
- Avoid simple answers to complex questions.
- Strive for precision of language.
- Strive to balance the perspectives that inform your study of the Holocaust.
- Avoid comparisons of pain.

- Avoid romanticizing history.
- Contextualize the history.
- Translate statistics into people.
- Make responsible methodological choices.

Resources

(a) Echoes and Reflections (https://echoesandreflections.org/) is a resource on Holocaust education created by the ADL, USC Shoah Foundation, and Yad Vashem. It provides lesson plans and trainings for teachers on the content they provide. Lesson plans are provided on the following topics: Studying the Holocaust, Antisemitism, Nazi Germany, the Ghettos, the "Final Solution", Liberation, Jewish Resistance, Rescue and the Righteous Among the Nations, Complicity and Responsibility, Justice, Life, and Memory After the Holocaust, Contemporary Antisemitism, and Teaching about Genocide.
(b) United States Holocaust Memorial Museum—Fundamentals of Teaching the Holocaust: https://www.ushmm.org/teach/fundamentals
(c) Yad Vashem (The World Holocaust Remembrance Center)—Education and E-Learning: https://www.yadvashem.org/education.html
(d) International Holocaust Remembrance Alliance—Recommendations for Teaching and Learning about the Holocaust: https://holocaustremembrance.com/resources/recommendations-teaching-learning-holocaust
(e) Centre for Holocaust Education—Teachers: https://holocausteducation.org.uk/teacher-resources/

Contemporary Antisemitism

Contemporary antisemitism is more difficult to recognize because it is not clothed in a Nazi uniform and does not openly claim hatred of Jews (Hirsh, 2018), Instead, it sees Jews as the oppressors and those who act against the Jews as the oppressed. The Boycott campaign against Israel beginning in 2003 with Israeli universities began with antizionists in Britain and spread into "Boycott, Divestment and Sanctions (BDS)" against Israel as an apartheid state using antisemitic tropes in their efforts (Hirsh, 2018).

Recognizing antisemitism is critical to stopping it. It involves understanding terms and expressions that are used to describe Jewish people. These are commonly shared through social media. The American Jewish Committee (AJC, 2024a) has compiled a glossary of antisemitic tropes and stereotypes that can help in recognizing antisemitism.

Conspiracy theories have a long connection with antisemitism with Jews historically having been viewed as seeking to dominate the world. They are easily spread through social media and are frequently accepted as true, particularly when they are pronounced by celebrities. Among the more recent claims are that Jews caused the

COVID-19 pandemic (Zipperstein, 2020) and claims that Jewish bankers are using lasers to start forest fires to finance railroads and claims that Jews remain a threat to society not because they are inferior but because they are too powerful and have too much control of the media and other institutions.

The impact of the conspiracy theories is increased antisemitism as they are accepted without discourse. Conspiracy theories contribute to antisemitic attacks as believers target Jews who are perceived as a pervasive threat to society and its institutions, and they undermine democracy itself. A poll made by the Southern Poverty Law Center (2022) found that those holding extremist far-right beliefs are also likely to mistrust the government and its policies. Consequently, such theories are threatening to both specific targeted groups such as Jews, as well as society itself.

Recognizing Antisemitism

Resource

(a) American Jewish Committee (AJC)—Translate Hate Glossary: Stopping Antisemitism Starts with Understanding It: https://www.ajc.org/translatehateglossary

Recognizing Conspiracy Theories

Resources

(a) UNESCO—Addressing conspiracy theories: What Teachers need to know: https://unesdoc.unesco.org/ark:/48223/pf0000381958
(b) Echoes and Reflections—Unit XI: Gringlas Unit on Contemporary Antisemitism: https://echoesandreflections.org/unit-11/?state=open#content
(c) Cox, C. (2023). Conspiracy theory: The demand for social work interventions, *Families in Society*, online first: https://doi.org/10.1177/10443894231174053

Antisemitism in Social Work Practice

Resources

(a) Cox, C. (2021). Addressing anti-Semitism in social work education, *Journal of Religion and Spirituality in Social Work: Social Thought*, 40, 111–125: https://doi.org/10.1080/15426432.2020.1871155

(b) Cox, C. & Marlowe, D. (2023). Antisemitism in Social Work: findings from an exploratory national survey, *Journal of Religion and Spirituality in Social Work: Social Thought,* published online: https://doi.org/10.1080/15426432.2023.2289435
(c) Cox, C. (2023). Antisemitism and social work: Challenges and opportunities for education and practice, *Journal of Ethnic and Cultural Diversity in Social Work*, published online first: https://doi.org/10.1080/15313204.2023.2291674

Countering Antisemitism

Resources

(a) Anti-Defamation League (ADL)—Fight Antisemitism: https://www.adl.org/what-we-do/fight-antisemitism
(b) Anti-Defamation League (ADL)—Resources to address and challenge antisemitism:https://www.adl.org/resources/tools-and-strategies/resources-address-and-challenge-antisemitism

Israeli-Palestinian Conflict

Resources

(a) Anti-Defamation League (ADL)—Ten ways to have conscientious conversations about the Israeli-Palestinian conflict: https://www.adl.org/resources/tools-and-strategies/10-ways-have-conscientious-conversations-israeli-palestinian
(b) The White House—The U.S. National Strategy to Counter Antisemitism, May 2023: https://www.whitehouse.gov/wp-content/uploads/2023/05/U.S.-National-Strategy-to-Counter-Antisemitism.pdf
(c) Encyclopaedia Brittanica (July 23, 2024)—Israel-Hamas War: https://www.britannica.com/event/Israel-Hamas-War
(d) American Society on Aging—Generations—Being an Israeli Mother in America Right Now: https://generations.asaging.org/being-israeli-mother-america-right-now

Additional Resources

Cox (2021) recommends three additional teaching models on antisemitism. Harrod (1996) developed a teaching model for sociology classes. This model, like others, can be used in social work courses as well. This model provides information through lectures and brief short movies focusing on three primary areas. These areas are: "Jews as the 'other'," "stereotypes and conspiracy theories," and "Jewish identity" (p. 196). This model used pre-tests and post-tests and showed that after three sessions students had increased knowledge of Judaism and of Jewish people.

Another teaching model was developed after the Tree of Life Synagogue shooting for public affairs courses (Levine Daniel et al., 2019). This model looks at oppression first in different levels of policies. It then looks at what the responses are that are related to bias and hate, then with a specific focus on antisemitism. This model shows the link between how individuals experience prejudice and hatred and a Jewish individual's experience. This then highlights the hate that exists in society. These lessons can be integrated in different topics. For example, a discussion of oppressive policies can be used when discussing workplace policies. This can also be integrated into a research class that focuses on data collection and tracking of antisemitic hate incidents.

UNESCO (2017) also created recommendations for guidelines for teaching about antisemitism as it continued to increase globally. A general recommendation was to use a human rights approach. Teaching about human rights and society's obligation to protect these rights should include a focus on antisemitism. Additional guidelines are to:

1. Help students to develop cognitive, social, and emotional skills that permit critical thinking that is necessary for counteracting antisemitism.
2. Build self-reflection in educators and students. Develop the ability to review their actions and beliefs and to identify their biases and prejudices.
3. Teach the complexity of antisemitism including its history and contemporary manifestations.
4. Teach intersectionality which illustrates how antisemitism can co-exist with other forms of discrimination and inequalities.

An innovative way to teach about antisemitism and racism focuses on the cases of Anne Frank and Emmett Till. Both were 15-year-old children murdered because of social hatred based on stereotypes and oppression. The comparison of the two cases vividly illustrates the similarities that hatred and social injustice can have on innocent people (Muller, 2022). The class stimulates students to explore their own assumptions and confront their biases and could be adapted into social work education.

We also recommend using Echoes and Reflections—Unit VIII—Rescue and Righteous Among the Nations (https://echoesandreflections.org/unit-8/) that can be used to discuss social workers' responsibility to fight social injustice. It is an important resource for strengthening professional identity and philosophies of helping.

The goal of this guide is to provide resources that can be integrated into teaching as well as contribute to improved practice. Education is a crucial factor in overcoming antisemitism and assuring that our profession is fulfilling its mission.

References

ADL. (2024). *U.S. Antisemitic incidents soared 140 percent in 2023-breaking all previous records*. https://www.adl.org/resources/press-release/us-antisemitic-incidents-soared-140-percent-2023-breaking-all-previous

Abrahams, I. (2005). *Jewish life in the middle ages*. Routledge.

American Jewish Committee (AJC). (2024a). *Translate hate glossary*. Retrieved from https://www.ajc.org/translatehateglossary

American Jewish Committee (AJC). (2024b). *The working definition of Anti-Semitism: What does it mean, why is it important and what should we do with it*. https://www.ajc.org/the-working-definition-of-antisemitism

American Psychological Association. (APA). (2023). *APA dictionary of psychology – Race*. Retrieved from https://dictionary.apa.org/race

Bergen, D. (2009). *War and genocide: A concise history of the holocaust: Critical issues in world and International History*. Rowman and Littlefield.

Browning, C. (2004). *The origins of the final solution: the evolution of Nazi Jewish policy*. Cambridge University Press.

Carey, A. (2022). *Amnesty accuses Israel of apartheid over treatment of Palestinians, prompting angry response*. CNN. https://www.cnn.com/2022/02/01/middleeast/israel-apartheid-amnesty-intl/index.htm

Clark, S. (2020). *How white supremacy returned to mainstream politics*. Retrieved from https://www.americanprogress.org/article/white-supremacy-returned-mainstream-politics

Council on Social Work Education (CSWE). (2022). *Educational policy and accreditation standards*. https://www.cswe.org/accreditation/policies-process/2022epas/

Counter Terrorism Guide. (2022, September). *Overview*. HAMAS, https://www.dni.gov/nctc/ftos/hamas_fto.html#:~:text=HAMAS%20emerged%20in%201987%20during,Palestinian%20state%20in%20Israel's%20place

Cox, C. (2021). Addressing antisemitism in social work education. *Journal of Religion & Spirituality in Social Work: Social Thought, 40*, 111–125.

Cox, C. (2023). Conspiracy theory: The demand for social work interventions. *Families in Society: The Journal of Contemporary Social Services, 0*(0). https://doi.org/10.1177/104438942311740

Curtis, M. (2024). *Is Israel committing Genocide in Gaza*. Retrieved from https://slate.com/news-and-politics/2024/01/israel-genocide-gaza-palestine-hamas-war-trial.html

Diament, J. (2023). *Anti-Jewish harassment occurred in 94 countries in 2020, up from earlier years*. Retrieved from https://www.pewresearch.org/short-reads/2023/03/17/anti-jewish-harassment-occurred-in-94-countries-in-2020-up-from-earlier-years/

Folley, A. (2020). FBI warns white supremacists encourage members to spread coronavirus to law enforcement Jews report. *The Hill*. Retrieved from https://thehill.com/blogs/blog-briefing-room/news/488919-fbi-white-supremacists-encouraging-members-to-spread

Greenblatt, J. (2023). *Antisemitism on the left is subtler than the right. But it's getting worse*. https://www.washingtonpost.com/outlook/2021/10/27/antisemitism-left-rising/

Halevi, N. (1983). The political economy of absorptive capacity: Growth and cycles in British Palestine under the British mandate. *Middle Eastern Studies, 19*, 456–469.

Harrod, W. (1996). *Teaching about antisemitism, teaching sociology* (pp. 195–201). https://www.jstor.org/stable/i256596
Hirsh, D. (2018). *Contemporary left antisemitism*. Routledge.
Human Rights Watch. (2023). *Extremist fact sheet, recycled Bigoty: Antisemitic conspiracy theories go mainstream*. https://humanrightsfirst.org/wp-content/uploads/2023/06/HRF-Fact-Sheet-Antisemitic-Conspiracy-Theories_6.29.23.pdf
International Holocaust Remembrance Alliance. (2016). *About the international Holocaust remembrance alliance*. Retrieved from https://holocaustremembrance.com/who-we-are
Jewish Virtual Library. (n.d.). *Anti-Semitism: Alfred Dreyfus & the affair*. Retrieved from https://www.jewishvirtuallibrary.org/alfred-dreyfus-and-ldquo-the-affair-rdquo. *Non-Jewish Victims*. Retrieved from https://www.jewishvirtuallibrary.org/non-jewish-victims-of-the-holocaust
Kampeas, R. (2020, April 23). *With white supremacists driven online by the pandemic, anti-Semitism trackers watch for new threats*. Jewish Telegraphic Agency.
Kramer, M. (2017). The forgotten truth about the Balfour declaration. *Mosaic*. Retrieved from https://scholar.harvard.edu/files/martinkramer/files/forgotten_truth_balfour_declaration.pdf
Levine Daniel, J., Fyall, R., & Benenson, J. (2019). Talking about antisemitism in MPA classrooms and beyond. *Journal of Public Affairs Education, 26*(3), 313–335. https://doi.org/10.1080/15236803.2019.1646581
Lowry, R. (2023). Israel is Not a Colonial State. *National Review*, Retrieved from https://www.nationalreview.com/2023/10/israel-is-not-a-colonial-state/
Muller, M. (2022). Anne and Emmett, university education students' reactions to a course in countering racism and antisemitism in the classroom. *Journal of Curriculum and Pedagogy*. https://doi.org/10.1080/15505170.2022.2098209
Montreal Holocaust Museum. (n.d.). *History of the Holocaust*. Retrieved from https://museeholocauste.ca/en/history-holocaust/
National Association of Social Workers. (2021). *NASW code of ethics*. NASW. https://www.socialworkers.org/About/Ethics/Code-of-Ethics/Code-of-Ethics-English
National Association of Social Workers. (2015). *Standards and indicators for cultural competence in social work practice*. NASW. https://www.socialworkers.org/Practice/NASW-Practice-Standards-Guidelines/Standards-and-Indicators-for-Cultural-Competence-in-Social-Work-Practice
Simama, J. (2023). The social construct of race that unnecessarily divides us. *Governing*. Retrieved from https://www.governing.com/now/the-social-construct-of-race-that-unnecessarily-divides-us
United States Holocaust Memorial Museum. (n.d.). *United States Holocaust memorial museum*. Retrieved from https://www.ushmm.org/
United States Department of State, Office of the Historian. (2018). *The Oslo accords and the Arab-Israeli peace process*. Retrieved from https://history.state.gov/milestones/1993-2000/oslo
UNESCO. (2017). *Addressing Antisemitism through education*. Retrieved from https://www.unesco.org/en/education-addressing-antisemitism
Welch, S. (2014). American opinion toward Jews during the Nazi era: Results from quota sample polling during the 1930s and 1940s. *Social Science Quarterly, 95*, 615–635.
Whitfield, S. (2020). *"The Protocols" Why the protocols of the elders of Zion is still used by Anti-Semites*. https://www.brandeis.edu/now/2020/september/whitfield-conversation.html
Wyman, D. (2018). *The abandonment of the Jews. America and the Holocaust, 1941–1945*. The New Press.
Yad Vashem. (n.d.). *Extermination camps*. Retrieved from https://collections.yadvashem.org/en/about/o6308
Zipperstein, S. (2020). *The conspiracy theory to rule them all, what explains the strange long life of the protocols of the elders of zion*. https://www.theatlantic.com/politics/archive/2020/08/conspiracy-theory-rule-them-all/615550/

Epilogue

Antisemitism remains a formidable threat in society. As described in the book, it is one of the oldest forms of oppression, but age has not impacted its virulence. Myths and stereotypes that feed antisemitism are easily spread through social media, reaching throughout society. As these are accepted and believed, they contribute to further prejudice and hatred. Although antisemitism focuses on Jewish people and institutions, it is often the precursor to oppression of other marginal groups that are perceived as a threat to those in power. Consequently, preventing and combating antisemitism must be a task for the social work profession.

Social work's focus on social justice and the dignity of all, in diverse societies, demands that it counter antisemitism and work to eradicate ignoring it only permits it to proliferate. Beliefs that Jews do not suffer from inequality or that they are white and integrated into society contribute to their being excluded from curriculum. But, this exclusion also enables antisemitism to continue. As noted in this book, Jewish social work students were often told they are privileged and did not have any problems after encountering micro-aggressions from both faculty and peers. Such statements and actions deny their experiences as well as their fundamental human rights of dignity and security.

The micro-level of practice demands that social workers are sensitive to self-reflection that helps them to identify their own assumptions and biases and beliefs about Jewish people. Such awareness is critical for both understanding one's own behavior and for working with Jewish students and clients.

Social workers must also be knowledgeable about the difference between antisemitism and anti-Zionism, prejudice against the state of Israel, its policies, and even its right to exist. Today, the two are closely intermingled as Jewish people are often treated as responsible for the policies of the Israeli government. However, blaming and attacking all Jews for a government's policies and actions is antisemitism.

Assuring that social work education includes a study of the Holocaust, the factors that contributed to it and its impact is basic to educating students as to the extremes that oppression and hatred can have on a society. It illustrates the dangers

C. B. Cox, D. B. Marlowe, *Social Work and Antisemitism*,
https://doi.org/10.1007/978-3-031-72771-9

that stereotyping and marginalization can have on individuals and groups. Studying the Holocaust and the trauma it inflicted can also be related to the experiences and stresses of those forced to flee their homelands today. Perhaps most important, the Holocaust documents the extremes that antisemitism can reach.

At the macro levels, social workers can use their advocacy skills to challenge conspiracy theories and the dispersion of myths and tropes that contribute to antisemitism. With social media playing a formidable role in the spread of antisemitism, social workers must be active in monitoring and rebuking false statements and accusations. Countering false statements by contacting the platform sources and associations and identifying the misinformation are tactics that can impede its spread. Joining with other groups in advocacy efforts that bring attention to the hate in society and its impact are positive actions that can work for social justice in societies.

The teaching guide (see Chap. 9) offers a framework for teaching about antisemitism as well as many resources that are available and easily accessible. It includes key issues that should be covered but, as with other teaching guides, it can be adapted to meet the needs of specific classes. The guide covers current issues with regard to antisemitism that can increase student understanding and sensitivity while helping them to identify oppression.

This book has been difficult to write. It began when antisemitism appeared to be increasing and was completed when antisemitism rose to historic levels across the globe. Unfortunately, this has occurred even with strategic plans to combat antisemitism developed in the United States and in Europe. This surge is frightening to Jewish people and must be a concern to all who desire socially just and diverse societies. It is important to remember that the UNDHR, written in 1948, was a response to the horrors of the Holocaust. Permitting antisemitism to flourish desecrates the document and its intent. Social work, with its focus on enhancing the dignity of all people and combating oppression, must intervene at all levels of practice to both challenge and combat it.

Appendix: Resources

ADL—Anti-Defamation League
https://support.adl.org

ADL fights all forms of antisemitism and bias, using innovation and partnerships to drive impact. A global leader in combating antisemitism, countering extremism, and battling bigotry wherever and whenever it happens, ADL works to protect democracy and ensure a just and inclusive society for all.

ADL investigates reports of antisemitic occurrences, assists law enforcement by sharing information, works to educate communities about threats, testifies at Congressional hearings and files federal lawsuits.

AJC—American Jewish Committee
https://www.ajc.org

AJC has 75 offices, institutes, and international partnerships, American Jewish Committee (AJC). It addresses the critical challenges facing Jews worldwide, seeks out opportunities on their behalf, and works to build a stronger global Jewish community.

They confront antisemitism in colleges and schools and provide information about relevant events all over the world with a specific section on human rights.

AMCHA Initiative
https://Amchainitiative.org

AMCHA Initiative is a non-profit organization dedicated to investigating, documenting, educating about, and combating antisemitism at institutions of higher education in America.

Campus Antisemitism Legal Line (CALL)
https://www.legal-protection.org/

Legal protection for students who have experienced antisemitism. This leads you directly to a website for reporting in-person incidents. It is associated with ADL and Hillel.

C. B. Cox, D. B. Marlowe, *Social Work and Antisemitism*,
https://doi.org/10.1007/978-3-031-72771-9

Hadassah – The Women's Zionist Organization of America
https://www.hadassah.org

Hadassah works to create leadership roles for women to advance justice and healing, including women's health, and fighting hate and antisemitism, supporting strong Israel and Jewish values.

Hillel International
https://hillel.org

Directed toward Jewish students, Hillel is the largest Jewish campus organization in the world. It explores and supports Jewish culture. It offers a newsletter. Help is available for reporting antisemitic incidents, navigating social media, and obtaining mental health support.

Hineni
https://hineni.org/

Offers messages of inspiration, faith, and strength online.

How You Can Fight Today's Antisemitism
https://uploads-ssl.webflow.com/5f207c2cb5e70085bd1bd76e/663e360b309f87e281b48379_Updated%20AntisemitismGuide%202F%205.9.24.pdf

Provides resources and information for standing up to antisemitism in the community.

Jewish Federations of North America
https://jewishfederations.org

The mission is to protect and enhance the well-being of Jews worldwide through contributions to community, Israel and civil society.

Kesher Shalom Projects
www.keshershalom.com

Founded by trauma therapists in response to the October 7th attack, the Projects aim to equip therapists worldwide to support Jewish clients during times of conflict.

More generally, they aim to combat the pervasive impact of antisemitism with courses and training.

Maccabee Task Force
https://www.maccabeetaskforce.org/

Formed in 2015 to combat the spread of antisemitism on college campuses. In particular, they are concerned about the BDS (Boycott, Divestment and Sanctions) movement, which in turn works to end "international support for Israel's oppression of Palestinians."

Basically, this is a social media outlet aiming to publicize the Jewish point of view.

Project Shema
https://www.projectshema.org/

Project Shema is a training and support organization built by progressives to help the Jewish community and allies challenge anti-Jewish ideas. This training aims to deepen understanding across lines of difference by nurturing empathy for Jewish identity, traumas, and lived experiences.

They hold training workshops for Jewish and non-Jewish allies, all professional settings, to help them discuss antisemitism.

Shine A Light
https://shinealighton.com/

Shine A Light is a purpose-driven convening platform for organizations, companies, institutions, and individuals to unite in shining a light on antisemitism in all its modern forms.

A resource mainly aimed at educators discussing roots of antisemitism. They have sections for all grades and programs for communities with many programs.

StandWithUs
https://www.standwithus.com/

StandWithUs is an international, non-partisan education organization that supports Israel and fights antisemitism.

StandWithUs empowers and energizes students and communities with leadership training and educational programs on hundreds of college campuses, high schools, and middle schools. StandWithUs informs through social media, print and digital materials, films, weekly newsletters, and missions to Israel.

Their main aim is to educate people about Israel without engaging in any special politics. They provide training and education for schools and communities.

The Jewish Therapist Collective
https://jewishtherapists.org

Its mission is to be a voice and vehicle of professional advocacy for therapists and those seeking therapy. It has 2000 associates across the globe. The Collective provides support and advocacy in coping with antisemitism in the professional community and in society.

Glossary

Anti-Racism, Diversity, Equity, and Inclusion (ADEI) Social work competency focusing on understanding how diversity and difference shape human experience and the impact of exclusion, discrimination, and oppression.

Antisemitism A certain perception of Jews, which may be expressed as hatred toward Jews. This includes rhetorical and physical manifestations directed toward Jewish or non-Jewish individuals and/or their property, Jewish community institutions, and religious facilities, and institutions. It is considered one of the oldest forms of oppression.

Apartheid A term used to describe the South African system of institutionalized racial segregation that existed from 1948 to the early 1990s. It ensured that the country was dominated politically, socially, and economically by the minority white population.

Bias Prejudice in favor of or against one thing, person, or group compared with another, usually in a way considered to be unfair.

Boycott, Divestment, and Sanctions (BDS) is a nonviolent Palestinian-led movement promoting boycotts, divestments, and economic sanctions against Israel. Its objective is to pressure Israel to meet what the BDS movement describes as Israel's obligations under international law. Critics accuse that it is antisemitic while supporters see it as a human rights movement.

Bullying Repeated aggressive behavior intended to hurt another individual, physically, mentally, or emotionally.

Collective Trauma The psychological impact of traumatic events experienced by a group of people, such as the Holocaust. This trauma can affect subsequent generations of the group.

Council on Social Work Education (CSWE) The accreditation body for schools of social work in the United States, which specifies competencies for social work education.

C. B. Cox, D. B. Marlowe, *Social Work and Antisemitism*,
https://doi.org/10.1007/978-3-031-72771-9

Cultural Competence The ability of social workers to understand, appreciate, and interact with people from cultures or belief systems different from their own.

Cultural Humility A lifelong process of self-reflection and self-critique whereby the individual not only learns about another's culture, but also starts with an examination of their own beliefs and cultural identities.

DEI (Diversity, Equity, and Inclusion) Diversity, equity, and inclusion are organizational frameworks that seek to promote the fair treatment and full participation of all people, particularly groups who have historically been underrepresented or subject to discrimination on the basis of identity or disability. The movements have been criticized for ignoring antisemitism.

Discrimination The unjust or prejudicial treatment of different categories of people, especially on the grounds of race, age, or sex. It can be used to refer to the treatment of Jews due to antisemitism.

Empowerment-Based Practice A social work practice that focuses on empowering individuals and communities to gain control over their lives.

Genetic Mutations Changes in the DNA sequence of a cell's genome, which can impact health and behavior, relevant in the context of social work when discussing coping strategies.

Genocide The deliberate killing of a large number of people from a particular nation or ethnic group with the aim of destroying that group. An example provided is the genocide of the Jewish people during the Holocaust.

Holocaust Denial Denying the fact, scope, mechanisms (e.g., gas chambers), or intentionality of the genocide of Jews during World War II by Nazi Germany.

Holocaust The genocide of six million Jews and millions of others by the Nazis during World War II, a critical historical context for understanding contemporary antisemitism.

Human RightsPractice Involves interactions at all levels of social work practice to ensure that rights are recognized and supported.

Human Rights Basic rights and freedoms that belong to every person in the world, from birth until death, fundamental to social work practice.

Intergenerational Trauma The transmission of historical oppression and its negative consequences across generations. This type of trauma affects descendants of those who have suffered major traumas, such as the Holocaust.

International Federation of Social Workers (IFSW) A global organization of social work associations that promotes social justice, human rights, and respect for diversities.

Intervention Actions taken to improve a situation, especially in social work, to address issues of antisemitism and support affected individuals and communities.

Jewish Social Workers Special Interest Group A group formed to address and support issues faced by Jewish social workers, including combating antisemitism within the profession.

Kinship Families Families in which children live with and are cared for by relatives other than their parents.

Micro, Mezzo, and Macro Levels of Practice The three levels of social work practice: micro (individual), mezzo (community or group), and macro (societal or policy level).

National Association of Social Workers (NASW) A professional organization in the United States that promotes social justice and human rights and sets ethical standards for social work practice.

Oppression Prolonged cruel or unjust treatment or control, often discussed in social work in relation to various forms of systemic discrimination.

Person-Centered Approach A therapeutic approach developed by Carl Rogers that focuses on the individual's capacity for self-direction and understanding of their own development.

Policy Sequence A series of courses in social work education that focuses on understanding, analyzing, and influencing social policies.

Protocols of the Elders of Zion is a book written in the early 1900s describing a Jewish plan for world domination. No evidence was ever given to support the claims but the book was influential in supporting Hitler's beliefs and continues to contribute to antisemitism.

Race is a categorization of humans based on shared physical or social qualities into groups generally viewed as distinct within a society.

Racism Prejudice, discrimination, or antagonism directed against someone of a different race based on the belief that one's own race is superior.

Rights-Based Approach An approach in social work practice that is based on the dignity and rights of individuals, emphasizing non-discrimination, inclusion, and participation.

Social Justice The objective of creating a fair and equal society in which each individual matters, their rights are recognized and protected, and decisions are made in ways that are fair and equitable. Social justice is a core value of social work, guiding professionals to fight against all forms of oppression, including antisemitism.

Stereotypes Oversimplified ideas about a group of people. In the context of antisemitism, stereotypes include negative character traits attributed to Jews.

Trauma Reminders Events or situations that trigger memories of past traumatic experiences. For many Jews, recent antisemitic attacks can act as reminders of historical traumas such as the Holocaust.

Trauma-Informed Care An approach in social work that involves understanding, recognizing, and responding to the effects of all types of trauma, aiming to avoid re-traumatization. Social workers are encouraged to use trauma-informed care to address the complex needs of Jewish clients who have experienced antisemitism and intergenerational trauma.

Universal Declaration of Human Rights (UDHR) A document adopted by the United Nations in 1948 that outlines the rights and freedoms to which all humans are entitled.

Vatican Council, Second A significant event in the Catholic Church held between 1962 and 1965 that, among other things, refuted the belief in Jewish responsibility for the death of Christ, which had fueled antisemitism for centuries.

Victim-Blaming Accusing victims of being responsible for the harm that has befallen them. In antisemitism, this includes blaming Jews collectively for actions committed by individuals or unrelated groups.

Index

C. B. Cox, D. B. Marlowe, *Social Work and Antisemitism*,
https://doi.org/10.1007/978-3-031-72771-9

The manufacturer's authorised representative in the EU is Springer Nature Customer Service Centre GmbH, Europaplatz 3, 69115 Heidelberg, Germany. If you have any concerns regarding our products, please contact ProductSafety@springernature.com

Printed and bound by CPI Group (UK) Ltd, Croydon, CR0 4YY
01/10/2026
02225982-0011